Studies in Brain and Mind

Volume 16

More information about this series at http://www.springer.com/series/6540

Francesco Marchi

The Attentional Shaping of Perceptual Experience

An Investigation into Attention and Cognitive Penetrability

 Springer

Francesco Marchi
Institut für Philosophie II
Ruhr University Bochum
Bochum, Germany

ISSN 1573-4536   ISSN 2468-399X   (electronic)
Studies in Brain and Mind
ISBN 978-3-030-33557-1   ISBN 978-3-030-33558-8   (eBook)
https://doi.org/10.1007/978-3-030-33558-8

This Springer imprint is published by the registered company Springer Nature Switzerland AG.
The registered company address is: Gewerbestrasse 11, 6330 Cham, Switzerland

For Serena and Niccolò

Acknowledgments

This book is the culmination of a 3-year PhD project developed at the Ruhr University Bochum, Germany. I would like to express my gratitude to the people who helped and supported me during this time.

I am grateful to Albert Newen for inviting me to Bochum to do my PhD and for his constant support as my advisor on the project. I am also grateful to Jakob Hohwy for his helpful insights on my work and for inviting me to visit his *cognition and philosophy* lab at Monash University. Some of the core ideas in this book would not have developed without the frequent discussions that we had during that beautiful Australian summer.

I would like to thank Peter Brössel, Sabrina Coninx, Beate Krickel, Tobias Starzak, and Pascale Willemsen for their detailed commentaries on the dissertation and for being awesome colleagues and office mates. Furthermore, I am grateful to Luca Barlassina, Erica Cosentino, Krzysztof Dolega, Judith Martens, Tobias Schlicht, Joulia Smortchkova, Markus Werning and all the former and current members of the Department of Philosophy II who have contributed to my project with discussions, comments, critical remarks, and many enjoyable moments together. A special thanks to Frances Egan and Carlos Montemayor for their suggestions on core parts of this dissertation.

A sincere thank you to my family and friends. I am especially grateful to my wife, Serena Bifolchi, who has endured my company during the most stressful times over the last 3 years and never ceased to cheer up and support me.

I am indebted to the *Barbara Wengeler Stiftung* and to the RUB Research School for their financial support.

Introduction

Setting the Stage

There is a long-standing debate in cognitive science about the interaction between what we believe or desire to be the case and what we experience to be the case. According to one strand of the debate, our beliefs, desires, and other similar mental states can shape how we experience the world through the senses. According to the opposite strand, our perceptual experiences of the world are determined by what we encounter in the world and immune to any influence from mental states like beliefs and desires. Questions raised in this debate concern, for example, whether negative thoughts make everything look darker, whether wearing heavy backpacks causes slopes to appear steeper, and whether an expert birdwatcher sees a moving bird differently from a layman.

In its modern version, the hypothesis that mental states like beliefs and desires can shape how we experience the world is usually referred to as the *cognitive penetrability of perceptual experience*. The label "cognitive" refers to the kind of mental states that are supposed to do the shaping, and "perceptual experience" refers to the way in which we experience the world through the senses, which is supposed to be shaped by those mental states.

Cognitive penetrability is receiving considerable attention in the contemporary philosophical and psychological debate. In the last few years, there have been no fewer than three collections of philosophical and empirical papers dedicated to the topic (Jenkin and Siegel 2015; Raftopoulos and Zeimbekis 2015; Newen et al. 2017) and that the University of Yale reports more than 170 empirical papers on the top-down effects of cognition onto perception in the last two decades (http://www.yale.edu/perception/Brian/refGuides/TopDown.html). To understand why this topic is such a pressing one, it may help to examine what the consequences would be if our perceptual experience were to be cognitively penetrable.

Stokes (2015) argues that there are three main consequences of cognitive penetrability. The first is relevant for scientific theorizing: if experience is cognitively penetrable, empirical observation could be *theory-laden*. This is a well-known issue in the philosophy of science as it poses serious problems for the possibility of evaluating the adequacy of competing scientific theories in the light of experiments.

The second consequence is epistemic: if perceptual experience is cognitively penetrable, one may be unwarranted in justifying some specific beliefs on the basis of that experience. A famous example of this problem is presented by Siegel (2012) and can be summarized as follows: suppose Jill believes that Jack is angry and this belief penetrates her experience of Jack's face making it appear angry to her. Now, Jill may take the experience as additional support for her very belief that Jack is angry. According to some prominent theories of justification, the epistemic status of this specific belief would have improved, despite having taken what seems like a rather epistemically pernicious route. While such an experience could still be used as a source of evidence for other beliefs, for example, the belief that Jack is looking at Jill, it seems epistemically unwarranted that the belief penetrating the experiences enjoys further support from the experience itself. Once again, this would be a problematic result, since perceptual experience is among the main sources of justification one has available for one's beliefs about the world.

The third consequence concerns the way in which we model mental architecture: if perceptual experience is cognitively penetrable, some modular models of the mind, whose main appeal has traditionally been identified with the straightforward explanation they offer for functional dissociations (Stokes and Bergeron 2015), must be rejected or deeply revised. This consequence is not necessarily undesirable, but it would require quite a radical revision of the way in which many scientists have thought about the architecture of the mind, since Fodor's (1983) original formulation.

The issue about modularity affects the delimitation of functional units and informational encapsulation when trying to model the architecture of the mind. Some modularity theorists have already put forward weakened versions of Fodor's original constraints on the delimitation of a cognitive module, giving up the requirement of informational encapsulation (Carruthers 2006), while others still hold on to such requirement (Sperber 2001). More recently, researchers have offered explicit discussions of modularity and encapsulation in relation to cognitive penetrability. Lyons (2015) argues that modularity does not require encapsulation and that cognitive penetration might not be so epistemically threatening for non-encapsulated modules. Burnston and Cohen (2015) argue for a version of modularity of Fodorian inspiration where the failure of a system to be encapsulated does not automatically entail penetrability. On the other hand, Mandelbaum (2018) defends a version of conceptualist modularity where the requirement of encapsulations is maintained and cognitive penetration is not allowed. In Mandelbaum's view, perception is conceived as having basic categorization among its proprietary functions. His account is very close to Fodor's original proposal and backed up by substantial empirical evidence about the shocking speed at which categorization occurs in both humans and other animals.

In light of these three consequences, it is clear how the interest in cognitive penetrability spans several disciplines and research domains. Therefore, understanding whether cognitive penetration ever occurs is of primary importance, because it has ramifications that tap deeply into some of the most relevant issues for the whole project of cognitive science. In this book, I focus on one specific problem in the *cognitive penetrability debate*, namely the relationship between *cognitive penetrability* and *attention*.

Attentional processes are one of the most important features of one's mental activity. It is in virtue of those processes that one is capable of selecting and prioritizing what information is behaviorally relevant among all the information available at any given time. Furthermore, attention is crucial for beliefs, desires, and perceptual experiences alike. By simply reflecting on everyday behavior, it is easy to see that attention is always at work. When we turn our head to visually detect the source of a noise, for instance, we are paying attention to that noise. When we focus our mind to understand a philosophical paper, filtering out background distractions, we are paying attention to the contents of the paper. When we want to find the car keys in an environment that is crowded with other objects, we are focusing attention on the features of the keys in order to find them.

If attentional processes constitute such a relevant and omnipresent aspect of our everyday mental life, it is important to understand whether and how their unfolding affects how we experience the world. Furthermore, given the relevance of the *cognitively penetrability* thesis for cognitive science, it is crucial to establish whether attentional processes may lead to cognitive penetration. If the answer to this question were positive, the scope of the consequences of cognitive penetration could potentially become extremely wide.

In line with these considerations, the relationship between cognitive penetration and attention has recently stirred the interest of many researchers who have offered detailed discussions of specific aspects of this problem (Raftopoulos 2007; Mole 2015; Gross 2017; Stokes 2018; Wu 2017). Building upon the work of these researchers, this book aims to offer a systematic treatment of this crucial aspect of the cognitive penetration debate and its potentially far-reaching consequences.

The Core Question: Can Attention Shape Experience?

It is sometimes assumed that attention and *cognitive penetrability* are independent and that attention is among those variables that must be kept fixed, in order for an experience to be genuinely cognitively penetrable (Pylyshyn 1999; Macpherson 2012; Siegel 2012). However, several scholars have recently raised doubts about this assumption (Mole 2015; Stokes 2018). In this book, I focus on this aspect specifically and examine whether *attentional processes* and *cognitive penetrability* do, in fact, exclude one another and whether cases of attentional shifts can be cases of cognitive penetration. The main research question that I seek to answer is the following:

> *Under what conditions, if at all, does attention lead to the cognitive penetration of perceptual experience?*

This question hinges on three further questions:

1. Whether and how perception is distinct from cognition?
2. What it means for a perceptual experience to be cognitively penetrated, and what kinds of cognitive penetrability are there?
3. What attention is and how attentional processes unfold?

The first set of problems concerns how the penetrating states or processes and the penetrated ones can be kept apart. Without a reliable way of distinguishing them, it would not make sense to ask questions about the possibility and nature of their interactions. The second set of problems concerns what sorts of interactions among such states and processes are relevant for the overall scientific projects of understanding how the mind works and how we should model perception and cognition. The third set of problems is related to the clarification of the nature of attention and attentional processes. This is, by itself, a fundamental issue in cognitive science, and its discussion is required to provide a compelling answer to the research question.

I take a step-by-step approach, addressing each set of problems in turn, before drawing the main conclusions about the relationship between *cognitive penetrability* and *attention*. Once each set of problems has been addressed, I argue that attentional processes can generate cognitively penetrated experience under specific conditions and that attention is one of the factors that must be considered when discussing *cognitive penetrability* and its foundational implications for scientific theorizing, mental architecture, and epistemology. Finally, I discuss how *attention* and *cognitive penetrability*, as well as their relationship, can be modeled within one of the most promising approaches to understanding the mind, namely, the *prediction error minimization* framework.

Plan of the Book

In Chaps. 1 and 2, I address the first set of problems. In Chap. 1, I begin by clarifying the notions of *cognition*, *perception*, and *perceptual experience* that I employ in the book. I then discuss three extant accounts of how a distinction between perception and cognition can be drawn. The first account is based on a distinction between *analog* and *digital* informational encoding (Dretske 1981). The second and third accounts concern a functional (Pylyshyn 1999, 2003) and temporal (Raftopoulos 2009) delimitation of perceptual processing, respectively. After discussing the three accounts, in Chap. 2, I argue that even if all of them were to be rejected and if draw-ing a sharp distinction between perception and cognition turned out to be impossi-ble, there would still be the possibility of drawing a graded distinction. I discuss the widely accepted notion of a mental processing hierarchy and, based on the spatiotemporal sensitivity of processes at different levels of the hierarchy, I propose a criterion based on the notion of *basic actions* for drawing such a graded distinction.

Once I have argued that a distinction between perception and cognition can be drawn and thereby settled the first set of problems, in Chap. 3 I move on to the dis-cussion of the second set. I start by reviewing the traditional problems that have driven the debate about *cognitive penetrability* and *top-down effects* of cognition onto perception in general. Afterward, I discuss how these problems are addressed in the contemporary philosophical debate. I provide four definitions of *cognitive penetrability* that capture the main issues that typically arise in the debate and that are based on the work of Macpherson (2012, 2015), Pylyshyn (1980, 1999, 2003), Siegel (2012), and Stokes (2014, 2015). Each definition focuses on a specific aspect of the phenomenon and is aimed at keeping these aspects apart, since at times they may be conflated in the debate. The first definition of *semantic cognitive penetrabil-ity* concerns the normativity of the relation between the cognitive and perceptual states involved in an instance of cognitive penetration. Similarly, the second defini-tion of *causal cognitive penetrability* requires such a relation to be causal. The third definition of *indirect nonconceptual cognitive penetrability* allows for the cognitive and the perceptual state to have conceptual and nonconceptual contents, respec-tively. Finally, the fourth definition of *consequentialist cognitive penetrability* focuses on the three main consequences that the actual occurrence of cognitive pen-etration would bring about. The four definitions allow me to discuss whether atten-tional processes, which I discuss next in the book, satisfy any of them. Finally, I present some evidence that has been proposed in the literature to support the *cogni-tive penetrability* hypothesis.

In Chaps. 4 and 5, I turn to the third set of problems and discuss the nature of attention and attentional processes. In Chap. 4, I initially focus on further clarifying the relevance of attention for the whole debate on cognitive penetration. I discuss two features that allow to qualify a mental phenomenon as attentional, namely, *selectivity* and *modulation* of information. On the basis of these two features and of a resource limitation constraint for biological systems, I elicit the main phenomena that a theory of attention must be able to explain. The requirement to explain a pre-cise set of attentional phenomena constitutes the *desideratum* on a theory of atten-tion. On the basis of the *desideratum*, in Chap. 5, I discuss four theories that are prominent in attention research, namely, the *filter model* (Broadbent 1958), the *binding model* (Treisman and Gelade 1980; Treisman 1998), the *selection for action* view (Wu 2011a, b), and the *biased competition* theory (Desimone and Duncan 1995; Duncan et al. 1997; Desimone 1998; Duncan 1998). I argue that the *biased competition* theory is the only one that meets the desideratum, and I focus on it as the most promising account of attention among those discussed. I present the main tenets of *biased competition* and add a new philosophical discussion of the nature of attention based on this theory. I argue that attention is the property of a mental representation of *being the current winner* of a competition process among mental representations.

Having addressed each set of problems that underlie my research question, in Chap. 6, I turn to the question itself. I discuss whether the instantiation of the property of attention, when understood as a consequence of the competition process, satisfies the requirements of the four definitions of *cognitive penetrability* introduced before. I start by explaining why attentional processes have usually been excluded from the relevant instances of cognitive penetration. The main reason is that attentional processes are typically taken to change the input to perceptual processes, while sameness of input is one of the main requirements of *cognitive penetrability*. I argue that if *biased competition* is the right account of attentional processes, such exclusion is unwarranted. On the basis of the *biased competition* theory, I argue that the attentional process of biased competition is a metacognitive process that regulates the allocation of resources, possibly at all levels of the cognitive and perceptual processing hierarchy. This constitutes a new way of understanding the role of attentional processes in perception and cognition. If attention emerges from competition among representations, its instantiation does not require a change in the input that led to the tokening of those representations in the first place. Concerning the four definitions, I discuss two cases (Carrasco et al. 2004; Liu et al. 2009) showing that attentional processes clearly satisfy the definition of *causal cognitive penetrability*. I then go on to argue that attentional processes can satisfy the definition of *semantic* and *indirect nonconceptual cognitive penetrability*. Finally, I argue that attentional processes have important implications for the justificatory role that perceptual experience can play for beliefs. I argue that, under specific circumstances, the epistemic consequences of attentional processes qualify them as instances of *consequentialist cognitive penetrability*.

Now that my research question has received a positive answer, I use Chaps. 7 and 8 to discuss whether my proposal is consistent with the *prediction error minimization* framework for modeling perception and cognition (Friston 2010; Gładziejewski 2016; Hohwy 2013, 2014; Kiebel et al. 2008). The reason for this move is that this framework is widely regarded as one of the most promising extant accounts of the mind. I retake each of the previous steps in the new context of *prediction error minimization*. In Chap. 7, I introduce the framework and discuss how *perception* and *cognition* can be distinguished in the framework as well as how *cognitive penetrability* has to be understood. In Chap. 8, I turn to the question of how attentional processes can be described according to *prediction error minimization*. I then return to the research question, arguing that *biased competition* fits naturally in the context of this particular framework and that attentional processes satisfy the currently most compelling definition of *cognitive penetrability* in the framework (Hohwy 2013, 2017). Finally, I discuss two experiments (Liu et al. 2012; Meng and Tong 2004), which show how cognitive penetrability is engendered through attentional processes, under a *prediction error minimization* interpretation of the experimental results.

References

Broadbent, D. E. (1958). *Perception and communication*. New York: Pergamon Press.

Burnston, D., & Cohen, J. (2015). Perceptual integration, modularity and cognitive penetration. In A. Raftopoulos & J. Zeimbekis (Eds.), *Cognitive influences on perception: Implications for philosophy of mind, epistemology, and philosophy of action* (pp. 123–143). New York: Oxford University Press.

Carrasco, M., Ling, S., & Read, S. (2004). Attention alters appearance. *Nature Neuroscience, 7*, 308–313.

Carruthers, P. (2006). *The architecture of the mind*. Oxford: Oxford University Press.

Desimone, R. (1998). Visual attention mediated by biased competition in extrastriate visual cortex. *Philosophical Transactions of the Royal Society of London. Series B: Biological Sciences, 353*(1373), 1245–1255.

Desimone, R., & Duncan, J. (1995). Neural mechanisms of selective visual attention. *Annual Review of Neuroscience, 18*, 193–222.

Dretske, F. I. (1981). *Knowledge and the flow of information*. Cambridge, MA: MIT Press.

Duncan, J. (1998). Converging levels of analysis in the cognitive neuroscience of visual attention. *Philosophical Transactions of the Royal Society of London, Series B-Biological Sciences, 353*, 1307–1317.

Duncan, J., Humphreys, G., & Ward, R. (1997). Competitive brain activity in visual attention. *Current Opinion in Neurobiology, 7*(2), 255–261.

Fodor, J. A. (1983). *The modularity of mind*. Cambridge, MA: MIT Press.

Friston, K. (2010). The free-energy principle: A unified brain theory? *Nature Reviews Neuroscience, 11*(2), 127–138.

Gładziejewski, P. (2016). Predictive coding and representationalism. *Synthese, 193*(2), 559–582.

Gross, S. (2017). Cognitive penetration and attention. *Frontiers in Psychology, 8*(246), 1–12.

Hohwy, J. (2013). *The predictive mind*. Oxford: Oxford University Press.

Hohwy, J. (2014). The self-evidencing brain. *Nous, 50*(2), 259–285.

Hohwy, J. (2017). Priors in perception: Top-down modulation, Bayesian perceptual learning rate, and prediction error minimization. *Consciousness and Cognition, 47*, 75–85.

Jenkin, Z., & Siegel, S. (2015). Cognitive penetrability: Modularity, epistemology, and ethics. *Review of Philosophy and Psychology, 6*(4), 531–545.

Kiebel, S. J., Daunizeau, J., & Friston, K. J. (2008). A hierarchy of time-scales and the brain. *PLoS Computational Biology, 4*(11), e1000209–e1000212.

Liu, T., Abrams, J., & Carrasco, M. (2009). Voluntary attention enhances contrast appearance. *Psychological Science, 20*, 354–362.

Liu, C.-H., Tzeng, O. J. L., Hung, D. L., Tseng, P., & Juan, C.-H. (2012). Investigation of bistable perception with the "silhouette spinner": Sit still, spin the dancer with your will. *Vision Research, 60*, 34–39.

Lyons, J. (2015). Unencapsulated modules and perceptual judgment. In A. Raftopoulos & J. Zeimbekis (Eds.), *The cognitive penetrability of perception: New philosophical perspectives* (pp. 102–122). New York: Oxford University Press.

Macpherson, F. (2012). Cognitive penetration of colour experience: Rethinking the issue in light of an indirect mechanism. *Philosophy and Phenomenological Research, 84*(1), 24–62.

Macpherson, F. (2015). Cognitive penetration and nonconceptual content. In A. Raftopoulos & J. Zeimbekis (Eds.), *The cognitive penetrability of perception: New philosophical perspectives* (pp. 330–358). New York: Oxford University Press.

Mandelbaum, E. (2018). Seeing and conceptualizing. *Philosophy and Phenomenological Research, 97*(2), 267–283.

Meng, M., & Tong, F. (2004). Can attention selectively bias bistable perception? Differences between binocular rivalry and ambiguous figures. *Journal of Vision, 4*, 539–551.

Mole, C. (2015). Attention and cognitive penetration. In A. Raftopoulos & J. Zeimbekis (Eds.), *The cognitive penetrability of perception: New philosophical perspectives* (pp. 218–238). New York: Oxford University Press.

Newen, A., Marchi, F., & Brössel, P. (Eds.). (2017). Cognitive penetration and predictive coding. *Consciousness and Cognition, 47*, 1–112.

Pylyshyn, Z. W. (1980). Computation and cognition: Issues in the foundations of cognitive science. *Behavioral and Brain Sciences, 3*(1), 111–132.

Pylyshyn, Z. W. (1999). Is vision continuous with cognition? The case for cognitive impenetrability of visual perception. *Behavioral and Brain Sciences, 22*(3), 341–365.

Pylyshyn, Z. W. (2003). *Seeing and visualizing.* Cambridge, MA: MIT Press.

Raftopoulos, A. (2007). Does attentional modulation of early vision entail the cognitive penetrability of perception? In *Proceedings of the European cognitive science conference 2007* (pp. 365–370).

Raftopoulos, A. (2009). *Cognition and perception: How do psychology and neural science inform philosophy?* Cambridge, MA: MIT Press.

Raftopoulos, A., & Zeimbekis, J. (Eds.). (2015). *The cognitive penetrability of perception: New philosophical perspectives.* New York: Oxford University Press.

Siegel, S. (2012). Cognitive penetrability and perceptual justification. *Nous, 46*(2), 201–222.

Sperber, D. (2001). Defending massive modularity. In E. Dupoux (Ed.), *Language, brain and cognitive development: Essays in honor of Jacques Mehler.* Cambridge, MA: MIT Press.

Stokes, D. (2014). Cognitive penetration and the perception of art. *Dialectica, 68*(1), 1–34.

Stokes, D. (2015). Towards a consequentialist understanding of cognitive penetration. In J. Zeimbekis & A. Raftopoulos (Eds.), *The cognitive penetrability of perception: New philosophical perspectives* (pp. 75–100). New York: Oxford University Press.

Stokes, D. (2018). Attention and the cognitive penetrability of perception. *Australasian Journal of Philosophy, 96*(2), 303–318.

Stokes, D., & Bergeron, V. (2015). Modular architectures and informational encapsulation: A dilemma. *European Journal for Philosophy of Science, 5*(3), 315–338.

Treisman, A. (1998). Feature binding, attention and object perception. *Philosophical Transactions of the Royal Society of London. Series B: Biological Sciences, 353*(1373), 1295–1306.

Treisman, A. M., & Gelade, G. (1980). A feature-integration theory of attention. *Cognitive Psychology, 12*(1), 97–136.

Wu, W. (2011a). Attention as selection for action. In C. Mole, D. Smithies, & W. Wu (Eds.), *Attention: Philosophical and psychological essays* (pp. 97–116). New York: Oxford University Press.

Wu, W. (2011b). What is conscious attention? *Philosophy and Phenomenological Research, 82*(1), 93–120.

Wu, W. (2017). Shaking up the mind's ground floor: The cognitive penetration of visual attention. *Journal of Philosophy, 114*(1), 5–32.

Contents

Chapter 1
A Play with Two Characters

Abstract In this chapter I introduce the terminology and concepts that are crucial for the development of my arguments in the book and discuss how the two key elements of my discussion, namely perception and cognition, can be kept apart in a mental processing system. In the overarching argumentative line of this book, which revolves around the cognitive penetrability of perceptual experience, keeping perception and cognition apart is a fundamental requirement. If perception and cognition cannot be separated, an issue immediately arises for the possibility of asking questions about their interactions. The structure of the chapter is as follows: Sect. 1.1 outlines the main theoretical commitments that form the backdrop of the discussion in this book. Section 1.2 is devoted to terminological clarifications and conceptual stage-setting. Section 1.3 explores how a clear-cut distinction between perception and cognition may be drawn.

1.1 The World and the Senses

We live in a dynamic world of rich and complex stimuli that we need to detect and decode in order to behave efficiently and, ultimately, to survive. Each of us is an integral part of that same world, but assuming for simplicity's sake that the body is the boundary between each subject and the outside world, what is outside the boundary may interact with what is inside the boundary thanks to our multimodal sensory channels. Smell, touch, taste, audition, and vision give us access to the world outside our body.

In this book, I adopt a naturalist perspective and construe the *subject* as a system composed of the brain and the body. The subject may also be thought to consciously operate from a first-person perspective. This means that a subject's conscious experience typically appears, through introspection, to be in first person.[1] With this stipulation, I do not intend to make any particular metaphysical claim about the subject. I only use the present terminology for clarity of exposition. In this chapter, I focus

---

[1] This may be due to the selectivity of some important components of the subject's cognitive system (e.g. some specific neuronal populations) toward changes in the environment that are relative to the subject's point of view. This feature has led some authors (Prinz 2012) to claim that these components are good candidates for the neural correlates of conscious experience.

© Springer Nature Switzerland AG 2020
F. Marchi, *The Attentional Shaping of Perceptual Experience*, Studies in Brain and Mind 16, https://doi.org/10.1007/978-3-030-33558-8_1

on the brain, which, in my perspective, is equated with an information-processing device.

Some of the terminology adopted in this book is taken from the framework of the computational theory of mind (CTM). CTM has been an extremely influential approach to the mind since the second half of the twentieth century. It has been developed in several directions to account for different aspects of the mind like mental content or the mind-body problem.[2] Here, however, I do not subscribe to any particular version of CTM.[3] In general, according to CTM, the mind can be modeled as a hierarchy of levels that, in the case of the human being, corresponds to a cortical processing hierarchy. Levels may be individuated on the basis of their spatial, temporal, and functional properties. I say more about the hierarchy below. For the moment, I simply assume the existence of such a hierarchy.

As a preliminary and very general characterization, *perception* is the process of acquiring and processing information about the world through the senses. Even though we are endowed with several efficient channels that convey perceptual information about the world, interacting with the world in a way that ensures the success of our actions, leading to self-preservation and well-being, is no simple task. Humans have a long learning phase in which they need to be supervised and helped by their elders in order to fully and adequately develop. In the learning phase, humans explore the world acquiring new information about it and slowly learning its regularities, what is stable and what is subject to change, and at what rate the changes usually happen. In other words, perceptual interactions with the world provide the basis on which we learn about the properties of the world.

It is hardly disputable that, once acquired, information about the world may guide subsequent perceptual interactions with it. One could, for example, skillfully scan a certain environment looking for a particular object that one knows to be there. Or one could pay close attention to one's steps and to the floor if the terrain is recognized to be difficult. This kind of background information allows us to use our tools so as to access the world in an efficient way. Thus, there is some information in the world that a subject may access through the senses and some other information that the subject has already acquired and stored somewhere.[4] The subject can recruit the stored information at a different point in time to interpret new sensory information, make judgments, acquire new beliefs, etc. The stored information can take the form of a belief, which may be true and justified,[5] but this need not be the

---

[2] Some of the most influential examples are Dretske (1981), Fodor (1983), and Dennett (1987). For a recent discussion of computationalism and the problem of mental content, see Piccinini (2004).

[3] In fact I only adopt some of the concepts of CTM, such as "information processing", since I find them to be commonplace in cognitive science and easy to follow and understand. I hold that, given that the present arguments are inspired by and anchored in neurophysiology, if it will turn out that the true account of the mind is not a computational one, most of the present discussion will be translatable into the terminology of the better theory.

[4] Later, it will become clear that the "level" at which information is stored is relevant for the debate about cognitive penetrability.

[5] This is the traditional definition of knowledge famously criticized by Gettier (1963).

case. For now, I subsume all information that has been acquired and stored by a subject under the label of "*background information*".

In the picture I have been presenting so far, the senses are considered to be instruments through which we acquire objective information about the world, and background information is like a user manual that explains how to properly use them. It is possible, however, that the role of background information in perceiving the world is deeper than that of a user manual. Background information may not simply orient our sensory devices; it might also change what it is like (Nagel 1974) to perceive the world through the senses, that is, our *perceptual phenomenal experience* of seeing, hearing, smelling, touching, and tasting something. The question of whether or not background information may change our perceptual phenomenal experience of the world is worth asking because it has important implications for theories of how the mind works and how we acquire knowledge. But before addressing this problem, I will clarify the terms that I will adopt during the course of this discussion.

1.2 Perception and Cognition: Definitional Issues

I have already mentioned the notions of *perception* and *perceptual phenomenal experience*. It is important to highlight the difference between them in a perceiving subject, and I will analyze them in turn, making use of some conceptual tools from CTM. *Perception* refers to the process or group of processes dealing with the information that enters the processing system, namely the brain in the case of humans, through sensory channels. For the moment, let us assume that after a certain amount of processing, perception ceases and any further information processing belongs to the domain of high-level cognition.

Of course, the matter is much more complicated than this, as will be elucidated in the following paragraphs. However, up to this point, there would be no fundamental difference, concerning perception, between a human subject and a machine endowed with some sort of surrogate sensory detector such as, for example, a digital camera. There could be differences in the architecture, physical substrate, kind of computations, etc. But both of these systems would be able to receive sensory-like information from the world and process it to a certain extent. Thus, both systems would be able to perceive.[6] Note that this notion of perception is also different from sensory detection. Very simple artificial systems, like automatic motion detectors, are capable of detecting the presence or absence of a certain stimulus, but without the ability to further process information, leading to, for example, a minimally integrated representation about that stimulus, they cannot be said to perceive it.

---

[6] Although, on closer inspection, this is not sufficient for perception. See the discussion of perception and action below.

Thus, information[7] processing is at the core of the present notion of perception. Such processing, however, is usually thought to involve states that are internal to the system and carry information about stimuli, namely *representations*. Here I adopt a rather broad notion of representation as a kind of information carrying state with accuracy conditions, i.e. they represent the world as being in a certain way, which may be accurate or inaccurate depending on whether the world really is in such way and to what degree. As a minimal characterization, I use the term "representation" to refer to internal states of a processing system (neural states in the case of the brain) that are about states of the world or other states of the system.

To say that a state of the system is about a state of the world or another state of the system means that the representing state reliably co-occurs with the represented state. In addition, the representing state must play some function for the system.[8] This usually happens because the represented state causes the tokening of the representing state. If the tracking state occurs in the absence of the tracked state, for example because it is caused by something else on that occasion, the system may be misrepresenting the tracked state. For example, in vision, the processing system operates on objects' projections onto the retina. Information about the retinal projection is in turn processed through the lateral geniculate nucleus of the thalamus and transduced into patterns of neural activation in early visual cortices.[9] The retinal projection and the corresponding pattern of neural activation are both representations of external objects and their properties, at least in the minimal sense that I adopt here. If such states of the system were not caused by some objects in the world impinging on the retina, but by other means, such as a hologram or a drug, the system would be misrepresenting the world. The specific nature of representations or of the representational vehicles is left open.[10] Throughout the course of this book, it will be assumed that perception is representational.

While a processing system can in principle represent many things, from objects and properties in the world to abstract or non-existent entities, in this work I am concerned with things to which the system has access through experience. Therefore, the notion of representation in this book applies to objects, properties, and events in the world that we can access through the senses and about which we can have perceptions and form perception-based beliefs and judgments. The notion does not apply to such things as abstract and non-existent entities or the objects of beliefs that are not perception-based. I hold that a story could be told to extend the arguments of this book to non-existent entities and beliefs that are not anchored in perception. To tell such a story, however, is not necessary for the task I pursue in this work and I leave it aside for the time being.

---

[7] Information is understood probabilistically (Shannon 1948; Dretske 1981).

[8] Where the function allows to specify the content of the representation (Shea et al. 2018).

[9] This does not mean that there are no external causes of those representations. External objects and states of affairs are causally linked to the patterns of neural activation in the brain that correspond to them.

[10] For example, one might think that representations in the human brain are just recurring patterns of neural activation (Prinz 2012).

Furthermore, I do not take a stance on the problem of the (naturalized) intentionality of mental representations. The arguments that I will develop are consistent with different positions on the matter such as pragmatist views on neural representations (Colombo 2013, 2014), computationalist views according to which all representational content is mathematical content and cognitive content is an intentional gloss (Egan 2014), or representationalist views where a causal chain between a (neuro)biological state and an object, property or event in the world suffices for intentionality (Searle 2015), or where content is specified by function (Shea et al. 2018). I further accept that there could be different kinds of representation in the same system, and later I discuss how to differentiate between them. However, one need not be a representationalist in order to inquire into perception. To be fair, there are theories of perception that are non-representational. I do not wish to engage with those theories. I hold that the discussion of the interactions between perception and cognition can be developed and understood more fruitfully in a representational framework, but at the same time it may be recast in non-representational terms.

As a final remark on the notion of perception, it is important to note that since perception is concerned with the information that reaches the system through the sensory channels, the current availability of such information is a necessary condition for each instance of perception. In other words, perception depends on an established causal link between the subject and the perceived object, property or event. Hence, illusions and hallucinations which may arise in the absence of the appropriate causal link or in the presence of an inappropriate causal link (hologram, drug) are states that represent the world as being in a way it is not, and, as such, they are cases of misperception (misrepresentation). As an example, take the famous Müller-Lyer illusion. According to the notion of perception introduced here, a subject who is under the illusion is misperceiving two lines of different length for there are no such things in the world. The two lines in the world are of equal length and, at most, one can say that the subject fails to perceive what is in the world, namely two lines of equal length. I will return to this point shortly.

Now that the notion of *perception* has been preliminarily elucidated, I can elaborate on the different notion of *perceptual phenomenal experience* (henceforth, simply *perceptual experience*). One immediate difference between perception and perceptual experience is that while perception can be unconscious, perceptual experience cannot. Furthermore, there is a particular *"what it's like"*, for a subject to represent the world in experience. According to the present terminology, an artificial computing device can be said to perceive; however, it is much less straightforward to think that such a device could be phenomenally conscious of the information it processes. One could argue that a very complex machine could in principle exhibit the same behavioral responses as a human being in the presence of certain stimuli and that we would have no way of telling whether or not it has perceptual experience of those stimuli.

To make the distinction, however, the complex matter of discussing the actual capabilities of such artificial devices is irrelevant. It is possible to imagine systems that are exact physical duplicates and complete functional equivalents of a human being, but which lack perceptual experience (Chalmers 1996).[11] Such systems could clearly perceive the world, in the sense of representing stimuli and acting upon them, albeit not with the correspondent experience of what it's like to perceive them. On some views, perceptual experience is construed as a set of perceptual representations that become *phenomenally conscious*. These representations may acquire their phenomenal character in virtue of having a particular kind of content (Jackendoff 1987), being processed in a particular way (Dehaene and Naccache 2000) or both (Prinz 2012).[12]

A third difference concerns the previously mentioned necessary condition for perception that the things perceived have a direct causal connection with their perceptual representation in the system. While one cannot perceive things that are not there, one can certainly have conscious perceptual experiences as if such things were there. For example, one can have an experience that presents one with what it's like to caress a cat, even if the cat is not there. This is what happens if one vividly dreams of caressing a cat. Perceptual experience can occur in the physical absence of the objects, properties or events experienced. Such is the case in illusions and hallucinations. Again, in the case of the Müller-Lyer illusion, the subject has an experience of two lines of different length. Such an illusory phenomenal state can be driven by hard-wired constraints on how the system processes information, but it can also be brought on by learned regularities in the environment (McCauley and Henrich 2006). The resilience and widespread presence of the Müller-Lyer illusion among humans seems to point to such a constraint. Nevertheless, even if these organizational principles of perception might exist for the purpose of reliably facilitating the processing of sensory information, they are not immune to failure as in the Müller-Lyer case.

Let me now turn to the notion of *cognition*. At the beginning of this section, I mentioned that through perception we acquire background information about the regularities of the world, which becomes independent from any particular perceptual encounter and is stored in the system. For example, by seeing the sun rising for many days one will infer that it will rise tomorrow as well. The belief that the sun will rise tomorrow, however, is independent from tomorrow's perceptual encounter with the sun. I assume that beliefs of this kind are also representational states, like those underlying *perception* and *perceptual experience*. For the purposes of the present discussion, I use the notion of *cognition* to refer to the set of representations that constitute a subject's background information about the world. The term

---

[11] The *zombie argument* is supposed to show that phenomenality is irreducible to the physical domain. As I said, I do not subscribe to this conclusion and endorse a physicalist view of the mind. I cannot discuss the argument here. I only note that a problem with the argument is that although exact physical duplicates of human beings without phenomenality might be logically possible, they could be nomologically impossible in our world. Thus, there could be some as yet undiscovered physical features of human systems that underlie and explain phenomenality. Nevertheless, the idea is useful to elucidate the distinction between *perception* and *perceptual phenomenal experience*.

[12] In Marchi and Newen (2016), we discuss this topic and argue for a processing approach to consciousness.

"cognition" is sometimes used to refer to the whole span of mental activities, of which *perception* and *perceptual experience* are subsets. For now, I adhere to a narrower notion of *cognition* that will be refined in the course of this chapter. Like perception, cognition involves states of the subject that represent the world (objects, properties, events, relations, etc.). But unlike perception and like perceptual experience, cognitive states can be instantiated and hold independently of the current perceptual availability of the things represented.[13] For example, one can firmly believe that last year's sunset at the seaside on the 7th of July was the most beautiful one has ever seen, or one can wish that there were an extra slice of this tasty cake on the plate. However, neither the sunset nor the cake is available, i.e. one does not have current access to them through one's sensory organs. Assuming that we can characterize the states involved in this example as a belief about the sunset and a desire about the cake, beliefs and desires can thus represent things to which one does not currently have sensory access and are, thus, prominent examples of cognitive states.

Cognitive states are often thought to have the same structure as propositions in a language, whose building blocks are concepts. Therefore, the format of cognitive states is supposed to be conceptual and the set of cognitive states is thought to include propositional attitudes. But are there cognitive states that are not propositional? This question is difficult to answer and how one may reply depends on one's notion of "conceptual format". As we shall see, equating cognition with conceptual propositional attitudes is too simplistic. I dedicate a section of the next chapter to tracing the distinction between perception and cognition in such a way that a clear-cut distinction of representational formats, e.g. the conceptual format for cognition, is not required. For the time being, however, the simple notion introduced here shall suffice to move us to the next point.

There is an issue that immediately arises from the tentative definitions of *perception, perceptual experience,* and *cognition* proposed here. The problem is that sometimes we have *perceptual experience* in the presence of an external object that causes the experience, and sometimes we do not. For example, it seems possible to have hallucinations that are subjectively indistinguishable from normal experiences, but which are caused not by an object or event in the world but by something else.[14] In this case, since such experiences represent something that is not currently available to our sensory organs, they would count as cognitive states according to my preliminary definition.

This is problematic because perceptual experiences are supposed to have certain properties that are not shared by most of the other higher-level cognitive states, such as beliefs and desires. A definition of cognition that groups together perceptual experiences with those other states seems to be too loose. For example, one could argue that cognitive states like beliefs and desires do not have essentially the same

---

[13] On this point, Searle (2015) argues that some representational states lack the indexicality of *here* and *now* that is an intrinsic feature of perception.

[14] Arguments form illusion and hallucination have been put forward by Ayer (1940) in support of sense data theory. See Crane (2005) for a recent discussion of the problem of perception raised by those arguments.

phenomenal component of perceptual experiences. One can believe that the Eiffel tower is a tall building even if one has no current perceptual experience of the Eiffel tower or even if one has never seen it. Furthermore, beliefs could be about things long gone; as an example, take my belief that the pyramids were built by ancient Egyptians. Perceptions, on the other hand, are about things that are available to the subject's senses here and now, like the laptop in front of me, for instance. Perceptual experiences seem to share this feature with perception. Take the case of hallucinations. It is true that one may hallucinate Napoléon Bonaparte sitting on the sofa, but even if Napoléon is long gone, the hallucination would presumably present him as being on the sofa now, which may lead the experiencer to notice that something is not quite right. Therefore, one needs an additional criterion in the definition of cognition that allows for distinguishing perceptual experiences from cognitive states proper. I will discuss how to provide such a criterion in the next section and in the next chapter.

Having provided a preliminary elucidation of the notions of *perception, perceptual experience,* and *cognition,* it is reasonable to begin asking some questions about the interactions between them. However, as we shall see, not every interaction is equally relevant for our purposes in this book. It is fairly straightforward to think that cognitive states interact with perception in some way, for example by orienting spatial attention or by constraining interpretations of perceptual output for identification and categorization (Pylyshyn 1999). Yet, as we have seen, the *cognitive penetrability* of perceptual experience would have radical consequences for theory evaluation, the architecture of the mind and perceptual epistemology (Stokes 2015), and the kinds of interactions in which I am interested are those that have been traditionally thought to be problematic in light of their consequences. A rather demanding example of such interactions is a semantic or otherwise logical connection between the contents of a cognitive state and the contents of a perceptual state (Pylyshyn 1999). A somewhat weaker example is a direct internal and mental causal connection between a cognitive and a perceptual state. The nature and requirements of the relevant interactions between *perception* and *cognition* are presented in greater detail in Chap. 3. For the time being, I need to discuss one important precondition for the possibility of any interaction between *perception* and *cognition,* namely that a clear distinction between perception and cognition can be drawn in the first place.

1.3   Is There a Real Distinction?

It is often assumed that the starting point of any discussion about possible cognitive influences on perceptual experience must be to provide a criterion for a distinction between *perception* and *cognition.* If *perception* and *cognition* were one and the same, how could one influence the other?[15] In the previous section, I sketched out provisional definitions of perception and cognition. In this section, I will discuss in more detail how the distinction can be drawn. The distinction relies on the notion of a hierarchy of mental processes that I introduced earlier. In fact, a hierarchy of processes is a presupposition for a distinction, as Raftopoulos and Zeimbekis write:

> The perception/cognition distinction is not immune to doubt. An extreme way to doubt it would be to adopt a view of the brain as devoid of any functional hierarchy (see Lashley 1929), but nobody today appears to be tempted by this position. (Raftopoulos and Zeimbekis 2015, p. 24)

There is a wide debate on whether perception and cognition are truly distinct or if there is only one continuous[16] flow of informational processing in a system such as the human brain. The latter view, which I call the *continuity view,* can be intuitively motivated by the fact that the vehicles that realize neural computations, namely the neurons, are similar throughout the brain. Of course, there are different types of neurons and the structure of the connections between them might vary quite radically in different regions of the cortex or at different cortical layers in the same region. More importantly, though, even assuming that the vehicles of information processing are the same throughout the processing system, the way in which information is encoded might still be different at different functional levels. In the next chapter, I argue that a clear distinction between perception and cognition can be defended even if we accept the *continuity view.*[17] In the following, I examine alternative accounts that propose a clear-cut distinction and that, therefore, reject the *continuity view.* Even if I may offer objections to the accounts presented here, my point is not to dismiss any of them. To the contrary, if any of these accounts holds, one can make sense of the distinction between perception and cognition and, thereby, ask fundamental questions about their interactions.

In his influential book *Knowledge and the Flow of Information*, Dretske (1981) illustrates this point clearly. He says that perception has a distinctive role in a hierarchy of processes and that the information encoded in perception has a radically different structure from the information encoded in cognitive states such as beliefs and desires. Dretske's idea is that two different types of information encoding correspond to perception and cognition, respectively, as I have construed them here. The two ways of encoding information are *analog* and *digital* encoding. To keep in

---

[15] As will become clear during the course of this chapter, this is not an obvious point. In a hierarchical processing system, it might be important to ask if and how processes high up in the hierarchy might influence processes at lower levels, even if all such processes are of the same kind.

[16] The term is borrowed from Pylyshyn's (1999) discussion of the same topic. His view will be addressed later in this section.

[17] It should be noted that the distinction I am interested in at this point is the one between perceptual and cognitive processing. It could still be maintained, for example, that perception and cognition may differ at the level of phenomenology and not at the level of processing, but issues of cognitive penetrability are primarily about the processes that underlie cognition and those that underlie perception. I am grateful to an anonymous referee for raising this point and highlighting the need for clarification.

line with the overall broadly representational framework that I adopt, I call them analog and digital representational formats. The *analog* format, which corresponds to perceptual encoding of information, is continuous,[18] whereas the *digital* format, which corresponds to cognition (beliefs, desires, etc.), is discrete. According to Dretske, *analog representations* are informationally rich and, at some point during the flow of processing, are transduced into informationally poorer *digital representations*, which may serve as the basis of beliefs and other such states that are composed by concepts. Digital (or conceptual) representations are representations that carry only very general information about the represented object or state of affairs, in a similar manner to the information carried by a sentence. For example, the sentence "there is a red chair in front of me" carries only the information that the thing in front of me is a chair and that it is red. If we take the sentence as a paradigmatic example of digital representation, no additional information except that the chair is red and in front of me is conveyed by the representation. Analog representations, on the contrary, always carry additional information about the things represented, similarly to the information carried by a picture. For example, a visual experience of the chair in front of me carries information about, among other things, the chair's shape, orientation, and material. In addition, representations in analog format are always more determinate than those in digital format; the visual experience of the chair does not only represent the color red, but a determinate hue of red.

Up to this point, it might seem that the distinction between analog and digital representations is only a matter of complexity. One could imagine construing a very complex digital representation (something like an extremely long descriptive sentence) that has the same degree of detail, determinacy, and informational richness of the visual experience. The construction of such a complex representation might not be possible for beings with a limited conceptual apparatus (Carruthers 2000, pp. 133–134), there might be nuances of experience for which we may not possess concepts. Nevertheless, the conceivability of the complex digital representation shows that the digital format, as described so far, is fundamentally the outcome of a process of generalization and simplification. There is, however, another important difference between analog and digital formats, namely that the former is continuous while the latter is discrete.

To illustrate the difference, consider a mechanical and a digital watch.[19] When the hand of the mechanical watch moves from 17.20 to 17.21, there are an indefinite number of intermediate positions that the hand transits through in order to reach its

---

[18] Note that this is a different usage of the notion of continuity. In the *continuity view,* "continuous" means that there is no difference in kind between information processing or representations at early stages of the hierarchy compared to later stages. This holds even if each level of the hierarchy is considered to be a separate discrete step. In the case of analog representations, on the other hand, "continuous" identifies a kind of informational encoding for perceptual processing that differentiates it from other processes in the brain. Unfortunately, the specificity of the terminology used in the literature does not allow for the employment of a different notion.

[19] This example is adapted from Carruthers (2000); Dretske (1981) makes a similar point by way of a speedometer.

destination from its starting point. Nothing of the sort is true of the digital watch where the new value just appears on the display. In this example, the mechanical watch represents the time continuously, whereas the digital watch does so in a discrete way. In general, one can describe the difference between the two representational formats by saying that there is always one value or property in between two values or properties of a continuous or analog representation, while there is no intermediate value or property between two values or properties of a discrete or digital representation. Continuity and discreteness are thus further criteria with which to distinguish analog from digital representations and thus perception from cognition.

An important aspect of the Dretskean view is that perceptual experience appears to be continuous. To illustrate, take the example of a patch of color that gradually changes from blue to green passing through all of the intermediate hues. Supposedly, our perceptual experience can track all (or the majority) of the changes in hue, while our belief about the color of the patch is limited by our conceptual apparatus, which may lack the resources to track the changes with the same degree of sensitivity or with the same fine graininess. Since continuity is one of the properties of the analog representational format, it follows that perceptual experience is underpinned by analog representation.

The distinction traced by Dretske is a neat way of separating perceptual from cognitive processes by means of positing two different representational formats for them. However, one critical problem with this view is that there seems to be no actual way in which the neurons could encode information in a truly analog format, as reported by Carruthers: "the processes subserving perception are almost certainly not continuous, but discrete – after all, any given brain-cell is either firing or at rest at any given moment" (2000, p. 134).

Since we are under the assumption that the vehicles of perceptual representations and cognitive representations are the same, it seems that, if neurons can only work in a discrete fashion, the format of perceptual representations must also be discrete, albeit very fine-grained. Carruthers proceeds to rephrase the notion of analog representation in such a way that it admits "significantly more variations" than our conceptual repertoire. Yet, this seems to be a quantitative difference between perceptual representations (including experience) and cognitive representations, and not a qualitative one. Perceptual representations just admit more discrete steps.

Other authors have proposed alternative strategies to defend a radical distinction between perception and cognition. In his famous 1999 paper, Pylyshyn argues that a significant part of visual perceptual processing, which he calls *early vision*, is not continuous with cognition, thereby rejecting the *continuity view*. He offers an extensive review of the evidence available at the time about the (im)plausibility of top-down effects from higher processing levels in the hierarchy onto lower ones, which would threaten the informational encapsulation, i.e. the cognitive impenetrability, of early vision. Pylyshyn systematically rules out alleged evidence in favor of such effects as cases of either post-perceptual modifications of judgment or pre-perceptual allocation of attention. He concludes that a significant part of vision "is best viewed as a separate process with its own principles and possibly its own internal memory, [...] isolated from the rest of the mind except for certain well-defined and highly circumscribed modes of interaction" (Pylyshyn 1999, p. 364).

In his paper, aside from discussing a series of experimental evidence in favor of its thesis, Pylyshyn proposes four general reasons for believing that a significant part of visual processing, which he calls early vision, is impenetrable by background knowledge and other higher-level cognitive capacities. First, many illusions, such as the aforementioned Müller Lyer illusion, persist even if the subject is provided with knowledge about the real properties of the stimulus. Second, the principle used by the system to analyze and process a visual input are very different from rational principles of inference. Pylyshyn gives the example of amodal completion in which two adjacent figures are usually interpreted as one figure occluding another figure in the background. Third, there is no direct evidence of top-down modulation of the visual system from higher-level processing areas that is sensitive to what the subject knows or what a stimulus means for the subject. And finally, there is a dissociation between vision and other cognitive functions, such as object recognition, shown in the condition of visual agnosia.

Regardless of the actual argumentative force of the four points, Pylyshyn's view has the merit of devising a clear distinction between a part of mental activity that is impenetrable to other mental states, such as beliefs and desires, and the rest of the mind, which could be completely interconnected.[20] In the context of the present discussion, one may adopt Pylyshyn's encapsulation criterion and call the encapsulated part of (visual) perceptual processing "perception" *proper* and the rest of mental activity "cognition".[21]

Since Pylyshyn's distinction between perception and cognition turns on the notion of cognitive impenetrability, it can only be accepted or rejected once we have clearly established that there is a set of mental processes that are functionally encapsulated from the rest of mental activities. However, if perception is limited to Pylyshyn's *early vision*, which is, by definition, cognitively impenetrable, questions about the cognitive penetrability of perception do not make much sense. And yet, if Pylyshyn's account turns out to be the right theory of visual perception, there is still an important question that is worth asking, namely whether the realization basis of visual perceptual experience is identical to the encapsulated part of visual processing, or whether it is wider. If the realization basis of visual experience is wider than the functionally encapsulated early visual module, it might incorporate functional units that are not encapsulated from other cognitive domains and, thus, cognitive. Since the influence of beliefs and desires on the operations of these functional units might have an effect on perceptual experience, it is still interesting to ask whether perceptual experience is cognitively penetrable, even if a dedicated part of perceptual processing is not.

---

[20] According to Pylyshyn, there may be other encapsulated domains like motor-control functions (Pylyshyn 1999), but they are not pertinent to the present discussion.

[21] Although Pylyshyn's discussion is limited to vision, if one has reason to posit a similar encapsulated functional unit for the other sensory modalities, the distinction may be extended to those modalities.

Even if one accepts Pylyshyn's impenetrability criterion, one might still wonder if it really suffices to ground a distinction between perception and cognition. Raftopoulos and Zeimbekis (2015) object that the impenetrability of a system does not grant that system belongs to a different kind of mental processes from other systems that are not encapsulated in the same way. They write:

> Granting the cognitive impenetrability of perception could at best be part of some way of securing a perception/cognition distinction. If an information processing system is cognitively impenetrable, that implies that it functions autonomously from certain other systems and can be defined without reference to them. But to secure the perception/cognition distinction, some explanation needs to be given of why the first system deserves to be called perceptual and the other cognitive. (Raftopoulos and Zeimbekis 2015, p. 24)

They argue that the required distinction can be secured on functional grounds and independently from the cognitive penetrability or impenetrability thesis.

In particular, Raftopoulos (2009) argues that *early vision*, i.e. the functionally encapsulated and cognitively impenetrable perceptual module envisioned by Pylyshyn, can be identified on the basis of processing latencies. Raftopoulos adopts the framework of Victor Lamme (2000, 2003, 2005; Lamme and Roelfsema 2000) who identifies three stages of visual processing. The first stage is a purely bottom-up stream of processing, called the *feedforward sweep*, which runs from the retina up to the inferotemporal cortex, lasts for about 100 milliseconds and is too fast to be affected by processes that happen elsewhere in the brain. After the *feedforward sweep*, other areas of the visual system start to send feedback signals to the early area of V1 in what is called the *local-recurrent processing* stage, lasting up until 120 milliseconds after stimulus onset. According to Lamme and Raftopoulos, *local-recurrent processing* does not involve higher-level areas of the brain and is limited to the visual system. As such, the feedback at this stage does not provide an instance of cognitive penetrability because no domain general cognitive information is supposedly involved. The third stage of processing, called *global-recurrent processing*, takes place at 150–200 milliseconds after stimulus onset. At this stage, feedback connections are involved from many areas of the brain including the frontal and prefrontal cortex. As such, *global-recurrent processing* is the first processing stage in which the operations of the visual system are sensitive to information that is being processed elsewhere. Therefore, this is the first and only cognitively penetrable stage of visual processing. Up to this point, however, much has happened in the visual system and Raftopoulos (2009) claims that the first two stages, which are cognitively impenetrable, can be identified with Pylyshyn's early vision. Presumably, the temporal criterion might be one further element to grant a distinction between perception and cognition, in addition to informational encapsulation.

One problem with Raftopoulos view is that there is evidence for feedback connections within the first 100 milliseconds of visual processing (Newen and Vetter 2017; Aru et al. 2016). But perhaps an even bigger issue is that the identification of early vision with the processing stages of *feedforward sweep* and *local-recurrent processing* cannot be used to ground a distinction between perception and cognition, on pain of circularity. The reason is that Raftopoulos proposes to identify early vision on the basis of processing latencies, but on closer inspection, in defining the second stage, the *local-recurrent processing*, as impenetrable by cognition and limited to the visual system, he is already presupposing that all the areas involved at this stage are perceptual and not cognitive areas. If such a definition of early vision were to ground the distinction between perception and cognition, then the fallacy would be something like the following: perception is defined by processing latencies because processes up to a certain point in time are limited to perceptual areas.

As what may be considered a way out of this problem, Raftopoulos and Zeimbekis (2015) write:

> *The set of processes that Lamme and Roelfsema call the feedforward sweep and local recurrent processing qualify as non-cognitive due to the priority of those processes relative to doxastic and personal-level processes, and as visual due to the traceability of the stimulus to the eyes. These seem good enough reasons to call them perceptual.* (Raftopoulos and Zeimbekis 2015, p. 25)

However, if this is the only argument for considering those processing stages as perceptual as opposed to cognitive, it is far too weak for this purpose. Neither the priority, which I take to be temporal, of these processing stages nor their traceability to the eye seem to be sufficient to dismiss the *continuity view*. Critically, there can be temporal priority and more or less traceability to sensory organs even in a system whose functional hierarchy is composed of processes that are all of the same kind or, to use the Dretskean terminology introduced at the beginning of this section, that encode information in the same format. In this case, the difference is merely quantitative and the distinction between perception and cognition becomes equivalent to that of early and late processing. In addition, Raftopoulos and Zeimbekis (2015, p. 27) recognize that even if one were to succeed in identifying a purely perceptual early visual module in functional terms or in terms of processing latencies, questions of the cognitive penetrability of perceptual experience would still be relevant if cognition could affect the *experiential output* of later processing stages.

1.4   Summary and Conclusion

If any of the views presented in this section turn out to be correct, there is a sharp distinction between perception and cognition that can be spelled out in terms of representational format, encapsulation, or temporal processing latencies. Therefore, in general, it would be perfectly sensible to discuss the possibility and the nature of the interactions between the two, even if such influence is limited to perceptual experience and leaves a significant bit of perception functionally encapsulated. All the views discussed here, however, have problems and it might turn out that none of them can establish a clear-cut distinction between perception and cognition. Even more radically, it might be the case that establishing such a clear-cut distinction is impossible and that the *continuity view* is the true account of mental processing. If this were the case, should we then abandon the very idea of making sense of the interactions between the high-level mental processes of believing and desiring and the lower-level mental processes of sensory processing and perceptual experience? The answer to this question can still be negative if one has a way of distinguishing between different functional levels in a continuous processing system. In the next chapter, I address this problem and argue in favor of answering this question in the negative.

References

Aru, J., Rutiku, R., Wibral, M., Singer, W., & Melloni, L. (2016). Early effects of previous experience on conscious perception. *Neuroscience of Consciousness*, niw004–10.

Ayer, A. J. (1940). *The foundations of empirical knowledge*. London: Macmillan.

Carruthers, P. (2000). *Phenomenal consciousness: A naturalistic theory*. Cambridge: Cambridge University Press.

Chalmers, D. J. (1996). The conscious mind. In *Search of a fundamental theory*. Oxford: Oxford University Press.

Colombo, M. (2013). Explaining social norm compliance: A plea for neural representations. *Phenomenology and the Cognitive Sciences* (online first).

Colombo, M. (2014). Neural representationalism, the hard problem of content and vitiated verdicts. A reply to Hutto and Myin (2013). *Phenomenology and the Cognitive Sciences, 13*(2), 257–274.

Crane, T. (2005). What is the problem of perception? *Synthesis Philosophica, 20*, 237–264.

Dehaene, S., & Naccache, L. (2000). Towards a cognitive neuroscience of consciousness: Basic evidence and a workspace framework. *Cognition, 79*(1), 1–37.

Dennett, D. C. (1987). *The intentional stance*. Cambridge, MA: MIT Press.

Dretske, F. I. (1981). *Knowledge and the flow of information*. Cambridge, MA: MIT Press.

Egan, F. (2014). How to think about mental content. *Philosophical Studies, 170*(1), 115–135.

Fodor, J. A. (1983). *The modularity of mind*. Cambridge, MA: MIT Press.

Gettier, E. L. (1963). Is justified true belief knowledge? *Analysis, 23*, 121–123.

Jackendoff, R. (1987). *Consciousness and the computational mind*. Cambridge, MA: MIT Press.

Lamme, V. A. F. (2003). Why visual attention and awareness are different. *Trends in Cognitive Sciences, 7*(1), 12–18.

Lamme, V. A. F. (2005). Independent neural definitions of visual awareness and attention. In A. Raftopoulos (Ed.), *Cognitive penetrability of perception: Attention, action, strategies, and bottom-up constraints* (pp. 171–191). New York: Nova Science Publishers.

Lamme, V. A. F. (2000). Neural mechanisms of visual awareness: A linking proposition. *Brain and Mind, 1*, 385–406.

Lamme, V. A. F., & Roelfsema, P. R. (2000). The distinct modes of vision offered by feedforward and recurrent processing. *Trends in Neuroscience, 23*, 571–579.

Lashley, K. S. (1929). *Brain mechanisms and intelligence: A quantitative study of injury to the brain*. Chicago: University of Chicago Press.

Marchi, F., & Newen, A. (2016). The cognitive foundations of visual consciousness: Why should we favour a processing approach? *Phenomenology and the Cognitive Sciences, 15*, 247–264.

McCauley, R. N., & Henrich, J. (2006). Susceptibility to the Müller-Lyer illusion, theory-neutral observation, and the diachronic penetrability of the visual input system. *Philosophical Psychology, 19*(1), 79–101.

Nagel, T. (1974). What is it like to be a bat? *The Philosophical Review, 83*(4), 435–450.

Newen, A., & Vetter, P. (2017). Why cognitive penetration of our perceptual experience is still the most plausible account. *Consciousness and Cognition, 47*, 26–37.

Piccinini, G. (2004). Functionalism, computationalism, and mental contents. *Canadian Journal of Philosophy, 34*(3), 375–410.

Prinz, J. J. (2012). *The conscious brain: How attention engenders experience*. New York: Oxford University Press.

Pylyshyn, Z. W. (1999). Is vision continuous with cognition? The case for cognitive impenetrability of visual perception. *Behavioral and Brain Sciences, 22*(3), 341–365.

Raftopoulos, A. (2009). *Cognition and perception: How do psychology and neural science inform philosophy?* Cambridge, MA: MIT Press.

Raftopoulos, A., & Zeimbekis, J. (Eds.). (2015). *The cognitive penetrability of perception: New philosophical perspectives*. New York: Oxford University Press.

Searle, J. (2015). *Seeing things as they are*. Oxford: Oxford University Press.

Shannon, C. E. (1948). A mathematical theory of communication. *Bell System Technical Journal, 27*, 379–423.

Shea, N., Godfrey-Smith, P., & Cao, R. (2018). Content in simple signalling systems. *The British Journal for the Philosophy of Science, 69*(4), 1009–1035.

Stokes, D. (2015). Towards a consequentialist understanding of cognitive penetration. In J. Zeimbekis & A. Raftopoulos (Eds.), *The cognitive penetrability of perception: New philosophical perspectives* (pp. 75–100). New York: Oxford University Press.

Chapter 2
The Cognitive Processing Hierarchy

Abstract In this chapter, I discuss how perception and cognition can be kept apart even in continuous processing systems. Section 2.1 discusses the desiderata of a gradualist approach to the mind, where there is no sharp distinction between perception and cognition. Section 2.2 is dedicated to the question of whether it is possible to keep perception and cognition apart in systems where the processing architecture is continuous and there is no strict distinction in representational format between different stages of processing. I propose a positive answer based on the spatiotemporal resolution of representations in the system. In Sect. 2.3, the resolution criterion is sharpened to capture the adequate resolutions for perception and cognition by the introduction of basic actions as an element of the criterion. The upshot of this chapter is that it seems possible to draw a sensible distinction between perception and cognition in systems with different processing architectures. This opens up the possibility of asking questions about the interaction of the two, and, specifically, about the cognitive penetrability of perception and perceptual experience, in a wider range of models of the mind.

2.1 A Gradualist Approach to Cognition

Suppose that the *continuity view* is true and that there is no difference in representational format or encapsulation between processes that take place in different parts of the mind. The *continuity view* implies that processes throughout the system are similar in the way they encode information. Following a Dretskean terminology, one might have a *digital theory* according to which all mental processes encode information in digital format. If one associates the digital format with a conceptual format, then conceptualist theories of perception (e.g. McDowell 1996) might be considered theories of this kind. Otherwise, one might propose an *analog theory* of the mind according to which the only representational format for mental processes is the analog format. Barsalou (1999) proposes that even higher-level conceptual processing involves simulations of sensory-like states and, as such, his perceptual-symbols theory could be considered as an analog theory. Both views might have their appeal and drawbacks, but regardless of which theory one subscribes to, they share the *continuity view*. Nevertheless, if either of these types of theories aspire to

© Springer Nature Switzerland AG 2020
F. Marchi, *The Attentional Shaping of Perceptual Experience*, Studies in Brain and Mind 16, https://doi.org/10.1007/978-3-030-33558-8_2

a degree of plausibility, they must not give up the possibility to account for a degree of functional specification and differentiation of mental processes.

Raftopoulos and Zeimbekis (2015) comment that no one would be tempted by a position that denies any functional hierarchy in the brain. They write:

> *Interactionists, who emphasize the existence of feedback from areas activated later by incoming information to areas which were activated earlier, do not deny that cognition has a functional cognitive hierarchy [...] As Peterson (2005: 189) describes them, 'these models maintain a hierarchical structure in that lower-level processes must at least be initiated before higher-level processes are initiated'.* (Raftopoulos and Zeimbekis 2015, p. 24)

The temporal criterion supposedly adopted by the interactionists, according to Raftopoulos and Zeimbekis, is one way to functionally differentiate among processes that are similar in other respects. A different and perhaps complementary approach is to characterize the functional hierarchy on the basis of architectural and biological differences in the vehicles that realize certain functionally specific mental processes.

Regardless of the criterion, what is important is that such a criterion must be in place. Dretske would also agree that there must be functional differentiations among mental processes within the same analog or digital domain. To claim the contrary would amount to the impossibility of accounting for a considerable set of functionally selective mental impairments as, for example, *akinetopsia,* i.e. the inability to perceive motion (Zeki 1991), *achromatopsia,* i.e. the inability to perceive colors (Remmer et al. 2015), and *visual agnosia,* i.e. the inability to recognize an object's identity (Alvarez and Masjuan 2016).[1] Furthermore, it is in principle possible to establish double dissociations between such selective functional impairments. Double dissociation between function A and function B requires that damage to a cortical area impairs A leaving B untouched, and damage to a different cortical area impairs B while leaving A untouched. Double dissociation is a widely adopted and potentially very useful tool to localize brain function.[2] However, if a criterion for functional specialization is absent from a theory of mental architecture, it is difficult to see how such a theory could account for selective impairments and double dissociations. Even more radically, a view that rejects any functional differentiation could fall short of accounting for the very difference between sensory modalities.

The upshot of the previous discussion is that any plausible version of the *continuity view* must not give up the idea of a functional hierarchy of processes. However, one needs to provide a reliable criterion for differentiating among functionally distinct processes in the continuous hierarchy. In what follows, I propose one such criterion. Once refined, the criterion will allow me to trace a line between perception

---

[1] For a general overview of these and further selective functional impairments, see Stashef and Barton (2001); Barton (2011); Martinaud (2017).

[2] For a discussion of the merits and limits of inferences from double dissociations to function, see Dunn and Kirsner (2003).

and cognition in a way that supports the possibility of the latter influencing the former as per the *cognitive penetrability* hypothesis.[3]

Mental processes can be conceived as articulated into a layered hierarchy of several levels. Levels may be individuated on the basis of their spatial, temporal, and functional properties, which may be characterized independently of the format in which they encode information. Levels that preform quick and highly context-sensitive functions, such as encoding of basic sensory features, are usually thought to be on the lower/earlier end of the hierarchy. Levels that perform more abstract and general functions, such as memory and language comprehension, are considered to be on the higher/later end of the hierarchy.

Early levels can be conceived of as levels in each sensory modality that are in close spatiotemporal proximity to sensory detectors and encode sensory properties such as shape and colors for vision, pitch for audition, texture for touch, and so on. Information encoded in such subsystems will, of course, change quickly and dramatically with rather subtle changes in sensory stimulation. Late levels that encode more abstract and general information are not as prone to change quickly and dramatically along with changes in sensory stimulation. The underlying idea here is that processes and states of the system at different levels of the hierarchy have different spatiotemporal sensitivity to changes in the environment.

Given the idea that different levels of the hierarchy have different spatiotemporal sensitivity, one can determine whether mental processes that are implemented by different levels are to be considered as *perceptual* or *cognitive* by adopting the following *sensitivity criterion* (SC):

> **SC:** Perception comprises processing levels that are sensitive to subtle changes in the sensory properties of the environment in a way that makes their operations quickly and radically affected by such changes. Cognitive levels are those that do not have such sensitivity.

According to SC, if I look at a red triangle and then I shift my gaze toward a blue square the operations of levels that encode shape and color are quickly and radically affected by the environmental change of gaze shift, which qualifies them as perceptual. Conversely, the operations of levels that encode my general beliefs about triangles and squares, e.g. that the former may only have one angle of 90° while the latter always have four, will not be affected in any way by such changes, which makes them cognitive. Furthermore, an important feature of SC is that it allows to distinguish between perceptual and cognitive processes, and the corresponding levels, regardless of whether those states and levels are described in terms of folk psychological notions (e.g. beliefs, desires, conscious experiences, etc.), functionally (e.g. the subsystems devoted to the processing of colors, shapes, motion) or neuro-anatomically (e.g. LGN, V3, V4/MT, etc.).

---

[3] As will become clear in Chap. 3, I favor the predictive processing (PP) approach to the mind, which belongs to the *continuity view*. The criterion proposed in this section is supposed to apply to the PP approach as well and will be recast in the appropriate terminology later in the book.

Of course, SC is an extremely simplified criterion and there are many exceptions to the straightforward distinctions that it establishes. For example, if my belief that there is a laptop on my desk is based entirely on my current sensory access to the laptop, for example by means of vision and touch, then I would be prone to change my belief quickly and dramatically if the laptop were to suddenly disappear into nothingness. In this scenario, my belief is subject to a quick and radical change along with the change in the sensory properties of the environment and the subsystem that encodes the belief would be qualified as perceptual according to SC. However, even in this case I might hold on to my belief and think that I'm under some kind of illusion, and that the laptop is still on my desk even if I no longer have sensory access to it. This shows that belief-like information encoded at some (cognitive) levels could still be less prone to changes than information about the sensory properties of the environment encoded at other (perceptual) levels. The case just described concerns a particular kind of mental states that we may call perceptual beliefs. Given the different results that evaluating them with SC can deliver, perceptual beliefs can be considered borderline cases between perception and cognition. Thus, SC may be too coarse-grained to adequately distinguish between perceptual and cognitive levels.

If the *continuity view* is correct and we still want to distinguish between levels of processing and, in addition, carve a distinction between perception and cognition, we need to introduce a more fine-grained criterion that allows for clear identification of perceptual and cognitive processes. Such criterion should still allow that such processes are of the same kind, e.g. encode information in the same format, and the difference between them is quantitative and not qualitative.

2.2   An Alternative to a Clear-Cut Distinction: The Resolution Criterion

A representational mental processing system is supposed to represent regularities in the world.[4] Such *worldly regularities* may be objects, properties, events, relations, etc. Worldly regularities persist and change at very different rates and different regularities have a different spatiotemporal resolution. For example, a bee's wing-flap is a regularity that changes at a much faster spatiotemporal scale than, say, the Earth's revolution movement around the sun. The concept of "worldly regularity" is meant

---

[4]Since some worldly regularities are the typical causes of the system's sensory stimulation, one may call them *causal regularities* (Hohwy 2013). To clarify a possible misunderstanding, such terminology is not supposed to limit the notion of representation to representation of causal relations (e.g. the *representation relation* between represented objects and representing processes). While this is a possible case of representation, since a causal relation is itself a regularity that the system can track, the notion of *causal regularity*, and by extension the notion of representation, is wider and usually applies to the *relata* of the causal relation. Indeed, the system can track not only regularities in the world, but also its own processes, and the relation between the two.

to highlight the spatiotemporal nature of the represented object, property or event, and, consequently, the spatiotemporal nature of the *representation*, i.e. the process or state in the system that represents the regularity.

Among all worldly regularities there is a set of regularities that the human processing system is more attuned to on the basis of the nature of its sensory detectors and, thus, of its phylogenetic history. However, our processing system can, in principle, represent all sorts of regularities either directly or derivatively. To illustrate, we are typically pretty good at detecting shapes and colors, sounds, flavors, textures, and smells. We are not so good at detecting the bacterial populations that live on a given surface or the molecules of which a given object is composed. We could, however, detect and subsequently represent those tiny objects, properties, and events by means of a sufficiently powerful microscope.

Shapes, colors, bacteria, and molecules are all regularities that exist at different spatiotemporal resolutions in the world. Those things, however, do not exhaust the set of worldly regularities that our processing system can represent. Even within the same sensory modality there may be differences between the regularities that can be represented by the system at different levels of the hierarchy. Within vision, for example, a process that tracks and represents the slow falling of a leaf from a tree has a different spatiotemporal resolution than a process that tracks and represents the shape of the leaf or the variations in wavelength distributions of the light reflected by the leaf's surface.

Very slow and stable worldly regularities can also be represented in the system. Although one cannot visually or haptically detect Earth's revolution movement, one can believe that this is the case. Information about the revolution movement is processed and stored somewhere in the system. Here, I limit my discussion to regularities that can be normally represented in experience. Earth's revolution movement is one such regularity because, even if it may be contingently excluded from a subject's experience in ordinary contexts, it is not so excluded in principle. The exclusion may be overcome by transducing the regularity at a different resolution, for example with the help of instruments (see above). The same cannot be done in the case of non-existing entities or entities that are believed to exist on grounds that are in principle different from experience, for example as a matter of faith. There are no instruments that allow us to transduce such "regularities" at the adequate spatiotemporal resolution, and thereby have experiential access to them.

According to the present discussion, our processing system is capable of representing worldly regularities at very different spatiotemporal timescales. Given the difference in the spatiotemporal resolution of the things represented, it is unsurprising that the representations themselves have their own spatiotemporal resolution. For example, when seeing an object from different perspectives the representations of some of its properties vary, e.g. its looking oblong or circular, while the representations of some of its other properties remain stable, e.g. its being a bottle. This reflects the idea of a spatiotemporal sensitivity of representations introduced in the previous section.

In this picture, however, the relevant difference between mental processes is a difference in their spatiotemporal resolution and not a difference in the kind of processes they are, in the format in which they encode information, in the latency at which they occur in the system, and/or in their encapsulated nature. In this framework, it is possible to devise a hierarchy of mental processes on the basis of their spatiotemporal resolution. We can, thus, introduce the following *resolution criterion* (RC) to distinguish between processes in the hierarchy, without positing a difference in informational formats or other features that could define a separate kind of mental processes:

> **RC:** Mental processes that represent worldly regularities at different spatiotemporal resolutions have different positions and functional roles in the mental processing hierarchy.

RC allows us to understand how processes of the same kind can nevertheless be distinct and have a different position and role in a processing hierarchy. Furthermore, it can be used to explain why processes in a continuous system can be functionally distinct and constitute a hierarchy in the first place. However, RC, by itself, does not allow for tracing a reasonable line between processes that belong to perception and processes that belong to cognition. In other words, RC does not presuppose a functional differentiation between processes in the hierarchy. Rather, it establishes such a differentiation, and yet it lacks the resources to draw a principled distinction between processes that may be labeled "perceptual" and processes that may be labeled "cognitive".

At this point, one might be tempted to combine RC with SC and simply say that among representations of worldly regularities in the system, some are more sensitive to subtle environmental changes than others and these are the regularities that are represented in perception. However, to say that certain changes in the environment may affect some regularities and not others, without specifying how high the resolution of perceptual representations is supposed to be, is too blurry a criterion. The question that arises is the following: how can one pinpoint the spatiotemporal resolution of the relevant environmental changes and, consequently, the sensitivity of representations affected by them? I try to answer this question in the next section.

2.3   Perception Has the Spatiotemporal Resolution of Action

I concluded the previous section with the question of how to identify the adequate spatiotemporal resolution for perception. I now attempt to offer an answer. Processing information about the world that is conveyed by sensory organs is not the only way in which a subject can access the world and relate to it. To behave efficiently in an environment detecting objects and properties of the environment through the senses is as important as interpreting sensory information in the light of our background information. This is the task of the processing system as we have described it so far. Equally important, however, is the possibility of acting in the environment, a task that involves the whole subject. In this section, I argue that *action* and, in particular, *basic action* is the key to understanding the spatiotemporal resolution of perception.

Before proceeding further, I provide some elucidations on the notion of action that I adopt here. For the purpose of my argument, I do not need to delve into specific theories of action. Rather, I employ a broad notion of action with some minimal constraint. Among all possible activities of an agent, the kind of actions that I am interested in are all activities that are *overt* and *controlled*. For an action to be *overt*, it must be performed in such a way that another observer could, in principle, detect it. This constraint is only aimed at excluding mental actions, assuming that such actions are genuine actions, from those relevant for the present discussion. The notion of *controlled* action is a notion that I want to characterize intuitively. Wilson and Shpall (2012) write:

> It is also important [...] that agents normally implement a direct control or guidance over their own behavior. An agent may guide her paralyzed left arm along a certain path by using her active right arm to shove it through the relevant trajectory. The moving of her right arm, activated as it is by the normal exercise of her system of motor control, is a genuine action, but the movement of her left arm is not. (Wilson and Shpall 2012, p. 6)

Of course, the matters of how to characterize the implementation of control over an action and the related concept of goal-directedness are very complex. Here, I do not wish to enter into such a debate and I minimally characterize the idea as follows: for an action to be *controlled*, the agent must in general be capable of directly initiating, stopping, and modifying the course of that action. In the case of one limb moving the other, an agent can initiate, control, and modify the action to a certain degree. However, the degree of control a subject exerts on the impaired limb of my example is by no means direct, insofar as it requires the mediation of the other limb.

A further point that is crucial for the present discussion is that, in what follows, I limit the set of relevant actions to *basic actions*. Basic actions are immediate and relatively short-term actions like grasping, kicking, taking a step, etc. In general, basic actions are typically thought to be actions that do not have other actions as their antecedents or components (Chisholm 1964; Stoutland 1968; Danto 1973; Sandis 2010). For my purposes, it is not required to provide very specific criteria to identify which actions count as basic actions. It suffices that a distinction can be maintained between an action such as "taking a sip from the coffee mug", which can be considered a *basic action*, and an action such as "preparing the coffee", which can be considered a complex action since it involves many other actions such as pouring water, opening the coffee can, etc. Nevertheless, one way to sharpen the distinction is to relate basic and complex actions to motor and prior intentions respectively (Pacherie 2000). Basic actions are those that may (but need not) have only motor intentions as their antecedents or causes. Complex actions are those that necessarily require prior intentions.

One important thing to note is that overt and controlled basic actions have their own range of spatiotemporal resolutions. It is possible that the spatiotemporal resolution of basic action spans from the few hundred milliseconds of a saccade[5] to the several seconds of a *tai-chi* movement. What is most relevant for my purpose here

---

[5] This is intended as a borderline case as it is debatable whether saccades count as actions at all.

is that an agent can perform overt and directly controlled basic actions that affect some of the system's representations about regularities in the world, but not others. For example, one might grasp an object, walk in a certain direction and turn one's head or shift one's gaze around. All these actions determine the way in which information about certain worldly regularities is conveyed to the system through the sensory organs.

Turning the head and shifting the gaze determine what objects and surfaces reflect light toward the agent's retina and from what angle the light is reflected. Picking up an object changes its position in the environment, while walking around changes the absolute position of the agent and the relative position of some object with respect to the agent. Similarly, we can also change the shape or color of an object. For the representing system, this means that by the performance of a basic actions, some of the representations in the system will change, while others will remain stable. A paradigmatic example is picking up an object and rotating it in one's hand, thereby looking at it from different visual perspectives. While the representation of the apparent shape of the object will change at any moment due to the rotations, the representation of the object as a member of a certain category of objects, e.g. that of bottles, will not change. Since basic actions have their own spatiotemporal resolution and some representations in the system are affected by the performance of a basic action, it follows that some representations in the system share the spatiotemporal resolution of basic actions. Following these considerations, I can add to the previously introduced *resolution criterion* (RC) the further ingredient that it needs to pinpoint the adequate resolution of perception. I call the new criterion the *action-resolution criterion* (ARC):

ARC: Mental processes that represent worldly regularities at different spatiotemporal resolutions have different positions and functional roles in the mental processing hierarchy. Perception comprises representations of regularities whose spatiotemporal resolution overlaps with the resolution of overt and controlled basic action. Cognition comprises representations of regularities at a lower spatiotemporal resolution than overt and controlled basic action.

Importantly, by including the notion of overlapping resolution in the definition it is implied that basic actions are not themselves perceptual states. Rather, basic actions occur at certain spatiotemporal resolutions, which can be used to individuate a set of perceptual representations that are affected by their performance by an agent. If the system represents regularities about shapes and colors, then according to ARC the processes that represent those regularities are part of *perception*, because we can perform basic actions that affect representations of colors and shapes. Conversely, *cognition* comprises all those regularities that are represented by the system and whose resolution is lower than that of basic action. If the system represents Earth's revolution or the passing of seasons, such representations are cognitive according to ARC because they will not change with the performance of any basic action, meaning that their spatiotemporal resolution is lower.

There are two important aspects in the definition of ARC. The first is captured by the notion of direct control, which highlights that the kind of *action* that is relevant for ARC involves a subjective feeling of agency. The second is that by limiting the discussion to *basic actions*, I ensure that the relevant actions are relatively short term and, as such, they may typically have a more reliable outcome, for there is less temporal room for interfering factors. These criteria are used to sharpen the notion of *action* that is used here to define the spatiotemporal resolution of perception.

To find out some of the regularities that can be represented by the processing system is a matter of empirical discovery and depends on contingent constraints about the system's structure and substrate. For example, we may accept that the human processing system represents shapes and colors because we discovered that there are components of the system (neuronal subsystems) that are selectively sensitive to such features. On the other hand, we can find out that the system represents regularities such as Earth's revolution and the passing of the seasons by reflecting on the fact that we can have beliefs and expectations about such regularities.

Now, while such examples are easy to accommodate using ARC, other cases are much more difficult to settle. An object's shape is a worldly regularity that has a spatiotemporal resolution which is very different from the resolution of Earth's revolution movement. Nevertheless, one can see an object's shape and believe that an object has a certain shape. In other words, there are two processes in the system representing the same regularity. Wouldn't ARC predict that seeing an object's shape and believing that an object has a certain shape are both perceptual processes or, even more radically, one and the same process?

To see why this is not the case we must accept that seeing an object's shape and believing that an object has a certain shape are processes that require different representations at different spatiotemporal resolutions. Consider the following example: There is an object in front of me. I see its shape and I believe that it has a certain shape. I can examine the object and move around it. I can grasp it and I can close my eyes or turn my head, thus removing the object from my field of view. All these actions only affect one of the two representations of the object's shape in the system. As a result of each of these actions, I always end up seeing a slightly different relative shape which is reflected in both the retinal projection of the object and in phenomenology, while I never cease to believe that the object has one and the same overall shape, regardless of how I act upon it.

The matter should become clearer if we think that one process represents an agent relative and perspectival regularity, which we may call $shape_1$. This regularity depends on such things as the retinal projection of the object, i.e. its relative position and angle with respect to the agent. The other process represents a different regularity, $shape_2$, which is centered on the object, insensitive to the current subjective perspective and independent of the object's relative position and consequent retinal projection. Intuitively, since the immediate overt and controlled basic actions we can perform only alter $shape_1$ while leaving $shape_2$ untouched, this means that only $shape_1$ is at the adequate resolution for action and thus only the process that represents $shape_1$ is a perceptual process.

Furthermore, consider performing an action that actually changes the overall shape of an object. Counter to intuition, this action will only affect $shape_1$, i.e. the agent-centered perspectival regularity, without altering the belief that the object has a certain shape. The reason is that the temporal resolution of the representation of *shape$_2$*, i.e. the belief that the object has *shape$_2$* also covers past and future states of the object and, as such, is not as fine-grained in temporal resolution as the representation of *shape$_1$*. If this were not the case, we would not be able to say that the object is now deformed or misshapen, compared to a previous point in time. Of course, at the same time, one is able to form a new belief representing the object's new overall shape.

Thus, ARC succeeds in isolating high-level processes leading to representations that are not affected by performing overt and controlled basic actions. These processes are differentiated from those leading to representations which change once an overt and controlled basic action is performed. On this account, cognitive processes represent things that one may believe to exist and have certain properties or that one may desire to be the case and so on.

Here one might object that my cognitive representation "that an object x is in the box in front of me" can be affected by the direct and controlled basic action of looking in the box, which would be a counterexample to my claim. While this is certainly true, it is also true that the action does not change the cognitive representation directly. The change requires one or more intermediate representations, which are directly changed by the overt action of looking in the box. To see why, imagine that y is inside the box, when looking in the box a light trick is played to my eyes so that y appears exactly like x in my experience. If the basic action of looking in the box could directly change my belief, one would expect the belief to change regardless of the light trick. Yet, in this case the belief would not change. However, the state of seeing does change quite a bit, e.g. from looking *at* the box from the outside to looking *inside* the box and such changes depend on the external stimuli and lighting conditions. For example, I now see x inside an open box instead of seeing the outside of a closed box. Since a lot of representations about what is in front of me can be directly altered by overt and controlled actions, this means that those representations share their resolution with basic actions and are therefore perceptual representations according to ARC. Since my belief that x is in the box does not directly change as a consequence of a basic action, the process of believing that x is in the box does not have the adequate resolution for perception. It is therefore a cognitive process according to ARC. For the belief to change, one would need an intermediate perceptual representation in which y is represented as y and not as x. The change in belief would then be a consequence of the change in perceptual representation and in the experience. The change in the experience is directly brought about by basic action and the change in belief only indirectly.

Furthermore, ARC only determines which regularities are perceptual among those regularities that a processing system can represent or is currently representing. However, the human processing system is not designed to represent regularities at each and every spatiotemporal resolution. There might be regularities that the human processing system is in principle incapable of representing, due to the limitations of its sensory apparatus. Importantly, I do not claim that ARC is immune to further objections or that it works perfectly to distinguish between perception and cognition. However, I hold that it can be used as a preliminary example of a clearly determined distinction that works in a continuous processing system.

The examples discussed above introduce one of the main virtues of ARC. According to ARC, perceptual representations share the spatiotemporal resolution of overt and directly controlled basic action. On the other hand, the spatiotemporal resolution of overt and directly controlled basic action depends on the action possibilities of an organism, which, in turn, depend on the organism's kind of body and its phylogenetic history. Thus, if the action possibilities of the organism were to change, the set of spatiotemporal resolutions of action would also change and the organism would be capable of perceptually representing new worldly regularities. Similarly, different organisms with different action possibilities are predicted to perceive worldly regularities at different spatiotemporal resolutions. Thus, one important feature of ARC is that it poses no principled boundaries on which processes in the hierarchy can be perceptual or cognitive. Beings with a different evolutionary history can perform basic actions, overtly and in a controlled fashion, at very different spatiotemporal scales and, in this way, they can perceive and cognize different things from us, provided that their processing system is representing those things.

Before concluding this section, I would like to discuss why ARC is different from other positions that address the interaction between perception and action. It has been famously argued that in vision, perception and action are subserved by different neural pathways in the brain. Goodale and Milner (1992) distinguished a *ventral pathway* devoted to identifying the stimulus and associated with conscious visual experience from a *dorsal pathway* devoted to analyzing the stimulus position from an egocentric perspective and coordinating immediate action towards it. The evidence for the dissociation comes from various sources, but one of the most compelling pieces of evidence adduced by Goodale and Milner was the case of subject DF affected by visual agnosia. After suffering extensive brain damage, DF was incapable of consciously recognizing the size, shape, and orientation of objects while retaining significant capacities to perform actions concerning the same objects. For example, the subject could estimate their size by the width of the gap between her index finger and thumb.

The philosophical significance of the dissociation (or lack thereof) between the two visual pathways has been highlighted by several authors. Ferretti (2016) argues for a fine-grained and compositional view of motor representations that allows them to emerge as complex representations built up from representational sub-components resulting from the interactions between the two pathways. This novel view solves several problems lurking in the philosophical literature aiming to characterize the function that motor representations are supposed to perform. Zipoli Caiani and Ferretti (2016) extend the "interactionist" approach to representation of action possibilities (or affordances), offering an extensive critical review of evidence both in favor of and against the dissociation between the pathways, concluding that:

> Evidence of a massive inter-stream interaction between the dorsal and ventral paths suggests that we should resist the temptation to conceive the process of detecting sensorimotor patterns and the process of selecting motor plans for action as two reciprocally independent tasks. In particular, the influence of the agent's semantic intentions and purposes on action

perception and guidance is not confined to higher planning levels alone, but rather extends
to the low-level stages of sensorimotor processing. (Zipoli Caiani and Ferretti 2016, p. 51)

Brogaard (2012) highlights that the original interpretation of Goodale and Milner, according to which egocentric properties are processed in the dorsal stream, which does not contribute to conscious experience, is at odds with the widespread intuition that mental states that inherit their content from visual experience represent egocentric properties. Brogaard argues that instead of giving up the intuition, we should reject the tenet of some standard construction of the dual pathway hypotheses that dorsal processing does not contribute in any way to ventral conscious representations. In a similar spirit, Briscoe (2008, 2009) argues that the contents of visual experience include 3d-egocentric space, which proponents of the two pathways hypothesis associate with the processing of the dorsal stream, and that this spatial information represented in experience contributes to motor planning (Briscoe and Schwenkler 2015).

A strict dissociation has also been called into question on purely empirical grounds and evidence has been accumulated for a close interaction between the two pathways, while evidence of a strict separation has been shown to be refuted or to offer only limited support. Schenk and McIntosh (2010) review and critically discuss much of the empirical evidence in favor of a strict anatomical and functional separation of the two pathways. One example is the prediction made in the original model that delayed actions should decrease in quality due to the fast decaying of visuomotor representation in the dorsal stream. The claim is that while online action is guided by the dorsal stream, delayed action can only be guided by the ventral stream as the dorsal stream's processing cannot rely on information stored in memory (Westwood and Goodale 2003). However, Schenk and McIntosh argue that reduced precision and kinematic changes in delayed actions are compatible with a single visual representation that decays over time in a similar way to many other memory-based tasks. Furthermore, they discuss evidence for the involvement of the dorsal processing in delayed action, supporting the view that the two pathways interact rather than substituting one another. On the basis of similar considerations for other claims present in the original model about the strict functional separation between the two pathways, Schenk and McIntosh conclude that "[v]isual functions of any significant complexity are likely to involve collaboration between the two visual streams, and other brain systems" (2010, p. 62).

Summing up, it has been suggested that, on the one hand, each stream can contribute, with respect to the context and the task, to the specific functional operations that were originally taken as being mainly subserved by the other one, as it is possible to have different kinds of interaction between the streams. This suggests that, at least in healthy individuals, it is very hard to isolate dorsal and ventral processing when it comes to complex visual tasks. Yet, on the other hand, this is not in conflict with the fact that, from a computational point of view, when studied in isolation, each stream has its particular functional, computational specialization (for a recent philosophical review, see Ferretti 2017).

Regardless of the reality and extent of the actual dissociation between the two pathways, ARC is not committed to the view that perception and action are realized by the very same substrate. As I have argued, the resolution of a given mental process determines its position and function in the processing hierarchy, but the hierarchy may include architectural constraints that distinguish between processes at the same resolution. For example, there could be auditory representations at the same spatiotemporal resolution as visual representations, and yet they may differ at the level of implementation and localization in the brain. Likewise, the neural implementation of the processes subserving action can be different from the neural substrate of vision and the other sensory modalities. The claim that follows from ARC is rather that whatever the neural implementation of motor control, vision, and the other sensory modalities, the eventual overlap between the spatiotemporal resolution of the processes underlying action and the processes underlying vision, etc. determines the scope of perception.

A separate discussion is due for theoretical approaches that tie together perception and action or even consider them to be one and the same. Here I will be mainly concerned with the embodied and enactive approaches to cognition. I do not refer to any specific view within these approaches and I only offer some general considerations in order to see how ARC might share some similarities with them, but ultimately come up as a different view.

Since my view highlights the role of action in perception it is quite sympathetic towards moderate versions of the embodied and enactive approaches. In the picture I propose, the action possibilities of an organism determine the scope of its perceptual vs. cognitive states, which makes my position akin to some mild forms of enactivism. At the same time, organisms with different kinds of bodies will be endowed with different action possibilities at different spatiotemporal resolutions, which confers to my view traits of embodied approaches to perception. It follows that the set of spatiotemporal resolutions that processes in a system can perceptually represent depend on the action possibilities of the organism in which the system is embodied. Therefore, ARC is not only compatible with some versions of the enactive/embodied theory of perception, but it entails some degree of enaction/embodiment.

ARC entails that, if a system is given different action possibilities, the landscape of its perceptual and cognitive processes can change quite radically. One example of this case is the aforementioned employment of instruments that allow the system to represent regularities that are normally outside of the scope of a human perceptual system at the adequate spatiotemporal resolution. Using such instruments, however, does not change the resolutions of the system's perceptual representations; it merely allows the system to represent new things at that resolution.

Another example is that of sensory substitution (Bach-y-Rita and Kercel 2003). If a person has lost the capacity to see, for example due to a retinal impairment, it is sometimes possible to provide the subject with devices composed of a sensory detector, like a camera, and a sensory stimulator that transforms visual information into information pertaining to other sensory modalities. This is possible with at least auditory and haptic substitution. The result of endowing the subject with such a

device, called a human-machine interface (HMI), is that, after training, the subject
shows certain behavioral capacities associated with the lost modality:

> *Sensory substitution studies have demonstrated the capacity of the brain to adapt to infor-*
> *mation relayed from an artificial receptor via an auditory or tactile HMI* (human-machine
> interfaces). *With training and with motor control of the input by the subject, percepts are*
> *accurately identified and spatially located. Thus, blind persons obtain visual information*
> *resulting in visual percepts (e.g. of a ball rolling across a table) and can produce appropri-*
> *ate motor responses (e.g. catching the ball).* (Bach-y-Rita and Kercel 2003, p. 544)

Regardless of the claim on whether subjects using sensory substitution devices
have a proper perceptual experience of the same kind as the impaired sensory
modality, the important fact is that the HMI allow them to act in a new way that
changes some representations in the system which would otherwise remain
unchanged. According to ARC, the new basic action possibilities, like grasping the
ball, which were not available to them before, add a new layer to the perceptual and
cognitive landscape of those subjects. If one accepts that external devices can extend
the action possibilities of an organism and thereby alter the set of representations at
the adequate resolution that a system embodied in such an organism can form, there
is a sense in which ARC predicts the possibility of extended perception and
cognition.

As an objection, one might think that a possible radical consequence of ARC is
that an organism that is incapable of acting is also incapable of perceiving. I think
that ARC commits me to the truth of this thesis for systems that never had the disposition to act. In Sect. 1.2, I said that artificial systems that detect and process
sensory-like information could be said to perceive the world according to the preliminary notion of perception I introduced there. However, in the light of ARC, if
those systems are designed without any capability to perform basic actions on the
world, they cannot genuinely perceive it. But let us consider human patients suffering from the full locked-in syndrome.[6] Should these patients be deemed incapable
of perceiving the world according to ARC? Provided that their sensory apparatus is
still functioning normally, the answer to this question is clearly negative. The reason
is that even if they happen to lose all of their action possibilities, they developed as
organisms that had those action possibilities in the first place. In other words, representational systems that have the disposition to act and represent can perceive, even
if their action performance is contingently incapacitated. Thus, according to ARC,
perception and action are not one and the same thing, for it is not the case that in
order to perceive the world one must also act upon it at the same time.

Finally, I hold that perception and action can be kept apart because of their different functional roles determined by their direction of fit (Hohwy 2013) – which is
world to mind for action and mind to world for perception – and direction of causation (Searle 2015) – which is world to mind for perception and mind to world for
action. This distinguishes ARC from radical enactivist approaches that posit the

---

[6] The full locked-in syndrome is a condition by which a subject is conscious but incapable of any
movement, including facial and eye movements.

identification of perception and action. Radical enactivist positions are also incompatible with the view advocated here because they typically reject any form of representationalism and information-processing views of the mind (Hutto and Myin 2012; Hutto 2013).

2.4 Summary and Conclusion

In this chapter, I have discussed ways in which perception and cognition can be kept apart in a continuous mental processing hierarchy, where all processes encode information in the same format and there is no strictly encapsulated unit. I have proposed a *resolution criterion* that allows for distinguishing between different processing levels in a continuous hierarchy on the basis of the spatiotemporal resolution of representations in the system. Even if the resolution criterion permitted to maintain a hierarchy of levels, the problem arose as to which of the levels may be called perceptual and which cognitive. I have introduced overt and controlled basic action as a further element for pinpointing the adequate resolution for perception and, by contrast, for cognition. The ensuing *action-resolution criterion* is designed as an example that is supposed to show how to construct a functional hierarchy and draw a line between perception and cognition even in a continuous model of the architecture of the mind. Having established that a line between perception and cognition can be drawn, it makes sense to ask questions about their interactions. In the next chapter, I discuss such interactions under the *cognitive penetrability* hypothesis.

References

Alvarez, R., & Masjuan, J. (2016). *Revista Clinica Española, 216*(2), 85–91.

Bach-y-Rita, P., & Kercel, S. W. (2003). Sensory substitution and the human-machine interface. *Trends in Cognitive Sciences, 7*(12), 541–546.

Barsalou, L. W. (1999). Perceptual symbol systems. *Behavioral and Brain Sciences, 22*(4), 577–660.

Barton, J. (2011). Disorder of higher visual processing. In C. Kennard & J. Leigh (Eds.), *Handbook of clinical neurology* (Vol. 102). Amsterdam: Elsevier.

Briscoe, R. (2008). Another look at the two visual systems hypothesis: The argument from illusion studies. *Journal of Consciousness Studies, 15*(8), 35–62.

Briscoe, R. (2009). Egocentric spatial representation in action and perception. *Philosophy and Phenomenological Research, 79*, 423–460.

Briscoe, R., & Schwenkler, J. (2015). Conscious vision in action. *Cognitive Science, 39*(7), 1435–1467.

Brogaard, B. (2012). Vision for action and the contents of perception. *The Journal of Philosophy, 109*(10), 569–587.

Chisholm, R. M. (1964). The descriptive element in the concept of action. *Journal of Philosophy, 90*, 613–624.

Danto, A. C. (1973). *Analytic philosophy of action.* Cambridge: Cambridge University Press.

Dunn, J., & Kirsner, K. (2003). What can we infer from double dissociations? *Cortex: A Journal Devoted to the Study of the Nervous System and Behavior, 39*(1), 1–7.

Ferretti, G. (2016). Through the forest of motor representations. *Consciousness and Cognition, 43*, 177–196.

Ferretti, G. (2017). Two visual systems in Molyneux subjects. *Phenomenology and the Cognitive Sciences, 17*(4), 643–679.

Goodale, M. A., & Milner, A. D. (1992). Separate visual pathways for perception and action. *Trends in Neurosciences, 15*(1), 20–25.

Hohwy, J. (2013). *The predictive mind.* Oxford: Oxford University Press.

Hutto, D. (2013). Exorcising action oriented representations: Ridding cognitive science of its Nazgûl. *Adaptive Behavior, 21*(3), 142–150.

Hutto, D. D., & Myin, E. (2012). *Radicalizing enactivism.* Cambridge, MA: MIT Press.

Martinaud, O. (2017). Visual agnosia and focal brain injury. *Revue Neurologique, 173*(7–8), 451–460.

McDowell, J. (1996). *Mind and world.* Cambridge, MA: Harvard University Press.

Pacherie, E. (2000). The content of intentions. *Mind & Language, 15*(4), 400–432.

Peterson, M. (2005). Object perception. In B. Goldstein (Ed.), *The Blackwell handbook of sensation and perception* (pp. 168–203). Oxford: Blackwell.

Raftopoulos, A., & Zeimbekis, J. (Eds.). (2015). *The cognitive penetrability of perception: New philosophical perspectives.* New York: Oxford University Press.

Remmer, M., Rastogi, N., Ranka, M., & Ceisler, E. (2015). Achromatopsia: A review. *Current Opinion in Ophthalmology, 26*(5), 333–340.

Sandis, C. (2010). Basic actions and individuation. In T. O'Connor & C. Sandis (Eds.), *A companion to the philosophy of action* (pp. 10–17). Oxford: Wiley-Blackwell.

Schenk, T., & McIntosh, R. D. (2010). Do we have independent visual streams for perception and action? *Cognitive Neuroscience, 1*(1), 52–62.

Searle, J. (2015). *Seeing things as they are.* Oxford: Oxford University Press.

Stashef, S., & Barton, J. (2001). Deficits in cortical visual function. *Ophthalmology Clinics of North America, 14*(1), 217–242.

Stoutland, F. (1968). Basic actions and causality. *Journal of Philosophy, 65*(16), 467–475.

Westwood, D. A., & Goodale, M. A. (2003). Perceptual illusion and the real-time control of action. *Spatial Vision, 16*, 243–254.

Wilson, G., & Shpall, S. (2012). Action. In E. N. Zalta (ed.), *The Stanford encyclopedia of philosophy* (Winter 2016 Edition). https://plato.stanford.edu/archives/win2016/entries/action/

Zeki, S. (1991). Cerebral akinetopsia (visual motion blindness). A review. *Brain, 114*(2), 811–824.

Zipoli Caiani, S., & Ferretti, G. (2016). Semantic and pragmatic integration in vision for action. *Consciousness and Cognition, 48*, 40–54.

Chapter 3
The Cognitive Penetrability of Perceptual Experience

Abstract In this chapter, I present the *cognitive penetrability* hypothesis in full detail. In Sect. 3.1, I offer an historical contextualization of the discussion of top-down effects of cognition on perception, of which *cognitive penetrability* is a special case. I discuss some of the most relevant objections to the occurrence of such effects and elucidate why the issue of whether *cognitive penetrability* occurs is considered a very pressing one in cognitive science. In Sect. 3.2, I present the recent developments of the *cognitive penetrability* debate. I narrow down four definitions of *cognitive penetrability* that are traceable to the most recent literature and reflect different aspects of the phenomenon that should not be conflated. In Sect. 3.3, I present some of the evidence that has been proposed to support the *cognitive penetrability* hypothesis.

3.1 The Influence of Cognition on Perceptual Experience

As a first step into the debate about cognitive penetrability it should be noted that there are two issues at stake. One issue concerns the cognitive penetrability of perceptual processing. Where perceptual processing is thought to be carried out by a specialized functional unit, which is separated from other parts of the system by means, for example, of positing a proprietary format for the representations it computes (see previous chapter), it makes sense to ask whether such a specialized functional unit is informationally encapsulated from the rest of the system and what the consequences of a failure of encapsulation might be. A separate issue concerns the cognitive penetrability of perceptual experience, where perceptual experience refers to the phenomenal feeling of what it's like to see, hear, touch, smell or taste something. The two issues are related by questions about how perceptual experience is related to perceptual processing; for example, one might ask whether the outputs of an early visual module as conceived by Pylyshyn are complex enough to fully underlie the contents of perceptual experience. In any regard, one kind of cognitive penetrability does not imply the other. Cognitive penetrability of perceptual experience requires that experience can be influenced by cognitive states such as beliefs and desires, independently of the details of the underlying processing.

In the course of this chapter I will mainly focus on the cognitive penetrability of perceptual experience, although I discuss penetrability of perceptual processing in

© Springer Nature Switzerland AG 2020
F. Marchi, *The Attentional Shaping of Perceptual Experience*, Studies in Brain and Mind 16, https://doi.org/10.1007/978-3-030-33558-8_3

the following section. The reason is that the majority of the evidence presented and discussed in the literature involves behavioral tasks that are supposed to assess whether something changes in a subject's perceptual, and specifically visual, experience as a result of the manipulation of the subject's background beliefs or other cognitive states, while holding other conditions fixed. However, I rely on the notions of "cognitive hierarchy" and "processing" to illustrate one of the central focal points of the debate on so-called *top-down* effects.

In the previous chapter, I established that a processing hierarchy and a distinction between perception and cognition could be defined even in systems whose processes at all levels of the hierarchy are of the same kind. Many cognitive scientists think of the mind as structured in a vertically organized hierarchy of processing subsystems. At the bottom of the hierarchy, one finds subsystems that are, in general, temporally active early on, specific for each sensory modality, and in the spatial vicinity of sensory detectors. At the top of the hierarchy, one finds subsystems that are, in general, active later on and multimodal or a-modal. This simple sketch suffices to introduce the important notions of *top-down* and *bottom-up* processing. The former refers to processing that runs from lower to higher subsystems and the latter refers to processing that runs in the opposite direction. Both forms of processing are ubiquitous in the brain.[1] Cognitive states are typically associated with higher-level processing while perceptual processes and perceptual experience are typically associated with lower-level processing. Such an association can be spelled out in terms of the criteria for distinguishing perception and cognition. As we have seen, these include proprietary analog vs. digital format (Dretske 1981), informational encapsulation vs. domain general informational access (Pylyshyn 1999), temporal priority (Raftopoulos 2009), and spatiotemporal resolution. In each of these cases, lower levels of the hierarchy are those that include representations in analog format, informationally encapsulated and temporally prior processing, and higher spatiotemporal resolution. Thus, the kind of effects that are relevant for the cognitive penetrability of perceptual experience are *top-down*[2] effects.

The debate about the possibility of *top-down* effects is a longstanding one. In this section, I explore some of the fundamental aspects of this debate, namely its historical context, the methodology employed to discover *top-down* effects, and the consequences of the occurrence of such effects. I focus on vision since the vast majority of classic and recent evidence for top-down effects revolves around this sensory modality. Furthermore, establishing that there is cognitive penetrability of visual perceptual experience is enough to raise worries about the potential far-reaching consequences of this phenomenon introduced at the beginning of the book. As such, I shall not be concerned with other sensory modalities, although I leave it open that the arguments that will follow about cognitive penetrability and attention could hold for other kinds of perceptual experience as well.

---

[1] When taking into account both adjacent and distant cortical regions.

[2] The *top-down* terminology is commonly adopted in discussions of these topics, albeit often in reference to different things. Here it refers exclusively to effects of cognition on perception, where the former is thought to be at a higher level than the latter in the mental hierarchy.

Bruner and Goodman (1947) presented a series of experiments on the effects of value attributions on the perception of size. Their results prompted a whole approach to psychology called the *new look*, which focused on the way in which various types of cognitive states could affect perception. During the flourishing period of the *new look*, the terminology of *cognitive penetrability* had not yet been introduced and the term was coined many years later by Pylyshyn (1980; see also Fodor and Pylyshyn 1981). Nevertheless, exponents of the *new look* were guided by the very same idea and were looking for background cognitive states that could affect how human subjects experience the world through their senses. According to *new look* psychologists, perception is an inferential process in which the system constructs a coherent percept starting from sensory stimulation and background information, in a way that is no different from problem-solving and thinking (Pylyshyn 2003). In other words, perception can be construed as a process of forming hypotheses and testing them.[3]

Despite enjoying some initial success, the *new look* was not immune to some significant worries. In particular, many experimental findings of *top-down* effects of cognition on perception are exposed to the same powerful objection. The methodology employed by those experiments, largely based on the subject's reports, is incapable of distinguishing between real changes in subjects' perceptual experiences and changes taking place merely in the perceptual judgments that subjects form about this experience (Pylyshyn 2003). Judgments, however, are typically thought to be high-level cognitive states. Therefore, the *new look* experiments merely served to demonstrate some fascinating but hardly surprising effects of cognition on cognition. In recent years, also due to the development of new experimental paradigms that moved away from subjective report, focusing on less controversial tasks like on-line perceptual matching (Levin and Banaji 2006; Witzel et al. 2011), the scientific community has once again become very interested in the possibility of *top-down* effects. A webpage of the University of Yale[4] reports more than 170 empirical papers on *top-down* effects of cognition on perception since 1995.

Despite the rather extensive list of alleged effects, this recent strand of the *new look* movement has encountered some powerful criticisms. In a recent paper, Firestone and Scholl (2016) expose several methodological worries about these experiments and individuate six pitfalls that could invalidate most of the recently purported top-down effects of cognition on perception. One of the pitfalls concerns an argumentative fallacy that, according to them, underlies many interpretations of the experimental results on top-down effects.

This so-called *El Greco fallacy* has its roots in the history of Renaissance art. In order to explain why the sixteenth-century Spanish painter El Greco used to paint oddly elongated shapes, it was posited that he had a perceptual disorder that made the world appear elongated to him. This story might seem to be a quite plausible explanation of the oddities in El Greco's paintings, but, on closer inspection, this

---

[3] In Chap. 5, I will discuss Bayesian approaches that start with the very same assumption. Importantly, in such approaches one of the ways in which hypotheses are tested is action and this provides the link between the inferential nature of perception and **ARC** (discussed above).

[4] http://www.yale.edu/perception/Brian/refGuides/TopDown.html

explanation is based on a logical fallacy. If El Greco had a general perceptual impairment, it is plausible that such a condition would make everything he saw look elongated. But if everything looked elongated to El Greco, not only the shape on the canvas, but also the canvas itself would have looked elongated. Now, if he painted an apparently elongated shape on an apparently elongated canvas, the picture would have looked perfectly fine to a normal observer. In other words: the distortion of the stimulus and the distortion of the frame of reference would cancel each other out. Firestone and Scholl (2016) apply this logic to several experiments about top-down effects, arguing that most of them fall prey to this pitfall.

To see how Firestone and Scholl (2016) apply the logic of the *El Greco fallacy* to the contemporary discussion of top-down effects, consider an experiment by Banerjee et al. (2012). The experimenters asked subjects to rate the brightness of the room they were in on a numerical scale and found that thinking about unethical actions made the subject rate the room as darker. The alleged top-down effect is that thinking about particular thoughts makes things look darker.

Firestone and Scholl replicated the experiment substituting actual patches of gray of varying darker and lighter hues to the numerical scale. They found that the effect reported in the original experiment is still in place in the new version with color patches. But if this is so, this effect cannot be a real top-down effect on the subject's perceptual experience. To think that it is would be to commit the *El Greco fallacy*. If thinking unethical thoughts makes things look darker, this should apply to both the frame of reference, namely the room, and to the experimental probes, namely the color patches. If one has to match a darker-looking room to a darker-looking patch of gray, one should supposedly choose the same patch that one would choose in normal conditions, since it would look as much darker as the room does. The fact that subjects selected color patches that were actually darker than those selected in normal conditions indicates that a top-down effect of thought on perceptual experience cannot be the explanation of these results.

While not all of their points are as striking as the *El Greco fallacy*, the criticism of Firestone and Scholl (2016) sets the bar very high for new experiments that purport to have discovered a genuine top-down effect. On the other hand, an experimental paradigm that would be capable of controlling for all the pitfalls will solidly establish the existence of top-down effects.

Despite the problems and methodological worries with the evidence of top-down effects, one might ask what makes the issue of the cognitive penetrability of perceptual experience such a pressing one, indeed, so much so that it has motivated many decades of heated discussion. On this point, it is believed that the truth of the *cognitive penetrability* thesis (henceforth CP) would have dramatic consequences for several branches of philosophy and cognitive science.

Stokes (2015) discusses what philosophers and psychologists have been most concerned with about the *cognitive penetrability* of perceptual experience. The scientific domains that are mostly concerned with the possibility of cognitive penetration are the evaluation of competing scientific theories, cognitive modeling, and perceptual epistemology. Stokes argues that the truth of the CP thesis would have three important consequences for these domains:

1. Theory-ladenness of empirical observation.
2. Problems for the epistemic role of perception for belief justification.
3. Rejection of modular models of cognitive architecture.

The first consequence concerns the philosophy of science: if perceptual experience is cognitively penetrable, empirical observation could be *theory-laden*. This poses problems for the possibility of evaluating the adequacy of competing scientific theories in the light of experimental evidence. The second consequence concerns perceptual epistemology: if perceptual experience is cognitively penetrable, then it could not play a reliable role for belief justification. Since perceptual experience is among the main sources of justification for one's beliefs about the world, this would be a problematic result. The third consequence concerns models of mental architecture: the cognitive penetrability of perceptual experience could entail a non-modular picture of the mind. This would require a radical revision, or even a rejection, of one of the received models about the architecture of the mind. I revisit all three consequences later in the chapter.

If Stokes is right, it is clear that the truth of CP and the extent to which penetrability effect may occur are determinant for the development and evaluation of theories of the mind and for epistemology. Accordingly, it is not surprising that the debate about CP, in one form or another, has been a very important topic in philosophy and psychology and has received such extensive and heated discussion up to the present time. Having explained why the debate about *cognitive penetrability* has endured for so long, I can proceed to introduce the currently most discussed views on this topic and the many complex issues related to them.

3.2 Cognitive Penetrability: Recent Developments

Elucidating the current status of the debate about cognitive penetrability (CP) is no easy task. The reason is that several authors have proposed different definitions of the phenomenon, tailored to highlight specific aspects of CP in different domains. In this section, I offer an overview of the main extant positions in the literature, explaining their motivations and clarifying their scope. As a general point, which may serve as an underlying condition for all of the different accounts of CP outlined below, cognitive penetration involves a change in a subject's perceptual experience that is brought about by a change in some cognitive state, while the external stimulus and other external conditions are kept fixed. For the remainder of this chapter and, indeed, of the book in general, it will be important to keep in mind this basic stipulation.

As I mentioned, the introduction of much of the current terminology in the debate about CP is due to Pylyshyn (1980, 1999). Pylyshyn discusses the idea of cognitive penetrability in order to be able to define *early vision*, i.e. a significant part of visual processing that is entirely impenetrable to other domains of cognition and, in particular, to higher-level and domain general information encoded, for example, in beliefs and goals. According to Pylyshyn (1999):

> *[...] if a system is cognitively penetrable then the function it computes is sensitive, **in a semantically coherent way**, to the organism's goals and beliefs, that is, it can be altered in a way that bears some logical relation to what the person knows.* (Pylyshyn 1999, p. 343, emphasis added).

Pylyshyn's notion of CP is closely tied to the third consequence of CP, namely how to model cognitive architecture and modularity, discussed at the end of the previous section. Importantly, the notion of penetrability adopted by Pylyshyn posits a direct relation of semantic coherence between the penetrating state or process and the penetrated state or process. Not only must a function computed somewhere in the system be sensitive to information stored elsewhere, but it must be sensitive to such information in a rational or otherwise normative (non-arbitrary and quasi-logical) way (Pylyshyn 1999, note 3). This requirement, which may be called the *semantic criterion*, specifies a notion of CP that I shall call *semantic* CP:

> **Semantic CP:** cognitive penetration occurs if there is a normative top-down relation between domain general information stored in the system and information processed locally by a subsystem.

According to Pylyshyn, there are reasons to think that the information processing of a specific subsystem, namely *early vision*, is not normatively sensitive to information stored elsewhere and is therefore semantically impenetrable. It is important to note that not all of the information stored in different parts of the system is equally relevant for the impenetrability thesis. Suppose that perceptual systems have a form of built-in perceptual memory and that information stored in, for example, auditory memory could affect early vision in a semantically coherent way. In such a case, no top-down process is involved, and we would speak of lateral or perceptual penetrability.

One might argue that, since no top-down relation is involved, perceptual penetrability might thus undermine the strict modularity of early vision but would not provide an interesting instance of an interaction between perception and cognition. This point is sometimes raised to dismiss alleged evidence of CP by reducing it to perceptual penetrability. However, note that in order for the argument to go through, one needs an independent characterization of perception and cognition that does not depend on the cognitive impenetrability of the former, which is not the case in my reading of Pylyshyn (see Chap. 1).

Semantic CP is arguably the strongest notion of CP. But while Pylyshyn is exclusively concerned with the impenetrability of early vision, *semantic* CP is a functional notion that can be applied at different levels. One could argue that, contra Pylyshyn, all of vision is semantically penetrable, or one could argue that, if perception is identified on the basis of a criterion different from its impenetrability, part of perception may be semantically penetrable and part of it may not be. Furthermore, one could argue that, even if early vision, i.e. perceptual processing, is semantically impenetrable, visual experience is semantically penetrable, with the consequence that visual experience would not be entirely determined by the processes that take place in early vision.[5] For visual experience to be semantically penetrable, a logical or otherwise systematic connection must hold between the content of the cognitive state and the content of the perceptual experience that is affected by the cognitive state. To give a simple example, if reading the word "red" written in black on white paper could make things look reddish to me, one may think that my experience is semantically penetrated by the cognitive processing of the meaning of the word, which is systematically related to the affected content. One way to understand this systematic relation is in terms of the reliable tokening of the same concept "red" in correspondence with both the typical occurrence of a red experience and that of the written word. On the other hand, if reading the word "red" makes things look taller to me, such systematic relation between contents does not hold and one may think that some interfering factor or intermediate states are generating the change in experience, rather than their being a direct result of the cognitive processing of the meaning of the word. Such a case, even if it would involve top-down effects, would not count as semantic penetrability of visual experience. A further example of a non-semantic influence of cognition on perceptual experience is when a belief about an important upcoming exam causes stress and an ensuing migraine, which in turn causes one to see flashing lights in the periphery of the visual field (Macpherson 2012).

However, not everyone agrees that such a strict constraint as the semantic criterion should be incorporated in the definition of CP. Some authors think that even relations between mental processes that are not normative may still be relevant for some core issues in the philosophy of mind. Siegel (2012) defines CP as follows[6]:

> *If visual experience is cognitively penetrable, then it is nomologically possible for two subjects (or for one subject in different counterfactual circumstances, or at different times) to have visual experiences with different contents while seeing and attending to the same distal stimuli under the same external conditions, as a result of differences in other cognitive (including affective) states.* (Siegel 2012, pp. 205–206)

According to the above passage, cognitive penetrability requires that two subjects have different visual experiences while all perceptual conditions, like stimulus, attentional focus, external lighting, and, one might add, the status of perceptual receptors, are kept fixed and the only difference between the two subjects lies in their cognitive states. It is important to keep all perceptual variables fixed so as to ensure that the only plausible explanation for the different experiences is a difference in cognitive states such as beliefs. This is all that is needed to raise some important philosophical worries about perceptual justification. Siegel does not argue for the actual occurrence of cognitive penetration and limits herself to offering some possible examples. What is important for her is that if cognitive penetration were to occur, it could sometimes undermine the possibility of justifying beliefs

---

[5] This does not imply that perceptual experience involves high-level or rich content, but only that its contents, whatever they are, are not exhausted by early visual contents.

[6] This is the second pass of Siegel's definition. It differs from the first insofar as in this second pass she includes a constraint on the allocation of attention. In the next section, I discuss how many authors in this debate consider attention not to be an interesting vehicle of cognitive penetrability. In the next chapter, I argue that this is not the case.

on the basis of perceptual experience, under a dogmatist account of the epistemology of perception. Thus, Siegel's discussion of CP addresses the second of the consequences specified by Stokes (2015), namely the problems that CP raises for justification of belief from perceptual experience.

To be more precise, Siegel's point is primarily targeted at one specific view about justification called *phenomenal dogmatism*.[7] Phenomenal dogmatism is a complex and widely debated topic in epistemology. An exhaustive review of this position would take us too far afield in respect of our present purposes. However, a brief illustration is due in order to understand the problem raised by Siegel. According to phenomenal dogmatism, perceptual experience confers immediate *prima facie* justification to some beliefs partially in virtue of how that experience makes things appear or "seem" to the subject (Pryor 2000; Chudnoff 2013; Brogaard 2018). Perceptual seeming can be understood in terms of representational contents: "it perceptually seems to you that p just in case you have a perceptual experience part of whose representational content is that p" (Chudnoff 2013, p. 84). What this means is roughly that a subject can be justified in believing that p, just by having an experience that makes it seem that p to him and in the absence of defeaters.[8]

Back to Siegel's point, CP raises a problem for phenomenal dogmatism as it leaves open the following possibility: a perceptual experience that could be somehow shaped, determined or influenced by the belief that p would, according to dogmatism, confer epistemic support to the very same belief that p. Siegel argues that cognitively penetrated experience does not, in fact, improve the epistemic status of the penetrating beliefs in the way that dogmatism requires them to and predicts that they would. Siegel (2012) proposes the following example:

> *Jill believes, without justification, that Jack is angry at her. The epistemically appropriate attitude for Jill to take toward the proposition that Jack is angry at her is suspension of belief. But her attitude is epistemically inappropriate. When she sees Jack, her belief makes him look angry to her. If she didn't believe this, her experience wouldn't represent him as angry.* (Siegel 2012, p. 209)

As the example goes, Jill takes an epistemically inappropriate attitude toward her experience and, instead of suspending her belief about Jack being angry prior to seeing him, she does in fact believe that he is angry and she allows such belief to

---

[7] It should be noted that Siegel (2012) speaks of dogmatism simpliciter, but she defines dogmatism as the conjunction of two claims the first of which is as follows: "having a perceptual experience with content p suffices to give you justification for believing p" (p. 208). As will become clear below, the notion of "seeming" at the core of *phenomenal dogmatism* can be construed in the same way. For this reason, and to keep technical complexities to a minimum, I do not make the distinction explicit in the text and simply talk about phenomenal dogmatism. Also, toward the end of the paper, Siegel discusses how the problem may generalize to other views in epistemology. I leave out this discussion as the issue about phenomenal dogmatism is enough to outline the relevance of CP for perceptual epistemology.

[8] A defeater can be, for example, a justified belief that things are not as they seem to me (undercutting defeater) or a justified belief that is inconsistent with the belief that enjoys *prima facie* justification from the experience (rebutting defeater) (Brogaard 2018).

shape her experience of Jack, perhaps by slightly modifying her experience of the expression on Jack's face.

If she takes her experience as of an angry face belonging to Jack as justification for her belief that Jack is angry, she would now be in an epistemically appropriate position to believe that Jack is angry. However, she would have reached that position through an epistemically inadequate route. The etiology of a justified perceptual belief that p would be viciously circular if the belief is justified on the cognitively penetrated experience as of p, where the experience is shaped by the previously unjustified belief that p. What is particularly striking is that in Siegel's definition there is no specification about the relation between the penetrating cognitive state and the penetrated perceptual experience. Accordingly, even if the relation were not rational, i.e. if the semantic criterion were not met, the problematic consequences for perceptual epistemology would follow nonetheless. In fact, Siegel explicitly says that cognitive penetrability is a kind of causal influence on visual experience.

Stokes (2013) also considers cognitive penetrability to involve a causal relation. His definition of cognitive penetration is the following:

> *(CP) A perceptual experience E is cognitively penetrated if and only if (1) E is causally dependent upon some cognitive state C and (2) the causal link between E and C is internal and mental.* (Stokes 2013, p. 650)

In Stokes' definition one finds again the requirement of a causal relation between a cognitive state and a perceptual experience, but with the specification that the link must be internal and mental. The requirement for the causal link to be internal and mental is supposed to rule out cases in which, for example, the causal route could involve certain non-mental internal states such as a fever that may cause pain, which in turn alters perceptual experience. While such a causal link is internal, it is not mental in the sense required by Stokes' definition.

Taken together Siegel's and Stokes' definitions provide a second notion of cognitive penetrability that I shall call *causal* CP:

> **Causal CP:** cognitive penetration occurs if there is a top-down causal (internal and mental) relation between a cognitive state and a perceptual experience, where the contents of experience are modified by the cognitive state, without a change in the perceptual input to the system.

According to *causal* CP, the contents of the experience are causally determined by some cognitive state. It follows that, as posited by Siegel's definition, two subjects might have experiences with different contents while being exposed to the same distal stimulus under the same environmental conditions as a result of a difference in the background cognitive state.[9] One first clarification is about the notion of a causal relation. Here I leave open what the specific notion of causation at play in this debate may be. I assume that the cognitive-perceptual relations that I talk about are compatible with different accounts of causation. As a minimal characterization,

---

[9] The causal internal and mental relation described here modifies the contents of experience. Since the contents of experience determine the "seeming" (see above), *causal* CP is enough to raise Siegel's worries for phenomenal dogmatism.

however, a causal relation of the sort involved in *causal* CP implies that the contents of the second *relatum*, the experience, would have been different, if the first *relatum*, the cognitive state, would not have occurred.

Secondly, in order to specify the notion of content I would need some constraints on representations. As I said, although a general form of representationalism is assumed in the background, I want to keep the notion of representation as non-committal as possible because the discussion in this book has a wider scope than specific versions of representationalism. For this reason, during the course of the discussion, I generally assume that experiences have contents of some sort. I will say something more on what sorts of contents these may be, but I do not endorse any particular view on representational contents.

The difference between *causal CP* and *semantic CP* depends on both the normativity and the nature of the cognitive perceptual relation. Suppose, for example, that one really likes the color green and that one's desire to see green causes one to see everything with a greenish hue. This phenomenon would qualify as an instance of *causal CP* and an instance of *semantic CP*, because the desire, whose content might be, for example, the concept "green", causally affects the content of the experience, which could be construed as the color attributed to the object. If one did not have the desire, things would have looked less greenish to one. Furthermore, the concept "green" of the desire seems to be normatively (semantically or otherwise) related to the experience of green, for example, by subsuming the adequate category for that specific hue.

On the other hand, suppose that it were true that reflecting upon unethical actions causes everything to look darker (Banerjee et al. 2012). Such a phenomenon would qualify as *causal CP* but not *semantic CP*, because the thought about unethical actions causally determines the content of the experience, but it is not normatively related to it. There is no immediately available normative connection, semantic or otherwise, between unethical actions and darker shades of color. Even if there might in fact be such a connection, the example is meant to illustrate the difference between the two forms of CP. In principle, *causal CP* could occur when the contents of the cognitive and perceptual state are loosely related or not related at all or if they are related in a completely arbitrary, idiosyncratic fashion. However, even if a semantic or otherwise normative relation is a too demanding requirement for CP, in order for a case of CP to be compelling, there must be some systematicity in the causal relations that may be at play in *causal* CP (Newen and Vetter 2017).

By focusing on the contents of experiences, *causal* CP highlights one important problem, namely that contents of experiences and the contents of cognitive states may be of very different kinds. In particular, the contents of experiences are often thought to be non-conceptual, while the contents of belief are thought to be conceptual. Thus, one problem that is closely related to the difference between *semantic* and *causal CP* is the problem of what kinds of contents cognitive and perceptual states may have.

Macpherson (2012, 2015) addresses the problem of cognitive penetrability in the light of a distinction between the conceptual contents of belief and the non-conceptual contents of experience. If one assumes that cognitive states and perceptual experiences have such different kinds of contents, a notion of CP that posits a direct causal link between a cognitive state with conceptual contents and a perceptual state with non-conceptual contents faces the problem of explaining how such a link is possible. Nevertheless, Macpherson argues that cognitive penetration of perceptual experience by cognitive states such as beliefs and desires does in fact sometimes occur. The kernel of her argument in favor of the occurrence of CP is that some experimental results[10] cannot be as well explained by alternative explanations to CP. Even if CP occurs, however, and even if the penetrating states, like beliefs and desires, have conceptual content, this does not imply, according to Macpherson, that perceptual experience must have conceptual contents as well.

Macpherson proposes that the actual occurrence of CP is compatible with experience having non-conceptual contents by positing an indirect mechanism involving the top-down generation of mental imagery. The key point is that our beliefs and desires are capable of generating states with a phenomenal character, such as mental images, dreams, and hallucinations. The top-down generated phenomenal states are not themselves beliefs and desires and, as such, they need not have the same kind of content as beliefs and desires, namely non-conceptual content. Moreover, since they have a phenomenal character, such phenomenal states seem to have the adequate kind of contents to interact with perceptual experience. If this is correct, sometimes the top-down generated non-conceptual phenomenal states may interfere with perceptual experience without the need for the contents of experiences to be conceptual. Of course, in order to see whether the argument goes through, one needs an account of the non-conceptual contents of experience. Macpherson (2015) examines several accounts of non-conceptual content and finds her version of CP, which is based on the indirect mechanism, to be compatible with most of them.

I shall label the kind of cognitive penetrability advocated by Macpherson *indirect non-conceptual* CP:

> **Indirect non-conceptual** CP: cognitive penetration occurs if there is a top-down causal (internal and mental) relation between: 1. a cognitive state with conceptual contents, 2. a top-down triggered process with non-conceptual contents and phenomenal character, and 3. a perceptual experience, where the non-conceptual contents of the experience are modified by the cognitive process (with conceptual content) in virtue of the intermediate process and without a change in the perceptual input to the system.

Note that the requirement of the causal link being internal and mental is incorporated here because the problem of causal chains that do not typically engender CP, such as, for example, pain caused by anxiety caused by fear, were first addressed in Macpherson (2012).

Against Macpherson's indirect view one might argue that the problem of a relation between conceptual and non-conceptual contents is not solved, but merely moved one step behind. In Macpherson's indirect mechanism there is still a causal link between a conceptual state and a non-conceptual state with a phenomenal

---

[10] In particular, Levin and Banaji (2006), who claim that knowledge about racial categories affects the perceived color of faces. See below for further details on this experiment.

character, namely a mental image, which needs to be explained. Now, if one does not have a good story to tell about how that link is established, then the same problem for direct CP arises for indirect CP. On the other hand, if one has a good explanation for the causal link in indirect CP, one may apply the same explanation to direct CP, effectively making the intermediate step irrelevant. Here, however, my task is not to object to Macpherson's view, but rather to frame the debate about CP by discussing the main accounts and problems that have been discussed in the literature. Thus, I will include *indirect non-conceptual* CP in the relevant definitions of CP.

The final definition of the CP thesis that I wish to discuss in this section is probably the most general form of the claim that cognition may affect perceptual experience. This view emerges from the work of Stokes (2015) and follows from his considerations about the three consequences of CP, which have piqued the interest of researchers since the beginning of the debate.[11]

Stokes devises a unified strategy to discern which mental phenomena are cases of CP on the basis of the consequence they have for other aspects of the mind. This *consequentialist* approach, at its core, marks an attempt to avoid reaching an impasse in the discussion of CP, by providing the criteria against which clear definitions of CP in different research domains may be developed. The ambitious aspect of consequentialism is that the criterion it proposes must be general enough to subsume phenomena that concern different aspects of the mind and are addressed with different methodologies, such as empirical psychology and philosophical analysis. At the same time, the criterion must be specific enough as to exclude those phenomena that have been dismissed in virtue of powerful objections like the El Greco fallacy (see above). In this respect, the consequentialist approach sets out to be a unified account for understanding CP. The success of such an endeavor is still open to debate, but its results in describing phenomena that have been discussed, accepted or dismissed as instances of CP in the literature look promising.[12]

To motivate consequentialism, Stokes observes that attempts at providing a definition of CP, and then reviewing empirical evidence that more or less fits with the definition, have proven to be instances of an unsuccessful strategy. As an alternative he suggests that we should consider as an instance of CP any mental phenomenon that involves a relation between perception and cognition and leads to one or more of the three consequences. I shall call this idea *consequentialist* CP.

Consequentialist CP: cognitive penetration occurs if a there is a top-down causal (internal and mental) relation between a cognitive state and a perceptual experience that leads to at least one of the three relevant consequences.

The first ingredient of *consequentialist* CP is, once again, a top-down causal, internal and mental relation, which excludes processes that take place outside the subject's mind. The second ingredient is the set of relevant consequences, individuated by Stokes on the basis of the worries that originally prompted the penetrability debate. As I have already reported above, the three consequences are:

[11] Part of the following two paragraphs have been adapted from Marchi (2017).
[12] See Stokes (2015) for discussion.

1. Theory-ladenness of empirical observation.
2. Problems for the epistemic role of perception for belief justification.
3. Rejection of modular models of cognitive architecture.

According to Stokes, a phenomenon involving a top-down, causal, internal and mental relation leading to at least one of the three consequences would be an instance of CP. The first consequence is that our empirical observations, in the simple form of perceptual observations, could be shaped by our background theories and could not serve as a deciding ground on which to establish, for example, which one of two competing and equally suitable[13] theories is true. This consequence is undesirable, for it may lead to an epistemological *impasse* that threatens scientific progress. The problem of theory-ladenness has a long history in philosophy of science and Stokes is not alone in highlighting its importance in relation to the cognitive penetrability debate. For example, Raftopoulos clearly states that: "discussions of CP of perception are related to the theory-ladenness of perception and CP is thought to pave the road for constructivism" (2014, p. 607).

Concerning the second consequence, the epistemic worry is the following: Perception and perceptual experience are among the available sources of knowledge about the world and, specifically, experience is among the sources of rational support or justification for those beliefs. But if experience is already shaped by the beliefs for which it is supposed to provide justification, the justification process becomes problematic. This is a problem for some prominent views in epistemology, such as phenomenal dogmatism (see above). At a first glance, this looks like a problem of circularity of justification.[14] However, it may not be a problem of circularity exclusively, but a more general one of rationality and irrationality of perceptual etiologies (Siegel 2013). I discuss this consequence in detail in Chap. 4.

The third consequence of CP concerns how we should model cognitive architecture. Some powerful models of the mind are built around the idea of modularity. Just like CP, and sometimes to accommodate for some forms of CP (Lyons 2015), modularity comes in various flavors (see introduction for a brief review of some current modularist positions). According to Fodor (1983), there are several requirements that have to be met by a processing subsystem in order for it to qualify as a module. Among these requirements, the most fundamental is that of informational encapsulation, which roughly states that the operations performed by a module are sensitive to its proprietary inputs but insensitive to information stored elsewhere in the system.

More recently, and even without calling CP into play, the original Fodorian notion of informational encapsulation has come into question. One of the main reasons is the increasing amount of evidence for close interactions between, for example, different sensory modalities (Kayser and Logothetis 2007; James et al. 2002; Shams et al. 2011) or hierarchically higher and lower areas of the brain (Bar 2003, 2007; Kveraga et al. 2007). Proponents of modularity have come up with different

---

[13] Given other constraints such as internal coherence, parsimony, etc.

[14] But see Ghijsen (2015) for a discussion of general epistemic problems related to internalism, of which cognitive penetration might be a specific token.

ways of retaining the modularity thesis by weakening, altering or abandoning the requirement of informational encapsulation (Burnston and Cohen 2015; Lyons 2015). Similarly, if CP happens, most of the theories and models of the mind that are built around the modularity thesis would have to be revised. However, Lyons (2015) points out that the consequences of the truth of CP for the modeling of cognitive architecture may not have to be taken too radically as to imply the complete dismissal of the modularity thesis.

I have introduced four accounts of the CP thesis, which I take to be the main positions currently under discussion. My interest lies not in evaluating these accounts and arguing in favor of one more than another, although I have offered some critical remarks. Rather, I come back to these accounts in the course of the book, when I argue that very well-established forms of interaction between perception and cognition, namely those mediated by attentional processes, meet the requirements of most, if not all, of them. For now, however, I shall conclude this chapter with a brief overview and discussion of some of the most relevant empirical findings that support the truth of the CP hypothesis, in one form or another.

3.3   Evidence of Cognitive Penetration

In this section, I discuss how CP could be supported on empirical grounds. The purpose of this section is to familiarize the reader with some of the strategies that have been adopted to tap into a subject's perceptual experience and its relation with a subject's high-level cognitive states. As the most studied sensory modality, vision offers the majority of examples of possible top-down effects of cognition on perception. Within vision research, color and shape perception arguably provide the most interesting evidence for the possibility of cognitive penetration. One example of such evidence are ambiguous and bi-stable pictures such as the well-known duck-rabbit picture or the Necker-cube:

Such images admit of two possible perceptual interpretations and they were already discussed during the golden age of the *new look* movement. The two possible interpretations of the images usually alternate and there seems to be a significant phenomenal difference in perceptual experience when either of the two interpretations becomes dominant. At first glance, it might seem that the subject's expectations, beliefs, desires or intentions about one possible interpretation of an ambiguous picture over the other may easily determine which of the two images is experienced. For example, it has been shown that subjects are capable of voluntarily altering the rate at which shifts in interpretations of ambiguous pictures take place without changing their fixation point (Meng and Tong 2004; Liu et al. 2012. I return to these experiments later in the book).

One could argue that in such a case a subject's voluntary and explicit intention or desire alters its perceptual experience through an internal and mental causal chain. In this case, the requirements of *causal* CP or even *semantic* CP could be met. However, such cases were soon rejected as evidence of cognitive penetration of perception for the reason that the influence that desires or intentions may exert in these cases is not an influence on perception, but rather an influence on the allocation of attention, which, under certain understandings of attention, seems to occur either pre-perceptually or post-perceptually. This opens up the problem of the nature of attention and the relationship between cognitive penetrability and attentional processes, which I leave aside for the moment, as it will be the focus of the next two chapters.

Further interesting findings come from research on color perception. In an experiment by Witzel et al. (2011), subjects had to adjust the color of a target stimulus to either gray or its typical color. Stimuli were highly familiar images such as the Smurfs or the Coca-Cola can. Stimuli were selected to be highly diagnostic of their typical color as well as being plausibly familiar to all subjects and were presented to subjects in a random color. Subjects could adjust the color of the stimulus by pressing keyboard keys thereby altering the stimulus hue along two color axes having opposing poles (greenish-reddish and bluish-yellowish) with perfect achromatic gray at the intersection. The aim of the experimenter was to test whether the subject's memory of the stimulus' typical color could affect the color adjusting task. The more interesting results emerged from the achromatic task, i.e. when subjects had to adjust the color of the stimulus to gray.[15] The reasoning of the experimenter was that, if knowledge of the stimulus' typical color could affect the way in which it appears to subjects, for example by making a randomly colored Smurf stimulus look bluish, the point at which they would settle for achromaticity should be slightly moved in the direction of the opposite hue from the typical one in order to compensate. The prediction was then that the subject would adjust the color of, for example, the Smurf to a slightly yellowish hue to compensate for the slightly bluish appearance, in order to perceive it as achromatic. The experimenters found that the prediction was confirmed by the results. The color to which the diagnostic stimulus was adjusted went in the opposite hue range from that of the typical color. Supporting the hypothesis that subjects were actually seeing the randomly colored Smurf as bluish, as a consequence of their knowledge about the stimulus' typical color. This experiment confirmed findings from Olkkonen et al. (2008) who originally developed the paradigm to test memory color effects for familiar fruit and vegetable stimuli.

On the other hand, an experiment of Levin and Banaji (2006) provides evidence for a complementary case, i.e. when the surface luminance of a stimulus that is not diagnostic of a typical color is perceived differently depending on background information and beliefs about racial categories. Here I focus on one particular version of this experiment, namely experiment 2, for reasons that shall become clear later as I introduce some criticism of the results. In experiment 2, subjects had to adjust a gray color patch to the neutral color of a target stimulus. The stimulus was a computer-generated picture of a human face with ambiguous facial traits between

---

[15] Note that for this task individual values for subjective achromaticity were previously independently assessed for each target, using gray disks as stimuli, and used to evaluate the effects.

typical Black (African American) and White (Caucasian) faces. The racially ambiguous face was presented in a neutral gray color (average surface luminance). The same ambiguous face was sometimes labeled "black" and sometimes labeled "white". This label was supposed to lead subjects to believe that the ambiguous face was an African American face in one case and a Caucasian face in the other. The result was that, in the "black" and "white" conditions, subjects adjusted the patch of color to a darker or lighter shade of gray respectively. The color mismatch here was in the same hue direction as the color label, as if subjects were seeing the face darker and brighter in the two conditions. This makes this case complementary to Witzel et al. (2011). Therefore, it seems that in the two experiments different subjects were experiencing different nuances of color depending in the first case on their knowledge of typical colors of certain stimuli, and in the second case on their background knowledge about race categories triggered by color labels.

These experiments are particularly interesting because they required subjects to perform an online perceptual matching task, therefore ruling out several possible objections related to introspection or verbal reports. Moreover, in both cases there was a categorical difference between the adjustable probe and the frame of reference. In Witzel et al. (2011) subjects had to adjust a randomly colored and highly color-diagnostic stimulus to achromatic gray, and the supposedly involved cognitive process, the beliefs about the diagnostic color, only applied to the stimulus. In the Levin and Banaji (2006) experiment 2, subjects had to adjust a uniform patch to a non-color-diagnostic and inherently ambiguous stimulus and, once again, background information about typical facial traits, recruited by the verbal label, only applied to the image and not to the probe. Since the probe and the reference were of different kinds and the proposed top-down effect in both cases only applies to one of those kinds, the *El Greco fallacy* cannot be adopted as an alternative explanation for these results since such fallacy only vitiates experiments where the supposed top-down effect may affect both the probe and the reference.[16] The same cannot be said for their experiment 1 where the reference stimulus and the target stimulus were both faces. This version of the experiment is exposed to the *El Greco fallacy* as well as other powerful objections like replicability with blurred stimuli (Firestone and Scholl 2015). I have chosen these two experiments because they seem to be the least exposed to the methodological worries and pitfalls highlighted by Firestone and Scholl (2016). This is not to say that alternative explanations are not available. Firestone and Scholl (2016) mention that a low-level explanation is possible for experiments on memory color effects such as those by Olkkonen et al. (2008) and Witzel et al. (2011), and very likely for Levin and Banaji (2006) experiment 1. Furthermore, Zeimbekis (2012) argues that the effects found in Olkkonen et al. (2008) and by extension those found in Witzel et al. (2011) are suitable for an alternative explanation that involves the subject shifting the boundaries of her concept of "gray" when adjusting the control stimulus and when adjusting the target stimulus.

---

[16] For example, Banerjee et al. (2012).

The conceptual shift explains why she settles on two different values for gray in the two cases. Such an explanation would involve a higher-level judgment effect that leaves visual appearances untouched. On the other hand, Gatzia (2019) argues, *contra* Zeimbekis, that the memory color effects found in similar experiments are best understood as phenomenological effects, but that the explanation need not involve cognitive penetration. Although such objections are reasonable, to my knowledge no knock-down counterargument is provided against a cognitive penetrability interpretation of effects such as those found in Witzel et al. (2011) and Levin and Banaji's experiment 2.

The studies presented in this section represent just a few examples of the strategy that has been employed to argue for the occurrence of top-down effects of cognition on perception that may qualify as CP under one or more of the four definitions. To summarize, the first step of the strategy is to devise an experimental paradigm that directly taps into a subject's perceptual experience. This could be reasonably achieved by having an on-line experience-based task such as color matching and adjustment. The second step is to manipulate a subject's background knowledge, desires or expectation. In Witzel et al. (2011) this was done by using stimuli that everyone experiences many times as having certain diagnostic properties, while in Levin and Banaji (2006) this was done using labels that recruit a subject's knowledge of typical facial traits associated with them. The final step is to argue that the manipulation of background knowledge best explains the eventual effects on subjects' experiences that are found in the experiment. Hence, arguments in favor of the CP thesis often take the shape of an inference to the best explanation.

A variation of this strategy consists in arguing that the occurrence of CP is also the best explanation for some already established phenomenon, which is shown to involve a cognitive perceptual relation on independent grounds. Marchi and Newen (2015) argue that emotion recognition in human facial expression is cognitively penetrable on the basis of this alternative strategy. They discuss an experiment by Carroll and Russell (1996), in which it is shown that manipulating a subject's beliefs and expectations might affect what emotion is recognized in a human prototypical facial expression. This experiment does not involve an on-line perceptual task and it is not supposed to directly tap into subjects' perceptual experience. Nevertheless, it is possible to argue that emotion recognition is a perceptual process on independent grounds (Carruthers 2015). For example, one can show that emotion recognition shares certain properties with other perceptual phenomena. One of these properties is the property of being subject to adaptation, the phenomenon by which a stimulus becomes less salient the more one is exposed to it (Block 2014).

On this basis, Marchi and Newen (2015) argue that the effects of background beliefs on the perceptual process of emotion recognition show a particular pattern of flexibility that is best explained as a change in perceptual experience rather than a change in perception-based judgments. Thus, they conclude that emotion recognition is a cognitively penetrable perceptual process.

In this section, I have discussed some empirical data that have been offered to support the conclusion that some aspects of perceptual experience may be influenced by a perceiver's background information in the form of beliefs, expectations, desires, etc. There are several other interesting results that could potentially be relevant evidence in favor of the occurrence of CP. As I mentioned, however, some of these results are typically quickly dismissed because the cognitive perceptual relations that they investigate involve the mediation of attentional processes. Changes in perceptual experience that involve shifts in attention are excluded as interesting instances of CP, because they are typically thought to cause a change of perceptual input.

This move, however, is more demanding than it seems. Since it is difficult to devise experimental paradigms that are completely devoid of any attentional effect (Van Boxtel et al. 2010), the claim that attentional effects exclude CP amounts to a form of radical skepticism about the possibility of CP. An opponent of CP would have to show that each and every case of attentional shifts is also a case of changes of perceptual input. On the other hand, a defendant of CP could claim that not all attentional shifts change the input to perception or that some attentional shifts change perceptual processing, perhaps in addition to a change in the input. To discuss these points in detail, one requires a clear understanding of attention itself. Providing a clear understanding of attention and inquiring into the relationship between attentional processes and CP, once such an understanding is available, will be the task of the next chapters.

3.4   Summary and Conclusion

The question about the cognitive penetrability of perceptual experience is considered to be a fundamental one because its answer may radically affect evaluations of competing scientific theories, models of cognitive architecture, and perceptual epistemology. In this chapter, I firstly addressed the historical roots of the debate about top-down effects on perception and some of the problems encountered by proponents of such effects. I then presented the recent developments of the debate, outlining the most prominent available accounts of cognitive penetrability. I narrowed down four possible versions of the hypothesis that perceptual experience is cognitively penetrable: *semantic* CP, *causal* CP, *indirect non-conceptual* CP, and *consequentialist* CP. Finally, I examined some of the experimental findings and argumentative strategies that have led researchers to believe that cognitive penetration may occur. The aim of the next two chapters is to show that according to one of the most influential current theories of attention, attentional phenomena meet the requirements of most, if not all, of the notions of cognitive penetrability presented here.

References

Banerjee, P., Chatterjee, P., & Sinha, J. (2012). Is it light or dark? Recalling moral behavior changes perception of brightness. *Psychological Science, 23*(4), 407–409.

Bar, M. (2003). A cortical mechanism for triggering top-down facilitation in visual object recognition. *Journal of Cognitive Neuroscience, 15*(4), 600–609.

Bar, M. (2007). The proactive brain: Using analogies and associations to generate predictions. *Trends in Cognitive Sciences, 11*(7), 280–289.

Block, N. (2014). Seeing-as in the light of vision science. *Philosophy and Phenomenological Research, 89*(3), 560–572.

Brogaard, B. (2018). Phenomenal dogmatism, seeming evidentialism and inferential justification. In K. McCain (Ed.), *Believing in accordance with the evidence*. Cham: Springer Verlag.

Bruner, J. S., & Goodman, C. C. (1947). Value and need as organizing factors in perception. *The Journal of Abnormal and Social Psychology, 42*(1), 33–44.

Burnston, D., & Cohen, J. (2015). Perceptual integration, modularity and cognitive penetration. In A. Raftopoulos & J. Zeimbekis (Eds.), *Cognitive influences on perception: Implications for philosophy of mind, epistemology, and philosophy of action* (pp. 123–143). New York: Oxford University Press.

Carroll, J. M., & Russell, J. A. (1996). Do facial expressions signal specific emotions? Judging emotion from the face in context. *Journal of Personality and Social Psychology, 70*(2), 205–218.

Carruthers, P. (2015). Perceiving mental states. *Consciousness and Cognition, 36*, 498–507.

Chudnoff, E. (2013). *Intuition*. Oxford: Oxford University Press.

Dretske, F. I. (1981). *Knowledge and the flow of information*. Cambridge, MA: MIT Press.

Firestone, C., & Scholl, B. J. (2015). Can you experience "top-down" effects on perception? The case of race categories and perceived lightness. *Psychonomic Bulletin and Review, 22*(3), 694–700.

Firestone, C., & Scholl, B. J. (2016). Cognition does not affect perception: Evaluating the evidence for "top-down" effects. *Behavioral and Brain Sciences, 39*, 1–72.

Fodor, J. A. (1983). *The modularity of mind*. Cambridge, MA: MIT Press.

Fodor, J. A., & Pylyshyn, Z. W. (1981). How direct is visual perception? Some reflections on Gibson's "ecological approach". *Cognition, 9*(2), 139–196.

Gatzia, D. E. (2019). Cognitive penetration and memory colour effects. *Erkenntnis, 84*(1), 121–143.

Ghijsen, H. (2015). The real epistemic problem of cognitive penetration. *Philosophical Studies, 173*(6), 1457–1475.

James, T. W., Humphrey, G. K., Gati, J. S., Servos, P., Menon, R. S., & Goodale, M. A. (2002). Haptic study of three-dimensional objects activates extrastriate visual areas. *Neuropsychologia, 40*(10), 1706–1714.

Kayser, C., & Logothetis, N. K. (2007). Do early sensory cortices integrate cross-modal information? *Brain Structure and Function, 212*(2), 121–132.

Kveraga, K., Ghuman, A. S., & Bar, M. (2007). Top-down predictions in the cognitive brain. *Brain and Cognition, 65*(2), 145–168.

Levin, D. T., & Banaji, M. R. (2006). Distortions in the perceived lightness of faces: The role of race categories. *Journal of Experimental Psychology: General, 135*(4), 501–512.

Liu, C.-H., Tzeng, O. J. L., Hung, D. L., Tseng, P., & Juan, C.-H. (2012). Investigation of bistable perception with the "silhouette spinner": Sit still, spin the dancer with your will. *Vision Research, 60*, 34–39.

Lyons, J. (2015). Unencapsulated modules and perceptual judgment. In A. Raftopoulos & J. Zeimbekis (Eds.), *The cognitive penetrability of perception: New philosophical perspectives* (pp. 102–122). New York: Oxford University Press.

Macpherson, F. (2012). Cognitive penetration of colour experience: Rethinking the issue in light of an indirect mechanism. *Philosophy and Phenomenological Research, 84*(1), 24–62.

Macpherson, F. (2015). Cognitive penetration and nonconceptual content. In A. Raftopoulos & J. Zeimbekis (Eds.), *The cognitive penetrability of perception: New philosophical perspectives* (pp. 330 358). New York: Oxford University Press

Marchi, F. (2017). Attention and cognitive penetrability: The epistemic consequences of attention as a form of metacognitive regulation. *Consciousness and Cognition, 47*, 48–62.

Marchi, F., & Newen, A. (2015). Cognitive penetrability and emotion recognition in human facial expressions. *Frontiers in Psychology, 6*, 828.

Meng, M., & Tong, F. (2004). Can attention selectively bias bistable perception? Differences between binocular rivalry and ambiguous figures. *Journal of Vision, 4*, 539–551.

Newen, A., & Vetter, P. (2017). Why cognitive penetration of our perceptual experience is still the most plausible account. *Consciousness and Cognition, 47*, 26–37.

Olkkonen, M., Hansen, T., & Gegenfurtner, K. R. (2008). Color appearance of familiar objects: Effects of object shape, texture, and illumination changes. *Journal of Vision, 8*(5), 13–13.

Pryor, J. (2000). The skeptic and the dogmatist. *Noûs, 34*, 517–549.

Pylyshyn, Z. W. (1980). Computation and cognition: Issues in the foundations of cognitive science. *Behavioral and Brain Sciences, 3*(1), 111–132.

Pylyshyn, Z. W. (1999). Is vision continuous with cognition? The case for cognitive impenetrability of visual perception. *Behavioral and Brain Sciences, 22*(3), 341–365.

Pylyshyn, Z. W. (2003). *Seeing and visualizing*. Cambridge, MA: MIT Press.

Raftopoulos, A. (2009). *Cognition and perception: How do psychology and neural science inform philosophy?* Cambridge, MA: MIT Press.

Raftopoulos, A. (2014). The cognitive impenetrability of the content of early vision is a necessary and sufficient condition for purely nonconceptual content. *Philosophical Psychology, 27*(5), 601–620.

Shams, L., Wozny, D. R., Kym, R., & Seitz, A. (2011). Influences of multisensory experience on subsequent unisensory processing. *Frontiers in Psychology, 18*(2), 264.

Siegel, S. (2012). Cognitive penetrability and perceptual justification. *Nous, 46*(2), 201–222.

Siegel, S. (2013). The epistemic impact of the etiology of experience. *Philosophical Studies, 162*(3), 697–722.

Stokes, D. (2013). Cognitive penetrability of perception. *Philosophy Compass, 8*(7), 646–663.

Stokes, D. (2015). Towards a consequentialist understanding of cognitive penetration. In J. Zeimbekis & A. Raftopoulos (Eds.), *The cognitive penetrability of perception: New philosophical perspectives* (pp. 75–100). New York: Oxford University Press.

Van Boxtel, J. J. A., Tsuchiya, N., & Koch, C. (2010). Consciousness and attention: On sufficiency and necessity. *Frontiers in Psychology, 1*, 217.

Witzel, C., Valkova, H., Hansen, T., & Gegenfurtner, K. R. (2011). Object knowledge modulates colour appearance. *I-Perception, 2*(1), 13–49.

Zeimbekis, J. (2012). Color and cognitive penetrability. *Philosophical Studies, 165*(1), 167–175.

Chapter 4
Attention and the Shaping of Experience

Abstract The aim of this chapter is to offer preliminary clarifications about how attention can be characterized in a theory-neutral way and, subsequently, what a theory of attention aims to explain. In Sect. 4.1, I relate this chapter to the previous one and the overarching theme of the book by discussing the importance of clarifying the notion of attention for the debate about CP. In Sect. 4.2, I discuss the theoretical problems related to attention. In Sect. 4.3, I specify what phenomena are relevant for attention research and outline a desideratum for an adequate theory of attention.

4.1 Why Attention Matters

Let me start with an extremely important question: Does attention participate in the shaping of experience? It is now rather uncontroversial that this question has a positive answer. This is obvious from everyone's personal experience; there are clear phenomenal shifts when one focuses attention on something rather than something else, say in the visual field, perhaps even without moving one's eyes. But there is also experimental evidence showing that this is the case (Liu et al. 2009; Carrasco et al. 2004) and assessing the extent of some attentional effects. From the philosophical point of view, a representationalist might easily accommodate these findings by holding that shifts in attention change the representational content by which the phenomenal character of the experience is determined. But even opponents of representationalism accept that shifts in attention can have quite relevant effects on the phenomenal character of an experience. On the basis of experimental findings such as those of the Carrasco lab, Block (2010) argues that covert shifts in attention, i.e. those that do not involve changes in the position and orientation of the sensory organs, change the phenomenal character of experience without altering either the experience-constituting aspects of the world (against direct realism) or the representational content of the experience (against representationalism). Changes in experience depend on a phenomenal component of the experience that is not determined by representational content and which Block calls *mental paint*. Regardless of one's position in this debate, there is widespread agreement in the philosophical literature about the quite radical influence of attention on perceptual experience. Now, given that attention does affect the way in which perceptual experience is shaped, one may ask a further question: Does cognition influence the way in which perceptual experience is shaped by attention?

The latter question also seems to have a positive answer. After all, one may voluntarily focus attention on something rather than something else and, as we have just seen, this often comes with clear modifications of one's phenomenal experience. It is also quite uncontroversial that voluntary attentional shift may involve cognitive factors such as desires or intentions of the attending agent.

If we could leave the discussion at this point one would think that this is already enough to prove that cognition interacts with perceptual experience in interesting ways and that CP is a real and rather common phenomenon. However, the matter is not so straightforward, because to assess whether the cognitive influences on perceptual experience that occur through shifts of attention are genuine instances of the kind of CP in which philosophers and psychologists are interested, one would have to answer the following question: How does cognition influence the way in which perceptual experience is shaped by attention? Unfortunately, this question cannot be answered in such a straightforward way as the previous two questions. In order to provide an answer, one must understand the nature and mechanisms of attentional shifts.

As introduced in the previous chapter, much of the alleged evidence of CP is explained away as attentional effects. The underlying thought seems to be that attentional effects do not threaten our established views about the mind and the way in which we gain knowledge from perceptual experience in the same way as genuine instances of CP. However, one cannot assess whether this strategy really works to rule out cognitive influences on perceptual experiences, unless one can clarify what attention really does and where in the cognitive hierarchy the effects of attention take place. I will postpone the discussion of the arguments against the possibility of attention-mediated cognitive penetration, i.e. what has been called "*the dismissive attitude*" (Mole 2015) until Chap. 6. But regardless of the truth of *the dismissive attitude*, it is already clear that a lot of weight in the CP debate hinges on attention.

If attentional effects are always post-perceptual or pre-perceptual (Pylyshyn 1999; Raftopoulos 2010), then the possibility of attention-mediated CP of perception is already excluded. The problem, however, is that attention is often regarded in the debate as a unified feature of the mind to which a specific function and place in the cognitive hierarchy can be assigned. However, as we shall see, attention is far more complex than what is implied by this simplistic picture. Once a better understanding of what attention does and where it exerts its role is in place, one may reassess alleged evidence of cognitive effects on perception and perceptual experience that are mediated by attention and whether they fit any of the definitions of CP introduced in the previous chapter.

If attention turns out to be something different or something more than what opponents of CP take it to be, several experimental results and interesting perceptual phenomena that have already been dismissed might be recruited again as evidence in favor of the reality of CP. Importantly, everyone in the debate, regardless of their position on CP, takes attention to be a very important and basic feature of the mind. Hence, if the possibility of attention-mediated CP is put back on the table, this would open up the door for a much wider set of fundamental interactions between cognition and perception that have yet to be discovered.

What should be clear from this discussion is that it is of the utmost importance to delve deeply into attention research and understand what attention is and how attentional processes unfold. This will allow us to reassess some arguments in favor of or against CP and to evaluate the real scope of this phenomenon. In the following exploration of attention, I adopt a theory-neutral strategy. In this chapter, I start by devising a working notion of attention based on some commonplace intuitions. On the basis of this notion I provide a series of types of mental phenomena that a theory of attention should explain. On the basis of the attentional phenomena that I individuate, which are widely accepted and discussed in the attention literature, in the next chapter, I evaluate extant theories of attention and offer my own version of one of the most popular theories.

4.2   What Is Attention?

In this section, I discuss the fundamental features of attention that are individuated on the basis of our everyday intuition in conjunction with some basic consideration about the human cognitive system. I offer a preliminary definition of attention, which serves as a guideline to introduce a taxonomy of mental processes that involve attention and that have been extensively discussed in the literature. On the basis of the taxonomy, I specify a criterion of adequacy for a theory of attention.

A canonic starting point adopted by many researchers on attention is the famous passage from James (1890), where he states:

> Every one knows what attention is. It is the taking possession by the mind, in clear and vivid form, of one out of what seem several simultaneously possible objects or trains of thought. Focalization, concentration of consciousness are of its essence. It implies a withdrawal from some things in order to deal effectively with others. (James 1890, p. 381)

Despite the overwhelming popularity of this quote in the literature, it is now clear that things are not quite as simple as James originally pictured them to be. Mole (2010) writes that:

> [...] a great deal of ingenious research succeeds in describing the ways in which various forms of attention behave, and succeeds in accounting for that behaviour by reference to its basis in the brain, but nobody knows quite how all of this adds up to an explanation of attention. (Mole 2010, p. vi)

Now, how could it be possible that everyone knows the nature of a phenomenon that nobody knows how to explain? There is a clear tension between the optimism of James' original inspiration and the complexities to which more than a century of attention research has led. Some researchers are even arguing that attention should be dismissed as a unitary concept and, ultimately, that there is no such thing as attention (Anderson 2011).

Despite the recent skepticism about a unified explanation of attention, there was some deep motivation to James' view that there is something common to all sorts of phenomena that we may label "attentional" and that such commonality can be easily grasped by anyone. This will be clear if we just spend some time reflecting on our everyday understanding of what the phrase "to attend" means. Intuitively, when one attends (or pays attention to something), there is a specific item or a small set of items that become more relevant for one's current purposes. The item or items to which one attends might be objects, properties or events[1] in the external world, as well as one's own mental states, for example one might pay attention to the voices in the corridor or pay attention to one's own thoughts and ignore the voices.

Now, if we think about ordinary cases in which we attend to something, we notice that to pay attention is a costly process. Attention sharpens our perceptual and cognitive capacities, but it is difficult to sustain it for a very long time. In other words, it seems that our cognitive resources are limited and that attention has the primary function of selecting where we preferentially allocate those resources. The necessity for selectivity is grounded in the observation that we are not able to simultaneously deal with all of the information that we ordinarily have available (Lennie 2003; Kastner and Ungerleider 2001), even in a very brief timespan.

Let us think about a couple of everyday examples. Imagine searching for a specific pen in a chaotically stuffed desk drawer. Without moving the objects in the drawer, one needs to slowly scan various objects or locations before the desired pen is finally found. If the cognitive system had unlimited capacity, it would not need to select which objects and locations to scan at a time. It would just process all of them at the same time and find the desired object immediately. As a second example, imagine reading a complex philosophical paper. In order to follow the argumentative line in the paper, one might want to focus attention and read each line carefully, instead of just quickly skimming through the text. After a while, this kind of careful reading causes fatigue and one might start to lose focus and need a short recovery time before one can start to focus again. In this example, attention is recruited for a different cognitive task than perceptual search. Like the previous example, however, the task is constrained in a way that points to the limited resources of the processing system (Liu et al. 2013; Chun et al. 2011; Carrasco 2011; Lennie 2003; Kastner and Ungerleider 2001). Indeed, the notion of limited capacity is the core idea behind quite a lot of attention research (Chun et al. 2011).

From the above discussion, we may conclude that "to pay attention" (to an object, property, event, mental state, etc.) is a contrastive notion. The item to which attention is paid is picked among the possible things that are currently available to the attending subject. Given the limited amount of our cognitive resources, whenever something is picked something else is thereby left out. Therefore, the expression "to pay attention" can be spelled out as *to pay attention to x while thereby ignoring y*. This way of phrasing is, as we shall see, partially wrong. Yet, it is helpful because it makes explicit the selective aspects of attention that underlie our everyday

---

[1] I clarify what kinds of objects, properties or events can be the target of attention below.

conception. Attention determines our capabilities to focus on a relevant item or, in other words, to select certain objects, properties, events or mental states among all those with which we are presented. This selective power of attention, for short *selectivity*, is one of the fundamental notions on which I establish my discussion.

A helpful way to phrase the problem of limited capacity and, thus, the necessity for selectivity is offered by Wu (2011) in the form of *the many-many problem*. Wu notes that at any given time we are presented with many different inputs (such as objects, properties, etc.) and there are many different outputs (in particular actions) that we may perform on the basis of the inputs. Among the many different possible outputs, we are able to actually produce only some of them. For instance, even if there are many possible ways that I could grasp the cup on the table in front of me, there is only one way in which I will eventually grasp it at a given time. Without an efficient selection and interface mechanism, which determines which inputs deserve to be dealt with first and which outputs are the most effective for dealing with them, even the most ordinary behavioral tasks would be impossible to perform because the system would be trapped in a stall between the many available inputs and the many possible outputs. The main task of attention is, thus, to achieve the kind of selection that is able to solve the *many-many problem*. I return to Wu's proposal later. For the moment, I take the *many-many problem* to be a helpful illustration of the fundamental function of *selectivity*.

Selectivity is perhaps the most fundamental aspect of attention. By itself *selectivity* entails that attention is an "all or nothing phenomenon": either something is selected or not. As it happens, however, sometimes one is forced to perform more than one action at a time or one has to pay attention to more than one object, property, etc. Furthermore, it might be that among the relevant objects, properties or events, not all are relevant to the same extent, and the amount of limited processing resources that should be dedicated to each selected item could differ.

Imagine a father watching his kid's football match. The kid is, of course, the most relevant target for the father's attention, but if he wants to understand what is going on, the father needs to pay attention to many other things such as the other players, the location of the ball, etc. Nevertheless, the kid seems to be a privileged target to which more resources are dedicated, compared to the other targets. At the same time, the father may fail to notice that the person sitting two seats to his left at the end of the match is different from the one who was sitting there at the beginning, meaning that the first person never captured the father's attention. In this case *selectivity* seems not to be flexible enough to account for the different degrees of attention that the father has to pay to his surroundings in order to behave efficiently in that context.

Thus, keeping in mind the limited capacity constraint, attention is nevertheless capable of selecting more than one item at a time (e.g. several football players currently engaged in an offensive move) and to sharpen the focus on the selected items to different degrees (e.g. one specific football player, the son, that is preferred among those currently attended to). In other words, attention is not only selective towards some items; it can also modulate how much resources are devoted to the selected items. The modulatory power of attention, for short *modulation*, is the second core notion of the present discussion. *Selectivity* and *modulation* are the two fundamental aspects that underlie our intuitive notion of attention (Chun et al. 2011). They are the tools that a system, such as the human brain, utilizes to optimize the allocation of its limited processing resources.

As I discussed above, different sorts of entities, such as objects, properties, and mental states, can be targets of *selectivity* and *modulation*. Given the idea of a functional processing hierarchy introduced in the previous chapters, we can conceive the different targets of attention as being processed at different levels in the hierarchy (Liu and Hou 2013). On the basis of these considerations, I offer a preliminary working definition of attention as follows:

> **Optimization:** Attention is the selective and modulatory optimization of processing-resources allocation at different levels of the cognitive and perceptual hierarchy

Optimized allocation of processing resources[2] appears to be a non-negotiable feature of a biological system such as the human brain, if we take into account the high metabolic costs of neuronal activity (Carrasco 2011; Lennie 2003). I would like to point out that by including the idea of a cognitive processing hierarchy in the definition, the current discussion of attention is limited to cognitive systems. It is, however, left open what sorts of information-processing systems may be cognitive.

One could argue that a possible exception to the need of optimization would be a case in which the available information that the system needs to process is so sparse that it does not exceed its processing resources. It is safe to assume that, for humans, in normal interactions with the environment, it is never the case that there is no need for selection. But we could think that such a case might happen in controlled conditions. Imagine, for example, that all that is presented before a subject's eyes is just a uniform color field that covers the whole visual space. In such a case, there seems to be no need for selection, because all that the visual system has to process is one uniform color hue. If we assume, for the sake of argument, that the subject can still be paying attention to the visual stimulus, then attention would not always involve selection and modulation. Hence, not every case of attention would be a case of selection and modulation, and *optimization* would fail as an adequate characterization of attention.

However, even if the available perceptual information does not exceed processing resources, it might still be the case that the system selectively prioritizes some parts of it in order to process it more efficiently. Furthermore, the system may be preferentially allocating resources to the processing of the visual stimulus, thereby "ignoring" other cognitive states, such as thoughts about the color, that may occur at the same time as the visual experience. In the uniform color field case there might be other cognitive processes, like thoughts or memories that compete[3] with color processing for neural resources. In other words, even assuming that perceptual information does not exceed the system's processing resources, there might be other

---

[2] In what follows I use "*optimization*" in italics to refer to the definition and simply "optimization" to refer to the process of allocating resources.

[3] In the following sections, the notion of competition will be spelled out in full.

relevant non-perceptual information that exceeds those resources. Thus, optimization may still be in place in cases in which available information does not apparently exceed processing resources.

But suppose that one can identify a clear case where only one input that does not exceed informational resources is present, and no other source of information, perceptual or otherwise, is available. I shall simply assume that, in such a case, attention is not involved. To think otherwise seems intuitively implausible and it would mean that attention is fundamentally equal to information processing. Such a notion of attention would not capture the contrastive cases in which some information is selected or preferentially processed among alternatives. In what follows I assume that all cases of attention involve a degree of selection and modulation of information that requires optimized allocation of processing resources.

Optimization is supposed to be a fairly uncontroversial definition of attention. Most researchers would agree that attention involves selection and modulation of information and that the target system, the human brain, has limited processing resources. As I mentioned, I use *optimization* as a guideline to identify the target phenomena, i.e. the *explananda* of a theory of attention. Afterwards I compare theories that try to explain such phenomena.

4.3 Varieties of Attentional Phenomena

The first requirement of a theory of attention is to get the extension of the term right. This means that an adequate theory of attention should capture all and only those phenomena that involve *optimization*. Using *optimization* as a minimal working definition I can now offer an overview of what sort of phenomena a theory of attention is supposed to explain. I do not claim that *optimization* is the only way in which we can characterize the *explananda* of a theory of attention. I do hold, however, that it is a reasonable starting point because it relies only on our intuitions about the selectivity and modulation of attention and some fundamental consideration about the processing constraints on biological systems that are capable of attending.

One first important point is that, given the general constraints on neural processing resources discussed above, optimization is in principle not limited to a single sensory modality. Optimization can target visual stimuli as well as haptic, auditory, gustatory, and olfactory stimuli. Attention may occur independently for each sensory modality or display cross-modal interactions (Ro and Rafal 1996).

If we carefully look at what happens when an object, property or event in the external world captures our attention, we will notice that optimization of the processing resource devoted to such item usually involves a shift in our body position, such that our sensory receptors are better oriented toward the target. This change of bodily posture to align the sensory receptors with the target is known as **overt attention**. If, for example, something suddenly makes a loud noise 10 m to my right, I might immediately turn my gaze to look at the source of the noise. However, one might ask whether each and every attentional task involves such a bodily shift. In the case of vision, for instance, one is capable of selecting a target stimulus within an array of stimuli without turning one's head or even without shifting one's gaze through saccadic movements. The capability of focusing on a target without any change in the position of the sensory receptor is known as **covert attention**.

In the present framework, covert attention can be described as a capacity to optimize resource allocation to information throughout the visual field without moving the eyes or the body. There is an extensive amount of research, dating back to the observations of Helmholtz, which supports the idea that we can pay attention, for example to our visual periphery, without shifting our gaze. Research on covert attention received a significant boost with the famous series of experiments by Michael Posner and colleagues (Posner 1978, 1980; Posner et al. 1980).

In the classical Posner paradigm, subjects are required to fixate on a cross located at the center of a display, on which a target object is presented on either the right or left side. Before the target a cue indicating its probable location is briefly flashed. The experiment measures how subjects' reaction times in target detection are affected by the cue. The result is that valid cues reduce reaction times without the subject changing fixation. This indicates that subjects are capable of selectively prioritizing some information on the basis of the cue without any bodily movement and, thus, the experiment demonstrates the effects of covert attention. In other words, subjects can covertly optimize allocation of processing resources to cued targets. In fact, most of the interesting results of current attention research target covert attention, involving experimental paradigms in which a subject's gaze position is carefully measured and is supposed not to vary. One further important distinction between overt and covert attention is that, since the former always involves a movement of the body or the eyes, its deployment is, therefore, necessarily serial, while the latter can be deployed "in parallel" (Carrasco 2011), e.g. across multiple items simultaneously.

Hence, attention does not always require a change in one's body position; on the contrary, optimization might happen in the complete absence of movement. This is even more evident if we think about the case of high-level cognitive attention, for example "paying attention to one's own thoughts" that I mentioned before. It is clear that in such cases no overt bodily movement is required in order to optimize allocation of processing resources to certain mental states over others. This first distinction between overt and covert attention is fundamental and it constitutes one of the most important phenomena that a theory of attention should explain.

A second general distinction concerns the question of what sorts of things can affect the optimization process in both covert and overt attention. If the system has to behave efficiently in a certain context, it is not sufficient that the system optimizes its resource allocation. The system also needs the optimization process to be sensitive to the goals and requirements dictated by the context. If optimization were to happen randomly, the system would display extremely inefficient behavior in any but the simplest of contexts, i.e. in a context where the amount of information does not exceed the processing resources.[4] But if optimization is not randomized, one can ask how it is regulated.

On the one hand, it seems that objects, properties, and events in the external world can automatically capture attention (recall the loud noise example) on the basis of their features. This usually happens if stimuli are presented abruptly or are salient enough, i.e. big, brightly colored, etc. On the other hand, a subject's current goals, expectations, and desires also play an important role in determining to which objects, properties or events attention is allocated and how. The former case, in which external objects, properties or events themselves strongly affect optimization, is a case of **exogenous attention.** Exogenous attention is also called "stimulus-driven" or "bottom-up". The latter case, in which internal mental states determine to what and how attention is directed, is a case of **endogenous attention.** Endogenous attention is also called "cognitively driven", "goal-directed" or "top-town" (Chun et al. 2011). To give an example, in classical versions of the Posner paradigm (e.g. Posner 1980), two types of cues can be used. One type of cue appears at the same location as the target object and, thus, exogenously drives optimization toward a specific location in the visual field by co-location. Another type of cue consists of arrows pointing either left or right that are presented in the center of the screen. This second type of cue requires a subject to identify the arrow and interpret its orientation. Thus, such cues endogenously drive optimization toward one visual hemifield by cue interpretation.

A third distinction concerns whether processing resources are allocated to only one item or more than one item at the same time. In this respect, forms of attention may be distinguished into **focal** and **distributed** (Eriksen and Hoffman 1972; Cohen and Dennett 2011) or **diffuse** (De Brigard and Prinz 2010). Focal attention occurs when optimization happens in such a way that practically all of the limited processing resources are devoted to a single target. Alternatively, if resources are optimized to suffice for more than one target, attention is diffuse.

One example of the transition between focal and diffuse attention is that of looking at fireworks. Before the fireworks start one is looking and attending to a quite extended and roughly delimited spatial location. In this case attention is distributed to the whole area. Once the fireworks start, single shots will initially capture one's attention and attention to each of them will be focal. Towards the end of the show, multiple shots will be fired at the same time and attention will again be distributed to several of them at the same time. In the present terminology, during the fireworks, *optimization* prioritizes allocation of resources firstly to an entire extended spatial location, secondly to single items at that location, thirdly to multiple items at that location. Given the limited processing resources, change in optimization will correspond to changes in visual resolution and detail in the three conditions. The problem of limited processing resources is again extremely important. In diffuse attention, targets are detected or experienced in less detail or resolution (Cohen and

---

[4]As I mentioned above, this may plausibly happen only in specific experimental environments.

Dennett 2011), whereas in certain cases of focal attention, very salient targets that are outside of the focus are not even detected (Simons and Chabris 1999).

A fourth general distinction can be made between **conscious** and **unconscious** attention. There is little doubt that we can consciously attend to certain things depending on, for instance, the perceptual saliency of those things or our expectations about those things. But is it possible to have optimization in a completely unconscious fashion? The problem here is whether attending to an object, property or event X necessarily involves phenomenal experience of X. In a famous series of studies based on the Posner paradigm, Kentridge and colleagues (Kentridge 2004; Kentridge et al. 1999, 2008) documented the effect of cueing attention on the behavioral performance of a blindsight subject. In blindsight, subjects cannot consciously experience a portion of their visual field, but they can still reliably perform certain perceptual tasks like, for example, forced-choice discrimination. Blindsight comes in two variants: in type 1 blindsight, subjects have no awareness of and cannot report anything about the affected portion of the visual field; in type 2 blindsight, a minimal degree of awareness is preserved and the subject can typically report that something changed in the affected visual field yet without being able to report detailed percepts. The blindsight condition makes it impossible for a subject of Kentridge's experiments to consciously experience the cue, but despite this impairment, experimenters found that the cue could still affect performance in subsequent discrimination tasks. What this evidence shows is that the processing advantages provided by attentional cues in normal subjects have the same effect on subjects who lack conscious experience of the cues. Thus, exogenous orientation of attention does not depend on conscious experience and can work in its absence, which supports the possibility of unconscious optimization. Further extensive evidence for the possibility of unconscious attention is reviewed by Van Boxtel et al. who write that: "attention can be directed toward and away from a stimulus or one of its attributes without the stimulus or attributes ever being visible"[5] (2010, p. 3). Hence, it seems that an unconscious cue can influence to which objects, properties or events attention is paid in a subsequent display.

The distinction of conscious and unconscious attention is closely tied to that of **voluntary** and **involuntary** attention. However, the two distinctions must be kept separate for there can be both voluntary or involuntary conscious attention as in the case of explicitly following an instruction to attend to something (conscious voluntary) versus a sudden loud noise 10 m to my right that immediately captures all my attention (conscious involuntary). A similar case can presumably be made for voluntary and involuntary unconscious attention.

Above, I have examined five distinctions between different phenomena that involve optimization and that, therefore, I have characterized as different forms of attention. Let me now turn to examine the targets of attention. So far, I have been talking about objects, properties, events or mental states as the kind of things to

---

[5] By saying that stimuli were not visible they mean that they were presented below the threshold for conscious detection.

which attention optimizes resource allocation. I shall now elucidate what exactly the targets of attention can be. In other words, I specify the sorts of objects, properties or events that can be selected and modulated by attention.[6]

Arguably, the most important targets of attention seem to be spatiotemporal features of objects and events around us. Attention has often been associated with a mental spotlight, capable of highlighting subsets of the sensory field and bringing them into the focus of the mind (James 1890). Although this *spotlight metaphor* is misleading in picturing attention as an independent device dedicated to spatial selection, it correctly highlights its sensitivity for spatial properties. In the Posner paradigm, for example, it is safe to assume that the kind of optimization that the cue triggers concerns the allocation of resources to the processing of spatial locations and can therefore be called **spatial attention**. In addition to spatial properties, attention can also be directed at temporal properties. **Temporal attention** can be paid, for example, to stimuli that occur at the same location but at different times (Coull and Nobre 1998).

Spatiotemporal properties are arguably among the most prominent targets of attention, but they are not the only ones. Properties or features of individual objects, such as color and shape (Wolfe and Horowitz 2004; Mole 2015), are also among the possible targets of optimization. **Feature-based** attention is an extremely important composite phenomenon, which determines the possibility of developing integrated representations of complex scenes (feature integration). Furthermore, optimization can target objects as wholes. **Object-based** attention (Scholl 2001; Duncan 1984) takes already integrated bundles of features of the same object (e.g. features within the same figural boundaries) as its targets. Finally, **cognitive attention** can be paid to internal mental states such as specific thoughts or memories (Mole 2015). For example, during mental rehearsal, one has to keep focusing attention on the rehearsed topic or sentence and disregard both internal and external factors of distraction.

On the basis of my preliminary definition of attention as *optimization*, I have discussed some of the most prominent distinctions that can be made in attention research. I take it that the distinctions outlined in this section are uncontroversial and accepted by most attention theorists. As such, they must be jointly explained by any adequate theory of attention. The present taxonomy is, of course, simplified. There might be other mental phenomena that involve optimization and that should therefore be included in the *explananda* of a theory of attention. A good theory of attention should explain those phenomena as well, but for the purposes of this book, it suffices to employ the above simplified taxonomy.

---

[6]This is not an exhaustive account of all the possible targets of attention. For reasons that will become clear later, there is no principled boundary to the scope of attention within all the information that is processed by a system such as the human brain.

4.4   Summary and Conclusion

In this chapter, I have clarified why the discussion of attentional processes and phenomena is crucial for the debate on cognitive penetrability, because of the rather entrenched *dismissive attitude* that characterizes this debate. As is now clear from the above discussion, clarifying the nature of attention is no easy task. I have outlined some fundamental constraints on the notion of attention by outlining basic everyday intuitions about attention and a variety of attentional phenomena that an adequate theory of attention is required to explain. In the next chapter, I discuss some of the most prominent extant views about attention. I evaluate these theories on the basis of a specific criterion of adequacy that takes the form of the following desideratum: a theory of attention must explain all and only the phenomena that involve optimization. These include, individually or in combination: overt and covert attention; exogenous and endogenous attention; conscious and unconscious attention; voluntary and involuntary attention; focal and diffuse attention; spatial, feature-based, object-based, and cognitive attention.

References

Anderson, B. (2011). There is no such thing as attention. *Frontiers in Psychology, 2*, 246.

Block, N. (2010). Attention and mental paint. *Philosophical Issues, 20*(1), 23–63.

Carrasco, M. (2011). Visual attention: The past 25 years. *Vision Research, 51*(13), 1484–1525.

Carrasco, M., Ling, S., & Read, S. (2004). Attention alters appearance. *Nature Neuroscience, 7*, 308–313.

Chun, M. M., Golomb, J. D., & Turk-Browne, N. B. (2011). A taxonomy of external and internal attention. *Annual Review of Psychology, 62*(1), 73–101.

Cohen, M. A., & Dennett, D. C. (2011). Consciousness cannot be separated from function. *Trends in Cognitive Sciences, 15*(8), 358–364.

Coull, J. T., & Nobre, A. C. (1998). Where and when to pay attention: The neural systems for directing attention to spatial locations and to time intervals as revealed by both PET and fMRI. *Journal of Neuroscience, 18*(18), 7426–7435.

De Brigard, F., & Prinz, J. (2010). Attention and consciousness. *Wiley Interdisciplinary Reviews: Cognitive Science, 1*(1), 51–59.

Duncan, J. (1984). Selective attention and the organization of visual information. *Journal of Experimental Psychology: General, 113*(4), 501–517.

Eriksen, C. W., & Hoffman, J. E. (1972). Temporal and spatial characteristics of selective encoding from visual displays. *Perception & Psychophysics, 12*, 201–204.

James, W. (1890). *The principles of psychology.* Reprint. Cambridge, MA: Harvard University Press, 1981.

Kastner, S., & Ungerleider, L. G. (2001). The neural basis of biased competition in human visual cortex. *Neuropsychologia, 39*(12), 1263–1276.

Kentridge, R. (2004). Spatial attention speeds discrimination without awareness in blindsight. *Neuropsychologia, 42*(6), 831–835.

Kentridge, R. W., Heywood, C. A., & Weiskrantz, L. (1999). Attention without awareness in blindsight. *Proceedings of the Royal Society of London B: Biological Sciences, 266*(1430), 1805–1811.

Kentridge, R. W., Nijboer, T. C. W., & Heywood, C. A. (2008). Attended but unseen: Visual attention is not sufficient for visual awareness. *Neuropsychologia, 46*(3), 864–869.

Lennie, P. (2003). The cost of cortical computation. *Current Biology, 13*(6), 493–497.

Liu, T., & Hou, Y. (2013). A hierarchy of attentional priority signals in human frontoparietal cortex. *The Journal of Neuroscience: The Official Journal of the Society for Neuroscience, 33*(42), 16606–16616.

Liu, T., Abrams, J., & Carrasco, M. (2009). Voluntary attention enhances contrast appearance. *Psychological Science, 20*, 354–362.

Liu, T., Becker, M. W., & Jigo, M. (2013). Limited featured-based attention to multiple features. *Vision Research, 85*, 36–44.

Mole, C. (2010). *Attention is cognitive unison: An essay in philosophical psychology.* Oxford: Oxford University Press.

Mole, C. (2015). Attention and cognitive penetration. In A. Raftopoulos & J. Zeimbekis (Eds.), *The cognitive penetrability of perception: New philosophical perspectives* (pp. 218–238). New York: Oxford University Press.

Posner, M. I. (1978). *Chronometric explorations of mind.* Hillsdale: Lawrence Erlbaum Associates.

Posner, M. I. (1980). Orienting of attention. The 7th Sir F. C. Bartlett lecture. *Quarterly Journal of Experimental Psychology, 32*, 3–25.

Posner, M. I., Snyder, C. R. R., & Davidson, B. J. (1980). Attention and the detection of signals. *Journal of Experimental Psychology: General, 109*, 160–174.

Pylyshyn, Z. W. (1999). Is vision continuous with cognition? The case for cognitive impenetrability of visual perception. *Behavioral and Brain Sciences, 22*(3), 341–365.

Raftopoulos, A. (2010). Ambiguous figures and representationalism. *Synthese, 181*(3), 489–514.

Ro, T., & Rafal, R. D. (1996). Perception of geometric illusions in hemispatial neglect. *Neuropsychologia, 34*(10), 973–978.

Scholl, B. J. (2001). Objects and attention: The state of the art. *Cognition, 80*(1), 1–46.

Simons, D. J., & Chabris, C. F. (1999). Gorillas in our midst: Sustained inattentional blindness for dynamic events. *Perception, 28*(9), 1059–1074.

Van Boxtel, J. J. A., Tsuchiya, N., & Koch, C. (2010). Consciousness and attention: On sufficiency and necessity. *Frontiers in Psychology, 1*, 217.

Wolfe, J. M., & Horowitz, T. S. (2004). What attributes guide the deployment of visual attention and how do they do it? *Nature Reviews Neuroscience, 5*, 495–501.

Wu, W. (2011). Confronting many-many problems: Attention and agentive control. *Nous, 45*(1), 50–76.

Chapter 5
Toward a New Theory of Attention

Abstract The aim of this chapter is to offer a new theory of attention which is based and expands upon the popular biased competition theory. The theory is introduced by contrast to alternative views and in the light of some basic intuitions about attention that have driven research on this topic since the beginning. I propose a philosophical account of attention that characterizes it as a property of competing representations. In Sect. 5.1, I discuss and evaluate three prominent theories of attention, arguing that none of them clearly meets the desideratum. In Sect. 5.2, I present the biased competition theory of attention in detail and argue that it meets the desideratum on a theory of attention. Section 5.3 expands upon the biased competition theory, toward an explanation of attention as the property of "being the current winner" of a biased competition process between representations. The picture of attention and attentional processes that emerges from this chapter serves as a basis for discussing their role in the interactions between perception and cognition as well as their relationship with the cognitive penetrability of perceptual experience.

5.1 Theories of Attention: An Unsettled Game

In this section, I provide an overview of some of the most prominent theories in attention research. I believe that most of these theories are compatible with *optimization* and that, therefore, they aim at explaining the same phenomena. I evaluate the advantages and shortcomings of each of the positions discussed here on the basis of the desideratum on a theory of attention presented at the end of the previous section. The guideline is that if a theory of attention is not capable of meeting the desideratum, such a theory does not offer an adequate explanation of attention[1]. The following overview, however, is not meant as a definitive dismissal of the theories addressed. The aim is rather to highlight some shortcomings of extant proposals in order to have a better picture of what a compelling account of attention looks like.

---

[1] A full explanation of attention should include something more. For example, a description of a causal mechanism that implements attention or of the function that the system computes during attentional processes.

© Springer Nature Switzerland AG 2020
F. Marchi, *The Attentional Shaping of Perceptual Experience*, Studies in Brain and Mind 16, https://doi.org/10.1007/978-3-030-33558-8_5

Let me start this overview with the *filter model* of attention proposed by Broadbent (1958). Driver (2001) highlights that, in proposing his model of attention, Broadbent was looking for an answer to two questions that had driven previous research on perceptual selection: 1. What differences are required between two stimuli presented at the same time in order for a subject to be able to clearly report one of them? 2. What do subjects know about the non-target stimulus? Previous research had used experimental paradigms such as selective shadowing, in which two spoken messages are presented at the same time and subjects are asked to repeat (shadow) only one of them.

In particular, experimenters had established that, in order for subjects to be successful at shadowing, there had to be some clear physical difference between the two stimuli. Furthermore, subjects were able to report only very little information about the physical properties of non-shadowed messages. Broadbent's explanation for this phenomenon was to posit two perceptual processing stages. In the early stage, all available information about the simple physical features of all incoming stimuli is processed in parallel. At the later stage, more complex features of stimuli such as identity and meaning are processed. Given that this stage requires increased detail and computational complexity, it was thought to have limited capacity and to be incapable of dealing with all the incoming information as the early stage does. In this picture, the task of attention is to filter what of the information available at the early stage is passed to the late stage for further processing or, as Driver puts it: "A selective filter protected the second stage from overload, passing to it only those stimuli which had a particular physical property, from among those already extracted for all stimuli within the first stage" (2001, p. 56). This model was capable of explaining why two stimuli are required to be physically different in order for a subject to clearly report one of them: the different physical properties are precisely what allows the system to filter out one of the stimuli. Moreover, the model could explain why very little is known about stimuli that are filtered out and the answer is simply because such stimuli have no access to further processing.

As simple and appealing as Broadbent's model might look, there is a problem that immediately presents itself and that is shared by all analog filter theories. The problem in question is where exactly to collocate the filter in the sequence of perceptual processing. The problem is straightforward: to what extent does the perceptual system process all information in parallel and what are the properties that need to be filtered out? For example, one may think that all physical properties of stimuli are encoded in the system and then a filter selects what abstract properties to extract. Alternatively, one may think that all properties are encoded and that the filter selects what properties are further encoded in memory and made reportable (Driver 2001). This problem gave rise to two different currents within the filter view of attention that are usually labeled "early selection views" and "late selection views" (Driver 2001).

According to early-selectionist views (Broadbent 1958) only very low-level physical properties are processed in parallel and the filtering process occurs early in the overall perceptual processing stream. However, late-selectionists (Deutsch and Deutsch 1963) objected that, since non-reportable stimuli can sometimes affect behavior, it is possible that all perceptual information about the stimuli is processed in parallel and can influence higher-level processing, but only a part of it is encoded in memory and is, thus, reportable.

A similar position is endorsed by Prinz (2012), who claims that the role of attention is to make information that is represented in the perceptual system at a specific processing level available for working memory encoding and as a consequence of such availability, attended representations would be consciously perceived. In this respect, Prinz's proposal qualifies as a form of late selection view insofar as all available information before the occurrence of attention is unconsciously processed (and not reportable) and it is capable of determining the behavior of the system to a certain extent. As a matter of fact, the debate between early-selectionist and late-selectionist views has not been settled and the precise place in which to locate the attentional filter remains elusive. At this point, one may ask whether the filter model, in any of the forms discussed above, meets the desideratum. In other words, does the filter model explain all and only those phenomena that involve optimization? The answer to this question seems to be negative.

What the different selectionist views have in common is that they posit a pre-attentional stage and post-attentional stage of processing and attention is supposed to be a partition between the two stages. If one adopts a hierarchical functional view of perceptual and cognitive processing, it seems that different levels of the hierarchy would correspond to the processing of different items. Lower levels would correspond to the perceptual processing of objects' features such as shape and color, while higher levels would correspond to the processing of more complex items like entire objects or even whole perceptual sceneries, which may include several objects. At even higher levels one may find processing of more abstract and long-term regularities that may be characterized as the contents of thoughts and judgments. In a cognitive system, such as the human brain, where the limited resources take the form of a fundamental metabolic constraint, one would expect that each of these different levels of processing needs its own optimization. Accordingly, different forms of attention, such as feature-based attention, object-based attention, and cognitive attention, would correspond to increasingly higher levels in the hierarchy.

Now, both early-selectionists and late-selectionists should specify at what levels the supposed filter of attention has to be located. But no matter what level they eventually settle on, it seems that other levels would thereby be excluded from the scope of attention. Suppose that early selectionists locate the filter at the very beginning of the processing hierarchy and that late selectionists locate it higher up in the hierarchy, for example after the processing of whole perceptual scenes. For early selectionists, attention would have the function of filtering out very early features of objects, whereas for late selectionists, attention would have the function of filtering out what elements of a perceptual scene are encoded in memory and may be reported by the subject. The two positions may therefore explain feature-based attention and some form of cognitive attention, respectively, but neither could explain both at the same time. This is, of course, an oversimplification, but it is already helpful to highlight one important limitation of such approaches, namely that they attribute to attention a functional role that is far too specific. Optimization seems to be needed for both the filtering of early features and for the filtering of what perceptual items are encoded in memory and an adequate theory should be able to explain optimization at, possibly, all different levels. Therefore, both theories fail to address some of the *explananda* and, for this reason, they fail to meet the desideratum.

Prinz's working memory theory of attention is an exception. As far as this theory is concerned, attention can make accessible to working memory information coming from all levels of the processing hierarchy (both bottom-up and top-down). In this respect, the theory may indeed account for all the different basic forms of attention that I have discussed. However, a striking shortcoming of Prinz's view is that, according to his proposal, if and only if a specific perceptual representation is attended is it consciously experienced, or, in other words, attention is necessary and sufficient for consciousness. If this claim were true, it would exclude the possibility of unconscious attention and, therefore, since unconscious attention figures among the *explananda*, it would also fail to meet the desideratum.

An alternative to selectionist views is the *feature-binding model* of attention (Treisman and Gelade 1980; Treisman 1998). According to the feature-binding theory, simple physical features of stimuli are quickly and pre-attentively processed in parallel but are unbound. Attention's task is to bind together into coherent objects features that co-occur at certain spatiotemporal locations (Treisman and Gelade 1980; Driver 2001). This theory presupposes *optimization* because binding seems to require optimized selective and modulatory processing of exactly those features that end up being bound together.

The theory is based on the much-replicated finding that subjects are capable of reporting what colors and simple shapes are presented when they are not paying attention, but they are not capable of reporting combinations of colors and shapes, unless they pay attention (Treisman 1998). This means that, contrary to early-selectionist views, there may be attenuated processing of unattended features to a certain extent. However, contrary to late-selectionist views, the task of attention is not simply to select certain features at a later point in the perceptual processing stream, but to select spatiotemporal locations that determine which features are to be bound together and belong to the same object. In other words, the functional role of attention is that of solving the binding problem (Treisman 1998), i.e. the problem of integrating together features of the same object and not of different objects concurrently available to perception. In this view, attention allows us to correctly integrate object features and to experience a world of coherent objects and scenes, instead of an array of disembodied or arbitrarily bound shapes, colors, etc.

Unfortunately, the feature-binding models appear to have the same explanatory inadequacy as selectionist views. Binding has to happen somewhere along the processing stream and once the locus of binding is identified, some lower and/or higher levels would be excluded from its scope. The problem is that *optimization* is needed at all levels of the processing hierarchy for which processing resources are limited, including those levels that are outside the scope of the binding functional role that is attributed to attention in this model. Furthermore, optimization is needed at processing levels where there are no features to bind, for example, when one focuses attention on one particular train of thought while writing a paper. Hence, the binding model is also incapable of explaining some of the explananda that figure in the desideratum.

The aforementioned *selection for action* view proposed by Wu (2011a, b) has a wider scope and, in this sense, may fare better than the models discussed above with regards to the desideratum. Wu agrees that *selectivity* is one of the basic functions of attention for both perceptual contents and contents of thoughts (Wu 2011a). However, by itself selectivity is not sufficient to characterize attention. What further characterizes attention over other possible selective processes is the fact that attention makes it possible for subjects to act in the world.

According to Wu, attention is what makes it possible to solve what he calls the many-many problem. Above I provided a sketch of the idea behind the many-many problem. The problem arises because in ordinary contexts, human subjects are typically presented with many inputs (objects and properties) from different perceptual channels and not all of them may be currently relevant. Furthermore, there are many actions a subject can perform in order to successfully deal with those inputs. Thus, selectivity is needed both for the many available inputs and for the many possible actions, in order to allow a subject to behave successfully. According to Wu, attention is the kind of *selectivity* that allows us to solve the many-many problem, i.e. attention is selection for action. Given the stress that Wu puts on the selective aspect of attention, I assume that his theory is also compatible with *optimization*. Importantly, Wu construes attention as a subject-level phenomenon specifically tied to agency by definition (Wu 2011a):

> But a worry now arises: is the required attunement at the level of the subject or is it rather the activity of a sub-personal perceptual system that is somehow distinct from the agent's own involvement. If the latter is the case, then selection as required to solve the Many-Many Problem is not a subject level phenomenon, and hence is not attention as we are conceiving it. (Wu 2011a p. 102)

When attention is conceived as selection for action, its scope is not limited to systems with limited processing resources, but to agents. Agents may have unlimited processing resources and still need attention to act. This insight is extremely important and I do not wish to reject it here. However, conceiving of attention exclusively as selection for action has, once again, a too narrow scope with respect to the desideratum. By defining attention by subject-level agency, it seems that Wu cannot account for selection that does not involve agency but that we would still call attention according to *optimization*. Not all of cognition is directly tied to agency. Many cases of cognitive attention, for example selecting certain thoughts or memories for current conscious access, may still involve *optimization* without requiring either action or action planning. One could, for example, remember a comforting memory to cope with depressive thoughts or just to enjoy the ensuing emotion of happiness without the aim or need to perform any related action.

Furthermore, in a limited resources system, such as the human brain, it is plausible to assume that there are sub-personal level processes that do not involve agency. To claim otherwise would be to generalize agency to the whole scope of cognition, which would trivialize the view. Still, we can plausibly assume that such processes are exposed to the same metabolic resource limitations that are due to the nature of the vehicle that implements them. If this is the case, the need for optimization arises at a non-agential sub-personal level, but Wu's theory would exclude these cases as attentional phenomena. Given the above discussion, I take Wu's theory to be highlighting one of the most important functions performed by attention, namely selection for action. Selection for action is achieved by a particular kind of optimization that is tied to agency and occurs at the subject level. The need for this kind of optimization may arise even in agents whose cognitive system is not constrained by limited resources. Yet, selection for action cannot be the whole story about attention, because optimization plausibly occurs at the sub-personal and non-agential level in a system where processing resources are indeed limited.

There are also some evolutionary considerations that support this point. Haladjian and Montemayor (2014) argue that attention may be one of the oldest evolutionary features of biological processing systems. This consideration is in line with the characterization of attention as *optimization*. In humans, for example, various forms of attention may have evolved at different times and for various tasks. This idea is plausible because the need for optimized selection and modulation of information would arise as soon as an organism with limited resources needs to behave flexibly and efficiently in a changeable environment. If this is true, it seems difficult to reconcile personal-level unitary views of attention with a process that may have a long complex evolutionary history in humans and that may concern many other organisms and systems. To conclude the discussion of the selection for action theory, it seems that even if this theory has a wider scope than the previous accounts and covers more of the *explananda* of a theory of attention, it can still not account for all the *explananda*, e.g. some forms of non-agential cognitive attention, because of its being tied to agency and to the subject level.

In reply to the objection of explanatory inadequacy, namely that positing too specific a functional role for attention does not explain all of the attentional phenomena that figure in the desideratum, proponents of the filter model, the binding model or the selection for action theory can argue that attention could be a very constrained phenomenon and that other phenomena that fall under *optimization* are not really instances of attention. In other words, they could say that the desideratum is too inclusive. But this would amount to having an ad hoc characterization of the extension, whereas *optimization* was motivated on the basis of some widely endorsed intuitions about attention and some minimal constraints on the processing system. I do not argue that this move is not available to these theorists. However, it seems that taking *optimization* as a starting point would yield a less controversial and arbitrary characterization of attention's extension and, thereby, of the functional roles that it may perform.

Some of the worries raised above about the problems of a personal-level agential view of attention apply to two other prominent views in the literature, namely the *cognitive unison* view (Mole 2010) and the *structuring* view (Watzl 2017). These views deserve separate treatment as they are primarily concerned with the metaphysical question about the nature of attention and depart form the conception of attention as *optimization* which forms the starting point of the present work.

Nevertheless, introducing them and comparing them to the account I defend might help in providing some context and preliminary clarifications for my view to be introduced soon.

According to Mole (2010), attention is an adverbial phenomenon, i.e. a way of doing something. In his view, adverbial phenomena are differentiated from processes; for example, for a phenomenon like *haste*, there is no process of haste, but only ways of doing something *hastily*. Thus, to understand the nature of haste one has to explain what it takes to do something hastily. Attention is supposed to work in the same way. As such, Mole asks what it is for something to be done *attentively*. To paraphrase his answer, an agent performs a task attentively if and only if the agent's performance of the task displays cognitive unison (Mole 2010, p. 51). Cognitive unison, in turn, is characterized by requiring all the cognitive resources in a task's background set to be dedicated to the performance of the task. The background set of a task is the set of resources that potentially serve the task and membership to this set depends on the subject's understanding of the task at hand.

Such a short introduction to Mole's view cannot do justice to the extensive and detailed discussion of attention in his book and to the argumentative force of his theory. However, a full illustration is beyond the scope and constraints of this chapter. This minimal introduction suffices to demarcate the difference between Mole's view and the view of attention that I shall put forward later. First of all, Mole explicitly rejects process-first accounts of attention, the primary reason being that for many proposed processes, like feature binding, for example, one might find real or hypothetical examples of those processes occurring without constituting attention. However, this only shows the limitations of extant process-first theories and hardly speaks against the process-first approach in general. Mole argues that the diversity of attentional phenomena, on which I also rely to frame the desideratum in the previous chapter, might make many if not all process-first views untenable. However, as we shall see later, I believe that there is one specific process-first view that meets the desideratum and, as such, should appear more promising in the light of Mole's criticism of the alternatives.

Moving to the second view that I want to address, in his recent book Watzl (2017) presents a view of attention that is also primarily dedicated to shedding light on the metaphysical nature of this phenomenon. According to Watzl, attention is a personal-level activity, i.e. an activity of the subject as opposed to some of her subsystems, that regulates priority structures. For example, in vision attention would structure visual experience according to center and periphery or foreground and background, as well as other priority relations. Watzl conceives of the role of attention as an organizational rather than a selective one and rejects the idea that attention is tied to resource limitations (2017, pp. 106–107). Watzl turns the idea of selectivity and resource limitation on its head claiming that rather than needing attention to select information due to resource limitations, selectivity is an outcome of our mental life being organized around priority structures. He discusses how his view is different from Wu's as according to him attention is itself an activity and, therefore, cannot be a form of selection that precedes and determines action.

Like Mole's view, an exhaustive illustration of Watzl's theory would require a much lengthier discussion, which is beyond the aims of this chapter. However, the snapshot offered here is enough to demarcate his view from my own. The idea that selection is an outcome of attentional process rather than a cause or precondition for attention is something that I also maintain, albeit in a different form. However, the idea that attention is an agent-level activity is in stark tension with the view that I want to put forward. The main problem, which echoes the one discussed for Wu's theory, is that sub-personal and non-agential subsystems might also need their own organization of priority structures. In other words, the idea that prioritization is necessarily executed at the personal agentive level might have the undesirable consequence of leaving many sub-personal phenomena that are still closely connected to selection and modulation outside the scope of a theory of attention.

Before concluding this section, I would like to discuss a final account of attention that goes in a much different direction from that taken by Mole and Watzl. The account in question is offered by Prinz (2012) and is different insofar as he claims that attention is identical with a specific neural process, namely synchronizations of some regular patterns of brain activations (vectorwaves) to the gamma frequency of 40 hz. According to Prinz, gamma synchronization makes the representations realized by vectorwaves available for working memory encoding. Making representations available for working memory encoding is the function of attention in his view. One problem with this account comes from Prinz's view of the relation between attention and consciousness. While he holds that attention is necessary and sufficient for consciousness, he also maintains that consciousness is intermediate between low- and high-level processes in the cognitive hierarchy. Summarizing his view, only representations that are both sufficiently integrated and anchored to the first-person perspective are suitable to become conscious. This idea goes back to Jackendoff (1987), but combined with Prinz's view on attention it entails that only intermediate-level representations could be attended. Intermediate representation involves egocentric and viewpoint-dependent features, from which something like object identities and other contents of thoughts and beliefs are excluded. It is immediately clear how this would not fare well with respect to the desideratum as this view has difficulties in accounting for high-level cognitive forms of attention.

The purpose of this section was to show that, even without taking the mechanisms into consideration, these accounts do not fully capture what we refer to when we talk about attention. Some of the theories fail to meet the desideratum by having too narrow a scope, while others face problems connected to restricting the target phenomenon to the personal level. Before beginning the endeavor of providing a full explanation of attention, it would be helpful to have, at least, a better starting model as a guideline, i.e. a model of attention that meets the extension desideratum. Providing such a model is the purpose of the next section.

5.2   Better Player in the Field: The Biased Competition Theory

In this section, I outline the *biased competition* theory of attention as a model of selective visual attention and attention in general. Furthermore, I argue that it satisfies the desideratum on a theory of attention introduced above, which makes it preferable to the alternative models discussed. The biased competition theory of attention originates in the work of Robert Desimone and John Duncan (Desimone and Duncan 1995; Duncan et al. 1997; Desimone 1998; Duncan 1998). Unsurprisingly, the whole approach revolves around the fundamental ideas behind most of recent research on attention mentioned above, namely (1) *limited capacity*: the cognitive system cannot process all of the information that is normally available to it at a given time (Broadbent 1958), and (2) *selectivity/modulation*: the cognitive system is selective as to what information is relevant in a given context and to which degree it is relevant. As we have seen, other theories of attention, such as the *filter model* (Broadbent 1958) and the *feature-binding model* (Treisman 1998), which identify attention with a specific process or feature of the system to be located at a specific place in the processing hierarchy, fall short of accounting for some of the distinctions between different forms of attention.

Proponents of the biased competition view take a different approach: starting from the observation that at any given time our perceptual system is presented with many different concurring stimuli and that it cannot efficiently process all of them (limited capacity), they conceive of attention as emerging from a distributed process, which can be implemented by different neural mechanisms in the brain. The different mechanisms share, however, one fundamental task: to resolve the competition for processing priority among the many available perceptual stimuli. Furthermore, competition is *biased*, i.e. it is sensitive to the relevance of different stimuli in the present context. Relevance, in turn, depends on both features of stimuli themselves like size, motion, and brightness or other environmental cues (bottom-up bias), as well as features of the perceiver such as goals, desires, and preferences (top-down bias).

The biased competition theory gets off the ground with the observation that if two stimuli are presented in the receptive field of the same neuron or group of neurons, the information that the system encodes about each of them declines. Since the system needs to develop a coherent interpretation of what it is presented with, one can say that stimuli in the same receptive fields compete for processing priority. Evidence for suppression of competing stimuli can be found both within the same sensory modality and across different sensory modalities (Woods et al. 1984; Sadato et al. 1996). The competition between stimuli for processing priority is necessary because of the limited system's resources, whereas the selectivity and modulation of relevant information depends on the possibility of having highly specific top-down and bottom-up biases in respect of which of the available stimuli should emerge as winners.[2]

Thus, the biased competition view conceives of optimization as a competition process between stimuli that fall within the receptive field of the same neuron or neural population. This particular kind of competition takes place at each level in the visual hierarchy[3] (West et al. 2011) and can in principle extend beyond vision, to other sensory modalities and to higher-level cognitive domains (Mather and Sutherland 2011; Duncan 2006). In fact, the competition process stems from some basic constraint on the functioning of neurons and, as such, it is in principle not limited to any specific place in the brain and, similarly, in other processing systems with limited resources. Taking vision as an example, at the lowest levels in the processing hierarchy, competing stimuli might be as simple as two points of light. At higher levels in the hierarchy[4], competing stimuli might be more complex visual features such as orientations, shapes, colors, etc. or they can be whole objects and even whole scenes (Mole 2015).

However, one of the most important aspects of the biased competition view is that the factors that determine the outcome of the competition at a given level are not limited to that level. The competition between stimuli for neural processing resources can be biased by top-down, bottom-up, and lateral factors. As I argue below, many of the distinctions between different attentional phenomena are captured by the sensitivity of the competition process to both bottom-up biases (stimulus properties) and lateral and top-down biases (factors internal to the system itself, including other cognitive processes). Another important feature of the competition is its integrated nature (Duncan 1998; Mole 2015). The possibility of having different directions of bias allows that whenever a clear winner emerges at any given level, the result of competition at that level can bias the competition at other levels toward the most consistent outcome. This means that an integrated and coherent outcome can be the result of several competition processes that bias one another at different levels.

Given the costs of neural processing, the need for optimization seems to be ubiquitous in the brain. Hence, if optimization is achieved through competition, one might think that the need for competition is not limited to perception, but arises over the whole span of the cognitive processing hierarchy. This is intuitively plausible. One can pay attention to one's own thoughts, for example one can focus on a specific train of thought to solve a problem, and when trying to recall specific memories one must select the relevant ones. Therefore, if competition is a good model of attention, it seems that the competition process should extend outside the domain of perception and into the domain of higher-level cognition (Chun and Turk-Browne

---

[2] Part of what follows in this section has been adapted from Marchi (2017).

[3] As often happens in cognitive science, vision is the primary focus of empirical research on biased competition. However, the idea of biased competition extends beyond vision.

[4] Following the terminology introduced in Chap. 1, we may refer to low-level competing stimuli as high-resolution (fast-changing) regularities and to higher-level competing stimuli as lower resolution regularities.

2007; Yi and Chun 2005). In accordance with this line of reasoning, Duncan (2006) provides comparative evidence for the occurrence of competition in several neural domains. Whether it is true that competition occurs outside perception remains an open empirical question, but there is evidence that competition operates outside perception at least in the domain of memory (Mather and Sutherland 2011).

There is now considerable empirical evidence in favor of the biased competition view, at least for visual areas of the brain (Beck and Kastner 2009). One of the most interesting sources of empirical support comes from the study of a perceptual disorder known as unilateral neglect, particularly in the form known as perceptual extinction. A subject suffering from unilateral neglect, usually caused by cortical damage, is incapable of detecting stimuli that are presented in one of its perceptual hemifields. In the case of vision, a neglect patient may be incapable of detecting stimuli in her left visual hemifield. If asked to bisect a horizontal line, she would draw the bisector too far to the right, as if she were not experiencing the left part of the target line. Similarly, if asked to evaluate the differences between two pictures that only differ on the left side, she would insist that they are identical (Driver and Vuilleumier 2001; Prinz 2012). A neglect patient seems to be incapable of performing tasks on the basis of how things look to her. Hence, unilateral neglect is likely a disorder that affects perceptual experience and phenomenology.

There is one particular form of neglect called unilateral extinction. In the case of vision, a patient suffering from unilateral visual extinction[5] would be in the same condition as in neglect concerning a given target stimulus **a**, presented in the impaired hemifield, but only when another stimulus **b** is presented in the opposite and unimpaired hemifield. In this case it is said that **b** extinguishes **a**. What is striking about extinction is that subjects retain a normal experience of their impaired visual hemifield, but only in the absence of competing stimuli in their unimpaired hemifield. In both neglect and extinction, visual areas of the brain in the occipital and temporal regions are usually fully functional. The cortical damage leading to both dysfunctions typically interests areas in the right parietal cortex (Raftopoulos 2014), some of which are associated with attentional networks and control (Shulman and Corbetta 2012). Accordingly, neglect and extinction are considered to be attentional disorders. Importantly, the peculiar competitive nature of the extinction disorder points to the competitive interactions that take place when attention is allocated.

The biased competition view offers a straightforward explanation for the competitive nature of impairments in extinction. Provided that the sources of certain relevant and hard-wired biases for the competition process can be located at specific levels in the cognitive processing hierarchy, and provided that those levels can be mapped onto relatively well defined areas of the brain, if such areas were damaged in one hemisphere but not another, when two stimuli are presented at the same time in both visual hemifields, the competition between them would be, so to speak,

---

[5]For simplicity I focus on vision, but neglect and extinction are found in hearing and touch and even cross-modally (Driver and Vuilleumier 2001).

unfair. The stimulus in the unimpaired hemifield would receive the correct biases, while the stimulus in the impaired hemifield would not receive any bias or the wrong biases. The outcome of the competition in this case would be invariably steered toward the stimulus in the unimpaired hemifield, which would explain extinction of the other stimulus.

Further support to this conclusion, and to the integrated nature of the competition, is provided by evidence that extinction decreases or disappears when stimuli presented in both hemifields belong to the same perceptual category or object (Mattingley et al. 1997). One explanation for the decreasing of extinction is that the system can derive the relevant biases, which are absent for the impaired hemifield, from other sources. Ward et al. (1994) found that extinction is greatly decreased if the stimuli presented in the two hemifields are of the same perceptual group (defined in terms of similarity, symmetry, etc.). Under the hypothesis that those stimuli are competing and that the competition is integrated, their findings support the view that the processing of stimuli in the unimpaired hemifield assists the processing of stimuli in the impaired hemifield if both stimuli belong to the same perceptual group. The same biases that drive the processing of the stimulus in the unimpaired hemifield may be used by the system to process the stimulus in the impaired hemifield, thus overcoming the impairment. In addition, Driver and Spence (1994) found a significant processing advantage for identification of concurrent visual and auditory stimuli if they were presented as coming from the same approximate spatial location. These results indicate that general biases such as perceptual category and spatial location may affect an overall underlying process of integrated competition both uni-modally and cross-modally.

The competition view seems to capture well the extension of attention defined by *optimization*. First, it can explain both covert and overt forms of attention because biased competition between stimuli can take place even in the absence of overt action. Second, the possibility of different directions of bias, especially top-down and bottom-up, can account for attention's exogenous and endogenous forms. Third, assuming that some very high and very low levels in the cognitive hierarchy are outside the scope of conscious experience,[6] and considering the fact that the competition could, in principle, take place at each level of the hierarchy, including these *unconscious extremes*, the biased competition view can also explain conscious and unconscious forms of attention.[7] Fourth, we have no reason to exclude that high-level processes such as those underlying subjective motivations, expectations, and desires may figure among the relevant biases. Thus, the competition view admits a significant degree of voluntary control, while still allowing for automatic and involuntary forms of attention, driven for example by automatic biases. Fifth, competition

---

[6] This is granted by several influential theories about the neural correlates of consciousness (Jackendoff 1987; Prinz 2012; Dehaene and Changeux 2011).

[7] The idea of top-down unconscious biases opens up the interesting possibility that attention can be endogenous and involuntary at the same time. This idea is not explored enough in the literature. Evidences of this kind of attentional modulation would support a theory that allows for this form of attention.

at different levels is by definition a graded notion. If certain levels are processing objects, competition at those levels can account for object-based attention. If other levels are processing features of objects, competition at those levels can account for feature-based attention, and so on.[8] Sixth, a competition process can in principle have one clear winner or several winners and this possibility reflects the distinction between focal and diffuse attention. Finally, the competition view does not constrain attention to any specific place in the brain. As such, attention can be a multimodal and multilevel phenomenon. As I have anticipated, the competition view can thus explain the most important phenomena and distinctions usually associated with attention and, in particular, it clearly meets all the requirements of the desideratum on a theory of attention introduced above. As such, it is preferable to the theories presented in the previous section, which fail or struggle to do the same.

It is worth mentioning that, concerning binding, integrated competition can explain how and why exactly those features that end up bound together are selected as winners at the same time. Once a feature of an object starts emerging as the winner of the competition among other features of other objects, the integrated nature of the competition allows for that feature to work itself as a bias in favor of the selection of other features of the same object. To give a simple example, the bias toward a specific color may act toward the selection of that color in the visual field. At the same time, selection of the color is integrated with other levels that process, for example, the spatial location where that color is present and the shape that bounds the areas where that color occurs. As a result, the location and shape that are currently related to the target color are also selected for processing. This shows, on the one hand, how different forms of attention, namely feature-based attention (color and shape) and spatial attention may interact and, on the other, how bounded objects start to emerge in the visual field on the basis of an integrated process of feature selection through competition. In other words, features that are related, for example by colocation, are mutually selected by biasing one another and this can account for feature binding.

If biased competition is not limited to one cognitive domain, one would expect to find evidence of its predicted integrative nature across different levels of the processing hierarchy. On this point, Rapp and Hendel (2003) found interesting evidence for cross-modal audio-tactile and visuo-tactile competition in patients affected by cross-modal extinction. The competitive interference they found among tactile stimuli on the one hand and auditory and visual stimuli on the other decreased significantly when the target features of competing stimuli involved different *levels of representation*,[9] that is, if processes tracking those stimuli and their features occurred at different levels in the hierarchy: e.g. physical properties vs. semantic properties. This suggests that the competition process can occur independently for each sensory modality, particularly when relevant stimulus features are of different levels of representation, or it can occur cross-modally both cooperatively, if there

---

[8] Clark (2016, pp. 74–76) outlines a similar view from a predictive processing perspective.

[9] The terminology is that of Rapp and Hendel (2003).

are strong general biases such as perceptual category or spatial location, or antago-
nistically, if features of competing stimuli are of the same level of representation.

Given the above discussion, the biased competition theory is preferable to the
alternative models of attention in virtue of its distributed and flexible nature.
Competition is not limited to one specific processing stage in the processing hierarchy. On the contrary, it appears to involve different levels of processing and different features of stimuli[10] such as spatial and temporal location, color, shape, full
objecthood, identity, as well as semantic properties. Therefore, the problem of
deciding at which specific stage in the processing hierarchy the relevant process
underlying attention has to be located, which is encountered by alternative models,
is solved by allowing for the selection mechanism to be located at many different
stages between perceptual input and motor output. Multidirectional integration and
the possibility of multimodal competition suggest that attention is a fundamental
feature of many aspects of cognitive processing, which is not constrained to a specific level of the perceptual/cognitive hierarchy.

On this point, the widespread nature of competition together with the possibility
of it occurring at different levels of the hierarchy is compatible with the evolutionary considerations about attention discussed in the previous section (Haladjian and
Montemayor 2014; see also Wiederman and O'Carroll 2013). The nature of neural
computation suggests that there is a need for selectivity and modulation for both
evolutionary older and evolutionary younger neural subsystems. Under the assumption that levels of the processing hierarchy are mapped onto specific neural subsystems, they would share the evolutionary history of those subsystems. If this is so,
different forms of attention must have appeared at different times in history. The
competition view can account for this fact in virtue of its flexibility and relative
level-dependence. Despite its integrated nature, competition can in principle take
place independently for each level, even if biases coming from other levels are not
available. As such, an evolutionary older subsystem could solve its selection problems via competition with the avail of, for example, bottom-up biases, before the
appearance of an evolutionary younger subsystem. The outcome of the competition
would become integrated once both systems are available and biasing each other.

As I presented it here, the competition view seems to be able to capture the phenomena that involve attention defined as *optimization*. However, like the previously
discussed models, as it stands this view does not provide an adequate explanation of
attention. For it to be an explanation of attention one should clarify what mechanisms are responsible for implementing biased competition at different levels.
Without further details on how the theory may be developed, it is little more than a
further metaphor by which we try to capture all and only the attentional phenomena.
Nevertheless, it seems to be a more helpful and adequate metaphor than those discussed in the previous section. One worry that arises here is whether the scope of
this metaphor is too wide. Given that it may capture all the phenomena that we label
attentional, how can one ensure that it captures only those phenomena? It seems that

---

[10]The original proponents limited their discussion to object-based attention and spatial selection.

there may be many forms of competition that are not instances of optimization. In the next section, I address this worry and provide further details on the competition view that may allow it to make some steps from being a helpful metaphor toward becoming a full explanation of attention.

5.3   Toward an Explanation of Attention

One preliminary clarification that helps in constraining the scope of biased competition to the relevant phenomena is that not all forms of biased competition are relevant for attention. Otherwise, a horse race could be an instance of attention, since there are several competitors and many biasing factors. The kind of competition that is relevant for attention takes place in cognitive systems. Now, to specify what counts as a cognitive system is beyond the purposes of the present discussion. One can in principle allow that different sorts of processing systems are capable of cognition[11]. This partially depends on what one is prepared to accept as the competing entities, a subject that I address below. Yet, regardless of this issue, all kinds of competition that are not internal to a cognitive system should be excluded from the scope of attention.

Let us now focus on the selective aspect of attention. According to *optimization* attention is required to select what stimuli should be allocated processing resources and to modulate the allocation of those resources. Biased competition is one form of selection and an initial way to further specify the competition view is to say how it distinguishes itself from other forms of selection. In general, one can say that in order for competition to take place there must be at least two competitors. Let us explore the difference between selection with or without competitors. Selection may be achieved without competitors if there are pre-existing rules that determine what entities are to be selected, let us call this *direct selection*. To make an analogy, monarchies are typically hereditary, which means that the first-born son of the king would become the head of the kingdom after the king's death or abdication. In this context, the way in which the head of the kingdom is selected is predetermined even before the first son is born. In fact, if no son were ever born to the king, the monarchy would usually have precise rules determining the next eligible candidate in many possible scenarios.

On the other hand, if the outcome is not predetermined with such systematicity, it might be that any of two or more candidates may end up being eventually selected at any given time. In this case, which I call *competitive selection*, one may say that the two candidates compete with one another. To make a similar analogy, think about the election of the president of a democratic nation. Of course, the competition need not be entirely fair and the outcome may be biased by various factors, like the promises made by the candidates, the current state of the national economy, the

---

[11] This is the wide notion of cognition that includes perceptual processing. See Chap. 1.

personal preferences of individual electors, and the success of the electoral campaign. In this case, one candidate may still be more likely to win, but the outcome of the competition would not be systematically predetermined.

Supposedly, a cognitive processing system could achieve selection of what stimuli to process in both ways. For direct selection, it would require stable rules to predetermine, in a systematic way, the target of its processing resources. For competitive selection, it would require the sensitivity of the competition process to various forms of biases that end up favoring one of two or more possible targets. For a biological system, it seems that competitive selection would be preferable, due to its flexibility, for behaving successfully in a changeable environment. Nevertheless, there is evidence that perceptual processing sometimes works according to some strict rules that are very hard to change as in, for example, the Müller-Lyer illusion.

The two ways in which selection is achieved are mutually exclusive. To illustrate, let us consider what happens when one becomes very skillful at a certain task, for example typing on a notebook keyboard. The first time one writes something in a word editor, one needs to pay careful attention to the keys, identifying the position of each character on the keyboard. After a certain amount of time, however, one becomes skillful enough that one can type without looking at the keyboard anymore and the writing process becomes faster and more efficient. This could be described as a transition from competitive selection to direct selection. Once one's typing skills are sufficiently developed, we can typically say that one is no longer paying attention to the keyboard because each key is directly selected, perhaps with the help of well-memorized motor schema that act as the systematic selection rules. If attention is indeed linked to competitive selection, this means that in cases where the targets of cognitive processing are directly selected, i.e. if there are no competitors, no attention is involved. This helps to further constrain the scope of competition to some but not all the phenomena that involve selection within a cognitive system. In other words, not all forms of cognitive selection would be cases of attention.

To see how the above discussion helps to constrain the notion, let us recall the hypothetical case discussed earlier in which the system might be processing only one bit of information that does not exceed its processing resources. As I said, such a case does not involve *optimization* and, therefore, an adequate theory should exclude it as an instance of attention. Now that attention is conceived of as involving competitive selection, it is clear that this case would not require attention according to the present theory, because there are no competitors. Still, the system may be processing the information, in which case one can say that the corresponding stimulus has been directly selected.

To further specify what kind of competition is relevant for attention one may ask what the competing entities are supposed to be in a cognitive processing hierarchy. So far, following Desimone and Duncan (1995), I have talked about competition among *stimuli* for processing resources.[12] However, something can be said to make

---

[12] Desimone and Duncan (1995) go even further to say that competition among stimuli is required to determine what stimuli are represented in the system. This is a radical view that makes attention

this point less general and to develop the competition view. If stimuli are considered to be individual elements of the external world such as external objects, properties, and events, they are the kind of things that may impinge on our sensory detectors, but they are not the kind of things that can engage in competitive interactions. What can actually engage in competitive interactions are the processes and states in the cognitive system – and their vehicles: neurons or neural populations (Reddy et al. 2009; Spivey and Huette 2014) – that encode and represent those individuals. If one is a representationalist, one may be then tempted to say that the competing entities are representations. The ensuing view would look like the following: representations at each level in the processing hierarchy compete for processing resources. Whenever a representation emerges as a winner somewhere in the system, given the current biases, it may contribute to the competition elsewhere in the system by biasing it toward a consistent outcome.

This move looks straightforward and appealing, but there are some nuances here that are worth exploring. If the competing entities were full-fledged representations, this would mean that the system is, at any time, already processing and representing all the items that are currently available to it. This seems to be incompatible with the limited processing resources of the system. If the system is already representing all the stimuli, what need would there be for competitive optimization of processing resources? Of course, to address this problem to its full extent one would need to specify what representations are, a task that I cannot pursue in this context. But even without committing to any particularly detailed view on representations, there are some things worth saying on the problem of representations and limited resources.

Let us take visual perception as an example. Whenever the cognitive system is presented with a visible perceptual scene, various elements in the scene may cause certain representations to be tokened in the system. However, by simply being tokened, such representations are not playing any specific functional role. To perform any cognitive operation on those representations, a system with limited resources would need to allocate those resources in an optimal way to the representations that are more relevant for the task at hand. This is where competition comes in. The tokened representations are the competitors and the biases determine which of them needs to be prioritized at any given time. At the lowest level the system may be, in fact, representing all currently available stimuli. To give an example, in vision the lowest processing level might be considered to correspond to the retina. Whatever impinges on the retina is already represented in a minimal sense and the visual system would be able to further process information that is currently available in the external environment only insofar as such information is conveyed to the retina. To

---

a necessary condition for representation. This may be true, for some levels of the cognitive hierarchy, under some specific commitments on what representations are. Here, however, I prefer a weakened version of the competition view where it can be maintained that the processing units are preferentially responsive toward some stimuli, but that leaves open what the implications are for the representational capacities of the system. Thus, the interpretation of biased competition that I propose is compatible with a broader range of representationalist positions.

generalize, at the lowest perceptual levels, the system is representing all the stimuli that are currently affecting its sensory detectors.

In this picture, competition may have a twofold role. On the one hand, competition may be among representations at different levels. For example, it can be among the representation of a specific object and the representation of a wider portion of the visual scene containing that object as well as other objects. The two representations may have a different relevance, depending on the cognitive task that the system has to perform at a given time. In this case, competition would determine what level of representation is the relevant one under the current biases by prioritizing the representation at that level. Inter-level competition may explain focal and diffuse attention as involving representations at different levels. On the other hand, competition may be among representations at the same level. For example, competition can be among representations of objects. If one object is more relevant for the task, the representation of that object is prioritized under the current biases. Intra-level competition may explain the distinction between feature-based attention, object-based attention, etc. Object-based attention, for example, may be caused by an object representation becoming the winner of competition with other object representations. The same line of reasoning applies to feature-based attention and to other forms of attention.

This account of competition is consistent with degrees of representation characterized by, for example, their fine graininess, i.e. their level of detail and by their level of integration or generality. This way of thinking about representations fits particularly well with the characterization of different levels of the hierarchy on the basis of the spatiotemporal resolution of the processes that take place at those levels introduced in the first chapter. Furthermore, this allows for some representations to be the integrated outcome of competition at different levels and the coherence of the representation may be reflecting the coherence of the biases that are involved in the underlying integrated competition processes. For example, if one is looking for a particular object in a crowded scenery, competition among object representations may require a degree of competition among feature representations, in order to prioritize those features that are diagnostic of the target object.

There are many complications to the above discussion that depend on specific commitments about what sorts of representations one is prepared to admit. I cannot settle these issues here and the above discussion is only an initial tentative approach to the specification of the entities that are engaged in competition. Nevertheless, I hold that, for the reasons just elucidated, the idea that competing entities are representations has some intuitive plausibility. Therefore, in this chapter and the next, I refer to the competing entities simply as representations.

The above discussion provides an example of how the competing entities may be conceived. By taking into account the kinds of systems in which we expect to find attention, I expect that a full explanation of attention would probably not depart too much from talking about competition among representational or quasi-representational states. Here, we could think that the kind of competition that is relevant for attention is competition among representations in a cognitive system and this excludes many kinds of competitions that are not plausibly tied to attention.

I have spelled out what optimization amounts to in terms of competition. Furthermore, I have clarified what distinguishes competition from other forms of selection and what kind of entities may engage in the competition that is relevant for attention. However, I have left unspecified what the relation between attention and competition is supposed to be and what it means for a competition process to be relevant for attention. Competition is a temporally extended dynamic process and the winners of the competition are representations. Importantly, one representation can be dominant while the underlying competition process is still ongoing. The biases that are driving the competition may constantly change but the overall balance of the biases could allow the same representation to win for a certain amount of time, before switching to a different representation. Now, the way to conceive of the relationship between competition and attention is to say that competition is the process that determines a winning representation and attention is the property of "being the winner" instantiated by the currently winning representation:

> **Biased competition:** Attention is the property of "being the current winner" of an ongoing biased competition process among representations.

According to the above definition, a shift in attention means that a new representation has become the winner as a result of the underlying competition process and it now instantiates the property of attention (being attended to). There are two important clarifications to make. First, it need not be the case that only one representation is dominant at a time. For example, one may be focusing on two alternative options while making a difficult choice. Competition can have one winner or a few winners depending on the current aims of the system. But, given the limited resources, if more than one representation is currently dominant, the amount of detail in which the content of such representation is represented would plausibly decrease. However, the resource constraint also suggests that there could be a limit on the number of concurrently attended representations (Liu et al. 2013).

An important upshot of this way of thinking about competition is that competition does not change what the system is representing. The task of competition is not to decide what is represented in the system at any given level of the hierarchy, but rather how the system represents something within the same level or among different levels. When one representation is prioritized over other representations, it means that the system is entertaining that representation in a particular way and that that representation has a property that other representations do not share. The changes that happen when a representation is winning in biased competition, and thereby instantiates attention, may be reflected in the phenomenal character that may be associated with the system's having that representation and in the pattern of activity in the vehicles of that representation.

To offer a clear example of how competition is supposed to work, consider, once again, the case of unilateral visual extinction. In extinction, the unimpaired hemifield always ends up as the dominant one. In a simple case of extinction, we may think that there are two competing representations of the stimuli presented in each hemifield, but the representation about the stimulus in the impaired hemifield is inevitably losing the competition with the representation about the stimulus in the

unimpaired hemifield.[13] This is precisely why one may say that the extinction subject is incapable of attending to the impaired hemifield. The representation of the
stimulus in the impaired hemifield is incapable of instantiating the property of being
attended to. This may be because the biases in favor of the unimpaired representation are too strong.[14] In a normal subject, representations about stimuli in both hemifields would compete with each other more fairly. Furthermore, if this were an
adequate preliminary explanation of what is going in extinction, one may expect
that bypassing the lack of biases in favor of the impaired representation would lead
to a decrease in the extinction phenomenon. One way to do this is to present objects
that recruit the same biases, for example by belonging to the same perceptual category, in both hemifields. Indeed, as I mentioned above, extinction decreases under
such conditions (Mattingley et al. 1997; Ward et al. 1994).

A final consideration concerns the possibility of finding out the competition
mechanisms and empirically testing the theory. Now, on the one hand, we have
empirical evidence of competitive interactions among certain neurons or neural
groups. This evidence has led the initial proponents of the competition view to
advance it as an explanation of attention. However, as we have seen, a full explanation of attention should cover many phenomena that span multiple levels of the
cognitive hierarchy. Under the assumption that different levels of the cognitive hierarchy map onto different areas or patterns of activity in the underlying implementation substrate, it seems plausible that biased competition among representations and
the ensuing property of attention can be implemented by a set of underlying mechanisms. This would mean that attention is not a natural kind at the level of implementation and, in the case of the brain, it is not a neurophysiological kind. To say the
contrary would be to identify attention with the product of one single neural competition mechanism, which may have the result of losing the possibility of explaining
some of the phenomena included in the desideratum.

If competition has to be an adequate explanation of attention, it seems more fruit-
ful to consider attention as a multiply realizable psychological kind, which could be
implemented by various underlying competition mechanisms. On the other hand, all
the mechanisms that may be grouped together as implementations of attention
should be expected to have the hallmark of a competition process. Here, one should
say what qualifies a mechanism as a form of competition. In order for a mechanism
to count as a biased competition mechanism, there must be competing entities and
the mechanism should be sensitive to internal or external factors that may count as
biases. In the brain, such a mechanism would plausibly involve the neural correlates
of representations at different levels and feedback and feedforward neural connections. Furthermore, the mechanism should be such that the emergence of an individual as a winner would cause some sort of disadvantage for the competitors and

---

[13] At least at the level that is relevant for phenomenology and reportability.

[14] Someone may suggest that extinction is a case in which competition is biased so strongly that it
would collapse into direct selection. However, in extinction there is a competitor, which may end
up winning in normal cases. With direct selection, on the other hand, I meant cases in which there
is only one representation, which is selected according to pre-existing systematic rules.

that a change in the biases could in principle steer the ongoing competition toward a different outcome. In the brain this may translate into inhibition or enhancement of neuronal activity. Identifying these mechanisms in the brain shall be the primary task of neuroscientific research on attention. On this basis the competition theory already predicts that whenever there is a shift in attention there should be some changes in the underlying competition process such that a different competitor, who must already have been engaged in competition, has now become dominant. If it turns out that it is not the case, for example because the underlying mechanism involves direct selection, the theory shall be refuted as a unified explanation of attention.

As an example of how the disconfirmatory process might look, let us discuss inattentional blindness. During inattentional blindness a subject who has been assigned an attention-demanding task, for example to count how many times a certain event occurs on screen, fails to consciously notice a salient stimulus, for example a moving gorilla (Simons and Chabris 1999), that appears in her visual field for a significant amount of time. Given the nature of the task, it is assumed that inattentional blindness is an attentional phenomenon. This is true if one adopts *optimization* as a baseline for defining attention: the available resources are exhausted by the processing of the representations that are relevant for the counting task. Competition seems to be an adequate explanation of this phenomenon. The instructions about the task act as a bias that favors one set of representations (the ball, the players, etc.) over other competing representations (the gorilla). For simplicity, we may suppose that the cognitive level of competition here is the level of conscious access and that the corresponding level of attention is conscious attention. But if this has to count as an explanation of conscious attention, we would expect that the underlying mechanism of inattentional blindness meets the requirements of a competition mechanism. We would expect the system to represent the unattended and overlooked stimuli at some level and the representations of those stimuli to become attenuated during the counting task. In this way, biased competition could be empirically validated or disconfirmed as an explanation of conscious attention once we look at what happens in the system during inattentional blindness.

5.4   Summary and Conclusion

In this chapter, I discussed the problem of attention and the requirements of an adequate theory that aims at explaining this phenomenon. I proposed the biased competition view as a model of attention that is preferable to some of the alternative views available in the literature. Furthermore, I have offered a preliminary version of a new theory of attention based on the competition model, which could be further developed into a full explanation of attention. Such an explanation, however, would require the description of specific mechanisms that realize competition. Since attention is supposed to be multiply realizable, the specification of what a bias or a competition mechanism looks like depends on the kind of system that one is considering.

The discussion offered here should help in bridging the gap between a helpful metaphor about attention and a compelling theory of an important cognitive phenomenon. As I mentioned, the competition view is becoming increasingly popular in cognitive science and all the aspects that I have addressed here are matters of ongoing discussion. But if competition were indeed the best explanation of attention, there are some implications that already follow from this theory that are relevant for the debate about the cognitive penetrability of perception and perceptual experience. To discuss this point in detail is the task of the next chapter.

References

Beck, D. M., & Kastner, S. (2009). Top-down and bottom-up mechanisms in biasing competition in the human brain. *Vision Research, 49*(10), 1154–1165.

Broadbent, D. E. (1958). *Perception and communication*. New York: Pergamon Press.

Chun, M. M., & Turk-Browne, N. B. (2007). Interactions between attention and memory. *Current Opinion in Neurobiology, 17*(2), 177–184.

Clark, A. (2016). *Surfing uncertainty*. Oxford: Oxford University Press.

Dehaene, S., & Changeux, J.-P. (2011). Experimental and theoretical approaches to conscious processing. *Neuron, 70*(2), 200–227.

Desimone, R. (1998). Visual attention mediated by biased competition in extrastriate visual cortex. *Philosophical Transactions of the Royal Society of London. Series B: Biological Sciences, 353*(1373), 1245–1255.

Desimone, R., & Duncan, J. (1995). Neural mechanisms of selective visual attention. *Annual Review of Neuroscience, 18*, 193–222.

Deutsch, J. A., & Deutsch, D. (1963). Attention: Some theoretical considerations. *Psychological Review, 70*, 80–90.

Driver, J. (2001). A selective review of selective attention research from the past century. *British Journal of Psychology, 92*, 53–78.

Driver, J., & Spence, C. J. (1994). Spatial synergies between auditory and visual attention. In C. Umiltà & M. Moscovitch (Eds.), *Attention and performance 15: Conscious and nonconscious information processing* (pp. 311–331). Cambridge, MA: MIT Press.

Driver, J., & Vuilleumier, P. (2001). Perceptual awareness and its loss in unilateral neglect and extinction. *Cognition, 79*(1–2), 39–88.

Duncan, J. (1998). Converging levels of analysis in the cognitive neuroscience of visual attention. *Philosophical Transactions of the Royal Society of London, Series B-Biological Sciences, 353*, 1307–1317.

Duncan, J. (2006). EPS mid-career award 2004: Brain mechanisms of attention. *The Quarterly Journal of Experimental Psychology, 59*(1), 2–27.

Duncan, J., Humphreys, G., & Ward, R. (1997). Competitive brain activity in visual attention. *Current Opinion in Neurobiology, 7*(2), 255–261.

Haladjian, H. H., & Montemayor, C. (2014). On the evolution of conscious attention. *Psychonomic Bulletin and Review, 22*(3), 595–613.

Jackendoff, R. (1987). *Consciousness and the computational mind*. Cambridge, MA: MIT Press.

Liu, T., Becker, M. W., & Jigo, M. (2013). Limited featured-based attention to multiple features. *Vision Research, 85*, 36–44.

Marchi, F. (2017). Attention and cognitive penetrability: The epistemic consequences of attention as a form of metacognitive regulation. *Consciousness and Cognition, 47*, 48–62.

Mather, M., & Sutherland, M. R. (2011). Arousal-biased competition in perception and memory. *Perspectives on Psychological Science, 6*(2), 114–133.

Mattingley, J. B., Davis, G., & Driver, J. (1997). Preattentive filling-in of visual surfaces in parietal extinction. *Science, 275*(5300), 671–674.

Mole, C. (2010). *Attention is cognitive unison: An essay in philosophical psychology.* Oxford: Oxford University Press.

Mole, C. (2015). Attention and cognitive penetration. In A. Raftopoulos & J. Zeimbekis (Eds.), *The cognitive penetrability of perception: New philosophical perspectives* (pp. 218–238). New York: Oxford University Press.

Prinz, J. J. (2012). *The conscious brain: How attention engenders experience.* New York: Oxford University Press.

Raftopoulos, A. (2014). What unilateral visual neglect teaches us about perceptual phenomenology. *Erkenntnis, 80*(2), 339–358.

Rapp, B., & Hendel, S. K. (2003). Principles of cross-modal competition: Evidence from deficits of attention. *Psychonomic Bulletin and Review, 10*(1), 210–219.

Reddy, L., Kanwisher, N. G., & VanRullen, R. (2009). Attention and biased competition in multivoxel object representations. *Proceedings of the National Academy of Sciences, 106*(50), 21447–21452.

Sadato, N., Pascual-Leone, A., Grafman, J., Ibañez, V., Deiber, M. P., Dold, G., & Hallett, M. (1996). Activation of the primary visual cortex by Braille reading in blind subjects. *Nature, 380*(6574), 526–528.

Shulman, G. L., & Corbetta, M. (2012). Two attentional networks. In M. I. Posner (Ed.), *Cognitive neuroscience of attention* (2nd ed., pp. 113–128). New York: The Guilford Press.

Simons, D. J., & Chabris, C. F. (1999). Gorillas in our midst: Sustained inattentional blindness for dynamic events. *Perception, 28*(9), 1059–1074.

Spivey, M. J., & Huette, S. (2014). The embodiment of attention in the perception-action loop. In L. Shapiro (Ed.), *The Routledge handbook of embodied cognition* (pp. 306–314). London: Routledge.

Treisman, A. (1998). Feature binding, attention and object perception. *Philosophical Transactions of the Royal Society of London. Series B: Biological Sciences, 353*(1373), 1295–1306.

Treisman, A. M., & Gelade, G. (1980). A feature-integration theory of attention. *Cognitive Psychology, 12*(1), 97–136.

Ward, R., Goodrich, S., & Driver, J. (1994). Grouping reduces visual extinction: Neuropsychological evidence for weight-linkage in visual selection. *Visual Cognition, 1*(1), 101–129.

Watzl, S. (2017). *Structuring mind.* Oxford: Oxford University Press.

West, G. L., Anderson, A. A. K., Ferber, S., & Pratt, J. (2011). Electrophysiological evidence for biased competition in V1 for fear expressions. *Journal of Cognitive Neuroscience, 23*(11), 3410–3418.

Wiederman, S. D., & O'Carroll, D. C. (2013). Selective attention in an insect visual neuron. *Current Biology, 23*(2), 156–161.

Woods, D. L., Hillyard, S. A., & Hansen, J. C. (1984). Event-related brain potentials reveal similar attentional mechanisms during selective listening and shadowing. *Journal of Experimental Psychology: Human Perception and Performance, 10*, 761–777.

Wu, W. (2011a). Attention as selection for action. In C. Mole, D. Smithies, & W. Wu (Eds.), *Attention: Philosophical and psychological essays* (pp. 97–116). New York: Oxford University Press.

Wu, W. (2011b). What is conscious attention? *Philosophy and Phenomenological Research, 82*(1), 93–120.

Yi, D.-J., & Chun, M. M. (2005). Attentional modulation of learning-related repetition attenuation effects in human parahippocampal cortex. *Journal of Neuroscience, 25*(14), 3593–3600.

Chapter 6
How Attentional Cognitive Penetration Works

Abstract After having presented the theory of attention that I endorse in this book, I can now turn to my primary research question, namely: can attentional processes generate cognitively penetrated experiences? In this chapter, I offer a positive answer to this question in the light of the biased competition theory of attentional processes and of the four definitions of cognitive penetrability introduced earlier in the book. Section 6.1 examines why attentional processes are typically dismissed from the possible interesting instances of cognitive penetration. In Sect. 6.2, I argue that attentional competition processes are metacognitive processes, which constitutes a novel approach to attention and helps to reject the dismissive attitude toward attention. In Sect. 6.3, I discuss whether attentional processes can satisfy the definitions of *semantic, causal, and indirect non-conceptual* cognitive penetrability. Section 6.4 is dedicated to the epistemic role of attention and the definition of *consequentialist* cognitive penetrability.

6.1 The Dismissive Attitude Concerning Attention[1]

As we have seen in the second chapter, there are various ways in which cognitive penetrability can be characterized, but for all of them, a cognitive-perceptual relation is crucial. In the third chapter, I discussed how competition at some levels in the cognitive hierarchy can be biased by processes or states of the system at other levels. Assuming that a distinction between perception and cognition can be drawn, this means that it is possible that competition at some perceptual levels may be biased by processes that take place at cognitive levels. In particular, the competition view allows that a perceptual representation instantiates attention, i.e. the property of being the current winner of the competition, in virtue of a top-down cognitive bias. The cognitive bias can be a representation at a much higher level of the hierarchy. Therefore, attention is a property that may clearly involve cognitive-perceptual relations for its instantiation.

Now, given the relevance of the penetrability debate for several fundamental domains of cognitive science, researchers should carefully scrutinize if among the

---

[1] This way of phrasing the problem is borrowed from Mole (2015).

© Springer Nature Switzerland AG 2020
F. Marchi, *The Attentional Shaping of Perceptual Experience*, Studies in Brain and Mind 16, https://doi.org/10.1007/978-3-030-33558-8_6

established cognitive perceptual relations there are some that may qualify as instances of cognitive penetration (CP). In this chapter, I adopt this strategy to discuss whether the cognitive-perceptual relations that underlie the instantiation of attention satisfy the requirements of different forms of CP. Now that I have introduced and clarified the theory of attention that I endorse, this is finally possible. This is an interesting problem to address, because most of the extant accounts of what a genuine case of cognitive penetration of perceptual experience would look like tend to exclude attentional phenomena (Siegel 2012; Macpherson 2012).

While talking about possible evidence of cognitive penetration of perception, I briefly introduced the problem of ambiguous pictures. When seeing a Necker cube, a subject might see the cube as being oriented upwards or downwards depending on which face of the cube is taken to be in the foreground. Moreover, for most subjects the two possible perceptual interpretations of the image alternate at a certain rate, unless they are instructed to maintain one interpretation over the other. If provided with such an instruction, however, subjects are capable of affecting the rate at which perceptual experiences of either orientation of the cube alternate (Meng and Tong 2004). At a first glance, it seems that this case may easily work as an instance of some form of cognitive penetration. In fact, a subject can have two noticeably different perceptual experiences while looking at the exact same stimulus, on the basis of an explicit verbal instruction, which plausibly involves some semantic processing and, perhaps, other cognitive factors. However, things are not so straightforward for advocates of cognitive penetration.

There is, in fact, an alternative explanation, namely that the alternation in experience is induced by a shift in the subject's attention to the picture. Some authors argue that a shift in attention is equivalent to changing the stimulus. If this were the case, even if one assumes that an attentional shift is driven by a higher-level cognitive bias, it might still be argued that such a phenomenon is not cognitive penetration of perceptual experience. Thus, attention enters the game as an apparently intermediate stage or a "partition" (Mole 2015) between the cognitive process that drives its instantiation and the ensuing perceptual experience. Now, having introduced the biased competition theory of attention, it is possible to reassess these claims and discuss whether some attentional phenomena are genuine cases of cognitive penetration.

Pylyshyn (1999) describes the possible role of attention in the interactions between high-level cognition and visual perception. On his account, such interactions are only of two kinds: cognition can either alter perceptual judgments made on the basis of the output of early visual processes, or it can affect the allocation of (spatial) attention prior to the operations of early vision, which is the informationally encapsulated perceptual stage envisioned by Pylyshyn. The second option leads to a change in the input to early vision. According to Pylyshyn's view, an attentional shift may, at most, alter the input to perception. If the input to perception changes then one of the most important requirements of cognitive penetration is not met. Therefore, under this construal of the role of attention, cognitive penetration is out of question.

Ever since Pylyshyn's discussion, attention has become a powerful tool in the hand of opponents of cognitive influences on perception and defendants of modularity. As we have seen, attention is a property that emerges from the system needs of dealing with overwhelming incoming information. Since the presence of some sort of attentional modulation of the brain's perceptual processing is widespread, it is difficult, if not impossible, to devise behavioral tasks that are completely devoid of possible attentional shifts (Van Boxtel et al. 2010). If attention is taken to exclude cognitive penetrability, its overwhelming presence in perception and cognition makes it very difficult to even conceive of what would count as compelling evidence in favor of the latter.

One eminent example of applying an attention-based strategy to rule out many possible alleged cases of cognitive penetration is that of Raftopoulos (2010), who discusses the problem of mutual exclusion of attention and penetrability precisely in the context of perceiving ambiguous pictures such as the duck-rabbit or the Necker cube. According to Raftopoulos, attentional processes take place at the stage of visual processing, corresponding to the activity of visual cortical areas V4 and IT, and which helps in disambiguating ambiguous images by selecting a certain shape[2] out of a neutral configuration. The neutral configuration, on the other hand, is delivered by an (attentionally) impenetrable early visual processing system. Raftopoulos' idea is, thus, another version of Pylyshyn's original claim that attention works outside early vision. In fact, Raftopoulos (2010) adopts Pylyshyn's notion of early vision to characterize the stage of visual processing corresponding to perceptual phenomenal experience. Taken together, these two positions ground the mutual exclusion of attentional effects and cognitive penetrability on the view that attentional modulation of perception can happen in two ways before or after early vision: (1) by fixating on different parts of the image, thereby changing the input to early vision, or (2) by selecting a certain possible shape in higher-level processing areas, in the human brain. In both cases, early visual processing is considered impenetrable by attention.

It is worth noting, however, that the two authors seem to have a different conception of early vision. Even if Pylyshyn only provides a functional characterization of early vision, and not a full account of its neural correlates, he points out many times that he considers early vision to include shape processing (Pylyshyn 1999, p. 343). Now, if attentional processes take place in V4, which, according to Raftopoulos, can be reliably associated with the encoding of shapes, this is already an attentional process that happens within early vision (in Pylyshyn's sense), thus threatening the modularity of such functional unit. Hence, Pylyshyn seems to have a broader conception of the impenetrable stage of early perceptual processing than Raftopoulos. Early vision in Pylyshyn's sense appears to be, in principle, sensitive to (cognitively driven) attentional modulation in Raftopoulos' sense.

---

[2] Raftopoulos (2010) assumes that these are the areas where shape is encoded. However, the role of V4 is sometimes associated with color processing (Prinz 2012).

As I discussed in the previous chapter, the competitive process that causes the instantiation of attention may involve cognitive processes. Therefore, I take it that the involvement of a cognitive-perceptual relation is non-controversial in many instances of attentional phenomena. Now, even if a cognitive-perceptual relation is involved, given the above discussion, one might think that the boundary of early vision and the locus of attentional processes is not so easy to draw. Regardless of where one is prepared to draw such boundary, however, both Pylyshyn's original view and Raftopoulos' more recent one heavily depend on the claim that the instantiation of attention changes the input to perception, which is based on a specific view of attention that is incompatible with the competition view. They both presuppose that attentional processes intervene at a particular place and perform a particular function. Various versions of the same strategy have been applied to rule out cognitive penetration for other kinds of alleged top-down effects (Firestone and Scholl 2015).

At this point, one might summarize the view that attentional processes and cognitive penetration are mutually exclusive in the conjunction of two claims:

1. A target cognitively driven shift in the perceptual experience is the result of a shift in the subject's attention.
2. A shift in attention either changes the input to the relevant early perceptual processing, or involves selection of its outputs, leaving early perceptual processing unaffected.

Given the competition theory of attention and assuming that claim 1 is true, it may be questioned whether or not attentional (competition) processes modulate perception in a way that would allow some form of penetration of perceptual experience by the states that drive the instantiation of attention. To argue for this possibility, one needs to undermine claim 2 and argue that attentional processes do not change the input to perceptual processing, and that they are not limited to output selection.

With the avail of the competition theory, I argue that the dismissal of all attentional phenomena as instances of cognitive penetration is premature. Claim 2 is composed of two disjuncts: (1) attentional processes change the input to early processing, and (2) attentional processes select the outputs of early processing. Let us focus for a moment on output selection. Raftopoulos' claim that attentional processes operate on the outputs of early perceptual processing (in particular, early vison) can be rephrased in this context as the claim that attention is a property of the outputs of early vision. This claim is certainly plausible in the competition theory, but the problem is that competition does not allow to limit the scope of attentional processes to this kind of selection. Raftopoulos may accept that attention emerges from competition, but in order to exclude cognitive penetration he needs the competition to be limited to the relevant outputs. If the competition theory is right, however, there is no principled boundary in the cognitive hierarchy for the scope of competitive processes that lead to the instantiation of attention. It then becomes an empirical question to see whether competition is limited in the way Raftopoulos claims it to be, for example to V4 in the human brain. This question is not settled here but there is already evidence that this is not the case (West et al. 2011). In what follows, I assume that the competition view does not warrant drawing principled boundaries for the instantiation of attention as required by the second disjunct of claim 2.

A more complex story must be told to reject the first disjunct, namely that attentional processes change the input to early processing. I address this matter in the next section, but before proceeding further it will be helpful to clarify how a plausible case of attentional cognitive penetration should look. Stokes (2014, 2018) offers a nice distinction between three possible attentional causal schemas that may look like cases of cognitive penetration, but only one of which may actually turn out to be an instance of attentional cognitive penetration. In each schema, a mental process causes a shift in attention that, in turn, causes a change in perceptual experience.

There are two important distinctions to be made here. The first is between the perceptual and the cognitive level of mental processing, which presupposes some criteria for distinguishing between perception and cognition, an issue that I already addressed in Chap. 1. The second distinction is between kinds of attentional processes that enter each schema as intermediate causes. For the current purposes the relevant distinction is between *overt* vs. *covert* attention.[3] What I mean by this distinction is, minimally, that *overt* attentional shifts involve an active modification (voluntary or involuntary) of, for example, bodily posture or gaze direction, whereas *covert* attentional shifts do not involve such modification and may occur while the overall external perceptual stimulation is held fixed (e.g. through a fixation cross).

With these clarifications in the background, I now present the three causal schemas adapted from Stokes (2014)[4]:

(a) *Cognitive process → Overt attentional shift → Perceptual experience.*
(b) *Non-cognitive processes → Covert attentional shift → Perceptual experience.*
(c) *Cognitive processes → Covert attentional shift → Perceptual experience.*

Schema **a** is the easiest to address. According to the above distinction, this schema involves an explicit active change in the posture, gaze, etc. of the subject. For example, if something suddenly appears in my visual field and I look in that direction in order to have a better view of the new stimulus, this would be a case befitting schema **a**. It goes without saying that such an occurrence is not an instance of cognitive penetration since the perceptual stimulation is clearly not the same before and after the gaze shift. Whenever one shifts one's gaze, even minimally, the amount and type of information available to one's perceptual system may change dramatically. Hence, any case befitting schema **a** is not an instance of cognitive penetration.

Things are slightly trickier with schema **b**. In schema **b**, one finds the required fixation of gaze and posture, which grants that the information coming to the perceptual system is always the same. Nevertheless, in this case experience can change over time due to a covert shift of attention. However, the states that drive the

---

[3] Stokes (2014) distinguishes between *intentional act of attention* and *non-agential (attentional) selection mechanisms.*

[4] For a more recent but less developed version of this idea, see Stokes (2018).

attentional shift are not cognitive processes and, therefore, cases that fit schema **b** fail to meet another fundamental requirement of cognitive penetration, namely that there is a top-down relation between a cognitive process and a perceptual process. Stokes proposes a particularly interesting empirical result as an example of schema **b**. The case in question is the experiment of Carrasco et al. (2004). In this experiment subjects were looking at a fixation point and they were perceptually (exogenously) cued to covertly shift their attention toward a contrast grating, which in turn was perceived as having increased contrast. I hold this to be a borderline case between schema **b** and **c** and I return to this experiment later on. For the sake of argument, since the cueing is exogenous and nothing indicates that a cognitive process is involved in this case, let's keep Stokes' interpretation and consider this example as a clear instance of schema **b** and, thus, not as an instance of cognitive penetration.

Let us now turn to schema **c**. Here we have all the right ingredients for cognitive penetration. The attentional shift is covert and, consequently, the external stimulus and other external conditions are held fixed. Furthermore, the process that drives the attentional shift is a higher-level cognitive process. Hence, schema **c** provides a valuable starting point for inquiring into the possibility of attentional cognitive penetration. However, going back to the first disjunct, still to be rejected, Pylyshyn's objection is meant to show that even if an attentional phenomenon satisfies schema **c**, it is still not clear whether a shift in the instantiation of attention would entail a change in perceptual input, which would automatically exclude cognitive penetration. This is when the competition theory comes in to help. In order to reject the dismissive attitude toward attention, one needs to argue that attention, once adequately understood as a property that emerges from biased competition, does not change the input to perception. Before arguing for this claim and for the full rejection of the dismissive attitude, I need to discuss a further aspect of the role that attention plays in perception that is relevant for the cognitive penetrability debate in general.

With the help of the three causal schemas I can now address another phenomenon that may be invoked to explain away some alleged cases of cognitive penetration. The phenomenon in question is *perceptual learning*. Perceptual learning refers to environment-driven long-term changes in a subject's perceptual system that facilitate the performance of some perceptual tasks (Goldstone 1998). While the improvement of some perceptual capacities with training have been known for a long time, the stage for contemporary research on perceptual learning has been most clearly set by Gibson (1963, 1969). Gibson focuses on ecological aspects of perception and construes perceptual learning as extracting previously available but unused information in the environment. Here, however, I will be mainly concerned with the mechanisms of learning internal to the subject and, specifically, with the role of attention in perceptual learning.

Goldstone (1998) discusses four main "internal" mechanisms that underlie perceptual learning: *attentional weighting, stimulus imprinting, differentiation,* and *unitization.* For the purposes of this chapter, I focus on the first mechanism. Attentional weighting concerns stimulus features (such as being red and being 3 cm long) and dimensions (such as color and length) and consists in the subject learning through practice or experience to automatically and systematically attend more to task-relevant features and dimensions and less to task-irrelevant ones (Goldstone 1998; Connolly 2017). In terms of biased competition, perceptual learning through attentional weighting can be understood as the system acquiring over time strong bottom-up biases that are deployed automatically in favor of certain features or dimensions of a stimulus to be represented.

Concerning cognitive penetrability, perceptual learning involves changes in perceptual capacities, and plausibly in perceptual experience, that are long-term and driven by the environment. As such, if a putative case of cognitive penetrability can be explained by perceptual learning through attentional weighting, nothing cognitive needs to be involved. In other words, this would be a case reflecting causal schema **b** and not causal schema **c**, which is the one needed to make a plausible case for cognitive penetration. However, it is important to note that, construed in this way, attentional weighting is a process that enhances perceptual capacities and is neutral toward the biasing source. While in perceptual learning such a source can be stimulus reoccurrence, nothing prevents that, in other cases, the source of bias can also be internal to the subject and involve a subject's knowledge or memory, for example by having the subject follow an instruction. Such a top-down-driven attentional weighting would then constitute a plausible candidate for causal schema **c**.

Furthermore, the reader should keep in mind that perceptual learning takes time (especially in adults) and, as such, it is poorly suited to explain cases in which the alleged cognitive effect on perceptual experience happens over a relatively short period or with relatively limited exposure to the stimulus. For example, the capacity of a subject to exert a degree of voluntary control on the rate at which percepts alternate in a bi-stable image (Meng and Tong 2004; Liu et al. 2012) does not necessarily require specific training or prolonged exposure. Later, I argue that such a capacity can be explained as an effect of a top-down cognitive bias on the attentional competition processes among representations of the two interpretations of the image, thereby constituting a plausible case of attentional cognitive penetration. What matters now is that, given that this effect does not require prolonged and repeated exposure, such an effect cannot be easily explained away as a case of perceptual learning.

6.2   Competition Is Metacognitive Regulation[5]

In this section, I argue that attentional shifts do not entail changes in perceptual input as the opponents of cognitive penetrability require. In the light of the biased competition view, attention is the property of "being the winning representations" that emerges from the competitive interaction of cognitive and perceptual processes in the system.

---

[5] This section is adapted from Marchi (2015).

If one grants that the competing entities are representations then, in a simple case, those representations may be about the individuals or states of affairs that they represent. Competition, on the other hand, is a process among the currently tokened representations of the system. One can say that, for example in perception, representations are about objects of the external world, whereas biased competition is about those representations. This, however, would only be partially accurate, because while representations may have contents, competition is not a representational process itself. In other words, although competition involves representations, it is not a process that represents. Rather, competition allows such things as contextual cues and internal background knowledge, which come in the form of biases, to determine which representation should instantiate attention (the property of being the current winner) at any given time given the biases. Looking at things from this angle highlights an important feature of competition, namely that competition is a meta-process, i.e. a process that involves other processes or states of the system, although it is not a form of meta-representation. As such, attention can be described as a form of metacognition,[6] in the sense that the system may use environmental cues or background knowledge to assess which of its ongoing cognitive processes or states best fits with the current context and tasks.

This novel approach to attention, which I call the *metacognitive view*, is not supposed to be a new theory on top of the biased competition theory that I already introduced. Rather, the metacognitive view works as a conceptual clarification of some of the implications of the biased competition theory of attention that are relevant for the problem of attention and cognitive penetrability to be discussed in this chapter. In particular, the metacognitive view allows us to: (1). rule out that attentional shifts are a form of input selection, and (2). help in shaping the arguments for attention being one of the possible ways in which cognitive penetration can occur.

If competition is a meta-process that involves representations, what may at first look like input selection, in the sense that is relevant for Pylyshyn's claim, is in fact a consequence of some representations becoming dominant in the competition. Since the competing representations are already engaged in competition once the process settles at a certain level of the hierarchy, this means that, at that level, the input that causes the tokening of those representations cannot be determined by the outcome of the competition, since the one temporally precedes the other. This line of reasoning applies to all levels of the cognitive and perceptual hierarchy. At some level, inputs are characterized by signals coming from the external world; at other levels, inputs are signals coming from other parts of the system. Nevertheless, in this picture attentional processes remain meta-processes that do not interest inputs directly; rather, they pertain to the system's representations triggered by those inputs. This is an important upshot of the metacognitive view of attention, because, if correct, many of the arguments that are based on the idea that attention works as input selection have to be revised or rejected. As I mentioned above, some of these arguments are at the core of the debate about attention and cognitive penetration. If

---

[6] See Hohwy (2015) for a similar view within the prediction error minimization framework.

the instantiation of attention is indeed a form of metacognition, the dismissive attitude based on the claim that attentional processes change the input to perception has to be rejected.

To lend plausibility to the claim that attention is a form of metacognition,[7] one preliminary clarification to make is that the occurrence of the term *cognition* in the discussion of metacognition has to be taken in a wide sense, denoting both high-level cognitive processes and low-level (perceptual) processes.[8] In a simple picture, a cognitive process, be it thought, belief or perception, is a mental representational process that is about something non-mental, e.g. objects or events in the external world, whereas a metacognitive process is a mental process that is about other mental processes, e.g. a thought about a thought.

In the literature, metacognition is often thought to involve a self-reflective process by which people assess what they know about their own cognitive processes and utilize such knowledge to modify their behavior (Koriat 2007). Given this specific conception, only conscious-explicit knowledge subjects have about their own cognitive processes can play a metacognitive role in evaluating those cognitive processes. Furthermore, it is sometimes assumed that proper metacognition requires some form of meta-representation. I believe that this notion of metacognition may be too restrictive. Some authors argue for the possibility of metacognition without meta-representation (Proust 2007) and of implicit and unconscious metacognition (Kentridge and Heywood 2000; see below). I employ the notion of "metacognition" to refer to a kind of cognitive processes, the meta-processes, that are directed, consciously or unconsciously, to other mental (including perceptual) processes, which are the object processes (Nelson and Narens 1990). In the course of this section, I clarify the function of attentional competition processes when understood as a meta-processes.

There is a distinction between two broad kinds of metacognitive phenomena: *metacognitive knowledge* and *metacognitive regulation* (Moses and Baird 1999; Fernandez-Duque et al. 2000a). In a paper, in which they try to link metacognition and executive function, Fernandez-Duque and colleagues (2000a) write:

> Metacognitive knowledge is knowledge people have about their cognitive abilities ("I have a bad memory"), about cognitive strategies ("to remember a phone number I should rehearse it"), about tasks ("categorized items are easier to recall") [...] Metacognitive regulation refers to processes that coordinate cognition. These include both bottom-up processes called cognitive monitoring (e.g., error detection, source monitoring in memory retrieval) and top-down processes called cognitive control (e.g., conflict resolution, error correction, inhibitory control, planning, resource allocation). (Fernandez-Duque et al. 2000a, p. 288)

In arguing that competition is a meta-process, one can ask whether it is a form of metacognitive knowledge or metacognitive regulation. According to Fernandez-Duque et al. (2000a), metacognitive knowledge implies awareness of one's own performance at certain cognitive tasks. Metacognitive regulation, on the other hand,

---

[7] Part of the remainder of this section has been adapted from Marchi (2017).

[8] See discussion below and Fernandez-Duque et al. (2000a).

is a more general cognitive phenomenon that involves the monitoring and control of other cognitive processes. Furthermore, metacognitive regulation includes perceptual processes such as color and word detection. Fernandez-Duque et al. (2000a) use the example of the Stroop task, in which subjects have to name the color of the letters of a color word (blue, red, etc.), the meaning of which may be congruent or incongruent with the color of the letters. In the incongruent condition, subjects report awareness of the conflict between word-color and word-meaning, whereas no such awareness is reported in the congruent one.

This means that explicit metacognitive knowledge of the conflict only arises in the incongruent condition. The authors, however, discuss data supporting the idea that a metacognitive regulative process of selection of word-color and word-meaning is present in both conditions. This result has three important consequences. First, metacognitive regulation can regulate low-level perceptual processes such as color processing. Second, the lack of awareness, either of the conflict or of the regulative process, in the incongruent condition opens up the possibility of unconscious and implicit metacognitive processes. Third, given that the Stroop task is a paradigmatic example of attentional selection, the authors explicitly associate the kind of metacognitive regulation in the Stroop task with attention and provide a starting point for the idea that the instantiation of attention is a metacognitive phenomenon. The biased competition theory of attention allows for a further development of this idea.

Fernandez-Duque and colleagues (2000a) describe metacognitive regulation in terms of, among other things, conflict resolution and resource allocation. In the previous sections, on the basis of the core features of selectivity and modulation, I outlined a preliminary definition of attention as optimization of resource allocation. Although the definition has now changed in virtue of the adoption of the biased competition view, the idea of optimization of resource allocation still captures the main task for which attentional processes emerged. The attended representation is the most relevant for the system's current needs and is allocated further processing resources. Thus, optimization of resource allocation is achieved through the competition process, which is itself a kind of conflict resolution. It appears that the function of competition and some functions of metacognitive regulation coincide.[9]

Furthermore, the "object processes" of competition are not, strictly speaking, elements of the external world (objects, features, spatial locations, etc.), which may figure among the contents of some cognitive representations, but the representations themselves. Therefore, the biased competition view allows for a preliminary understanding of competition as a regulative meta-process that optimizes resource allocation to the winning representations, i.e. the representations that instantiate attention. Competition regulates representations, relative to the current biases.

The main difference between competition and other forms of metacognition is that competition, as we have seen, spans the whole cognitive hierarchy. Under the assumption that consciousness does not encompass the whole hierarchy, competition

---

[9] In this account, all instances of competition would be cases of metacognitive regulation, but not all instances of metacognitive regulation would be instances of competition. It is left open that regulation can happen by other means.

can operate outside consciousness and attention can be a property of unconscious representations. This is a potential problem for the view that competition is a form of metacognition that depends on the answer to the following question: can metacognitive regulation be unconscious? On this point, Fernandez-Duque et al. (2000b) are very careful in allowing only some metacognitive processes to be unconscious in a limited set of circumstances. However, if biased competition were a form of metacognitive regulation, its pervasiveness, including its unconscious form, would provide instances of unconscious metacognitive processes in a much wider set of circumstances.

This idea seems quite challenging, but as Fernandez-Duque et al. (2000b) note, it is not inconsistent with the existing literature. Moreover, although it is often assumed that metacognitive processes imply a form of conscious awareness, the idea of implicit and unconscious metacognitive processes is not unprecedented (Reder and Schunn 1996; Kentridge and Heywood 2000; Spehn and Reder 2000; Koriat 2007). In particular, Kentridge and Heywood clarify that "there is nothing inherent in metacognitive regulation that demands consciousness" (2000, p. 308). Along the same lines, Koriat states:

> [...] much of the experimental research in metacognition is predicated on the tacit assump-
> tion that the metacognitive processes studied entail conscious control. Nonetheless,
> although the term metacognition is generally understood as involving conscious awareness,
> it should be acknowledged that monitoring and control processes can also occur uncon-
> sciously. (Koriat 2007, p. 293)

One of the main reasons behind the link between metacognition and conscious awareness is that awareness is often a prerequisite for adopting metacognitive regulatory strategies. For example, in the case of minimizing the occurrence of errors, subjects have to be aware of their error-making in order to adopt a *slow down* minimization strategy (Fernandez-Duque et al. 2000b). However, experimental findings from Kentridge and Heywood (2000) demonstrate that this need not be the case, by showing that a change in strategy that leads to better performance can happen implicitly and unconsciously.

By adopting a target detection task, they were studying how the instantiation of spatial attention on the basis of unconscious cues affected the reaction times of a patient with blindsight, a perceptual impairment that makes one effectively blind in a significant portion of one's visual field. They serendipitously discovered that the patient was capable of implicitly shifting his strategy for detecting targets after being presented with a series of unconscious cues in his impaired visual field.

In one experimental condition, they found improved reaction times for detection of validly cued targets. Critically, both targets and cues were presented in the subject's impaired hemifield and the subject was informed of the likelihood of a target appearing at the cued location being twice as high as that of the target appearing at the non-cued location. In another experimental condition, the blindsight subject was informed that the previously high likelihood of a target stimulus being presented at the same location of the cue was now inverted, i.e. targets were now more likely to occur at the opposite location from the cue. The change meant that the contingent relation between the occurrence of cues and targets that the subject had previously learned was no longer correct. The subject was aware of the rule change and, due to his condition, unaware of the locations of the targets and cues. However, at the beginning of the experiment, the subject was incapable of voluntarily switching his strategy according to the new rule and his detection reaction times for validly cued targets[10] were slower, despite his knowledge of the rule change. His reaction times were quicker only for targets presented at the same location of the cue (low likelihood), i.e. only if they satisfied the previously learned rule.

However, as the experiment proceeded, the subject was able to change his strategy, and his reaction times improved for targets presented at the opposite location of the cue (high likelihood). The idea is that if explicit knowledge of the rule change were sufficient for a conscious metacognitive shift in strategy, this would have happened right at the beginning of the experiment. Since this was not the case, it is plausible that the implicit statistical properties of the new cue-target relation were the key factor driving the subject's gradual change of strategy. If this is correct, since the subject reported no awareness of either the cues or the targets, "the substitution of an effective schema in replacement of one which had become ineffective as circumstances changed does not therefore appear to necessarily engage consciousness[11]" (Kentridge and Heywood 2000, p. 311). Critically, the authors were interested in the attentional capacities of a subject with blindsight and the paradigm they used is one of the most widely adopted to study attention. Therefore, it is likely that the implicit strategy change is an attentional phenomenon and, in the present context of biased competition it can be explained with the acquisition of new biases regarding the relationship of targets and cues. This case may then constitute an interesting instance of attentional unconscious metacognitive regulation. Thus, according to Kentridge and Heywood (2000), metacognitive processes can occur without awareness.

The biased competition view can explain their findings and link metacognitive regulation to attention. Keeping in mind that what follows is supposed to happen outside of the subject's conscious awareness, in biased competition terms the experimental task could be described as the system entertaining two competing spatial representations about the most probable location of the target: r1: "cue location" and r2: "opposite location from the cue". In the first condition, however, on most occasions the target appeared at r1 and we might stipulate that the subject acquired a bottom-up bias in favor of r1. The critical finding is that, at the beginning of the second condition, where r2 was the more likely representation of the target location and the subject knew about the rule change, the subject was unable to use his knowledge of the reversal of the rule to improve performance. Translated again into biased competition terms, this means that the top-down bias about the known rule change,

---

[10] Opposite locations, according to the new rule.

[11] Similarly, Spehn and Reder (2000) discuss further experimental evidence of strategy selection, and, thus, metacognitive regulation (monitoring and control), that occurs outside subjects' awareness. On the basis of their findings, they argue that "metacognitive judgments are relatively basic cognitive components which sometimes become conscious" (Spehn and Reder 2000, p. 192).

favoring r2, was not sufficient to override the strong bottom-up bias in favor of r1, to the effect that r1 still ended up as the attended representation. As a consequence, the subject's performance decreased.

Over the course of the task, however, the now incorrect bottom-up bias that caused suboptimal performance would gradually undermine itself. While a new, inverse and correct, bottom-up bias in favor of r2 is being formed, the top-down bias in favor of r2 became more and more relevant, to the point at which r2 became dominant and attention is shifted, causing a new increase in performance. Furthermore, the biased competition view does not face serious problems in accounting for the unconscious nature of this process. If attention emerges from competitive metacognitive regulatory processes of this kind, one might sometimes be aware of one's voluntary control over the competition (voluntary attention) but typically not aware of the competition itself and of its biases.[12]

In this section, I have introduced a specification of biased competition as a form of metacognitive regulation that spans the cognitive hierarchy and has the basic function of determining the representations that should instantiate attention and thereby be prioritized in processing. This approach is made consistent with literature on metacognition, on the assumption that metacognitive regulation interests other mental processes and can be driven unconsciously. The biases driving regulative meta-processes must not always remain unconscious. In fact, once recast in the present terminology, the kind of cases that are most relevant for the cognitive penetrability debate are those in which an explicit high-level cognitive process of a subject, which may be described as a belief or desire, acts as a bias that drives the meta-processes of competition at some perceptual levels. Such cases equate specifically to voluntary endogenous covert attentional shifts, which are also the kind of attentional shifts required in the adequate causal schema **c** for cognitive penetration discussed in Stokes (2014) and in the previous section of this chapter.

If the above discussion is correct, the instantiation of attention does not change the inputs to perception and the dismissive attitude toward attention and cognitive penetrability, based on this claim, has to be rejected. Furthermore, the idea that competition is a form of metacognition casts light on the nature of the cognitive perceptual relation invoked by different forms of cognitive penetrability. Such a relation holds between a high-level bias that drives the meta-process and a low-level representation that becomes the winner in virtue of the bias. In the relevant cases this qualifies as an (internal and mental) causal[13] relation because if the bias were absent or impaired, the representation would not be dominant at that time. The metacognitive regulation view allows us to say this much: there are causal internal

---

[12] A separate story needs to be told for attention in vision for action. Although I cannot offer a detailed account here, as it is not my primary focus and it would break the flow of the chapter, I believe that unconscious metacognitive regulation of a form similar to the one described for blindsight could be extended to account for the role of attention in action-oriented vision and in the "unconscious" dorsal stream.

[13] I assume that this is true on different accounts of causation, e.g. counterfactual and interventionist.

and mental relations that can hold between high-level cognitive biases and low-level perceptual representational processes, while the input to the system remains the same. So far, however, I have not shown that attentional phenomena, even when driven by high-level cognitive biases, qualify as any of the different forms of cognitive penetrability discussed in Chap. 1. In the next section, I discuss whether attention, when adequately conceptualized as a representational property that emerges from competitive metacognitive regulation, meets the conditions of the four definitions of cognitive penetrability.

6.3 Attention and Cognitive Penetrability: A Second Look

There are some general considerations about attention and perceptual processing that stem from the biased competition theory and the metacognitive view discussed in the previous section. In particular, there are three fundamental conclusions that one may take from the discussion so far. First, competition is a meta-process that does not alter the input to perception. Second, competition at each level of the cognitive hierarchy is sensitive to biases from the external world as well as from other levels of the hierarchy, both higher and lower. Third, competition is possibly ubiquitous in the hierarchy. These three claims have been independently motivated in the course of this chapter and the previous one. What follows is that processing throughout the cognitive hierarchy can be regulated by the meta-process of biased competition. If one holds the view that the competing entities are representations, one may say that representations at each level of the hierarchy or integrated complex representations that span over multiple levels compete among one another for priority (allocation of limited processing resources) and the competition is regulated by top-down, bottom-up, and lateral biases.

Now, the way in which one categorizes different processes or levels of the hierarchy into perceptual or cognitive processes depends on the criteria one adopts to distinguish between perception and cognition. As discussed in Chap. 1, one may say, for example, that if some level encodes representations in analog format, then that level is perceptual, and if it encodes representations in digital format, that level is cognitive. In this case, competition among analog representation engenders the instantiation of perceptual attention, while competition among digital representation engenders the instantiation of cognitive attention. Regardless of how one characterizes the distinction, however, as long as a distinction is in place it seems that competition at perceptual levels may be, in principle, sensitive to biases coming from the cognitive level. If this is correct, it follows that perceptual processing is cognitively penetrable in a general sense: if a cognitive bias can alter the way in which perceptual attention is instantiated, it does so by affecting the underlying competition process among perceptual representations. An attentional shift of this sort does not imply a change in the input to perception or a change in what the system is representing, but rather a change in what representation is prioritized.

I can now return to the specific types of cognitive penetrability of perceptual experience that I singled-out in Chap. 1. Let me start by examining *causal* CP. To facilitate the discussion, I rehearse the definition offered in Chap. 1:

Causal CP: cognitive penetration occurs if there is a top-down causal (internal and mental) relation between a cognitive state and a perceptual experience, where the contents of experience are modified by the cognitive state, without a change in the perceptual input to the system.

Now, the possibility that the instantiation of attention may sometimes qualify as an instance of *causal* CP depends on whether or not biased competition allows for a top-down relation of the appropriate kind between a high-level cognitive bias and a perceptual experience that changes the contents of the experience. As I have argued above, the relations between biases and representations that occur in biased competition are internal and mental. Furthermore, the relations are causal, because the winning representation would not win if the biases that favor it were absent or impaired.[14] In the previous section, I argued that competition is a meta-process that does not alter the input to the different levels of the cognitive hierarchy. Hence, given these considerations it follows that the relations involved in the instantiation of attention are of the appropriate kind for *causal* CP and that the requirement of sameness of input is met. But do the contents of the experience change when attention is driven by a cognitive bias in this way?

The answer to this question partially depends on what kinds of contents one admits for perceptual experience. As mentioned previously, I do not take a particular stance on the contents of experience, but there are nevertheless some general considerations that are worth exploring. If one looks at the phenomenal character of ordinary perceptual experiences, it seems that experiences are complex phenomena, in the sense that they usually integrate several aspects of the world that are related to different sensory modalities. If perceptual experience has contents, one may think that such contents are complex and integrated, as is reflected in ordinary phenomenology. In other words, experience represents complex states of affairs that may involve a multiplicity of (multimodal) sensory features. Furthermore, experience is not only integrated across different sensory modalities but within the same modality as well. For example, we do not experience individual disembodied perceptual features such as shapes and colors floating around, but coherent bundles of features that we attribute to objects. Representations of individual features can be thought of as lower-level representations that are integrated into a more complex representation that underlies an overarching coherent experience.

Under the biased competition view, attention is a property of representations. If this is correct, concerning perceptual experience, attention can be a property of the whole complex integrated representation that underlies integrated experiences or a property of the lower-level representations that are the components of the complex one. It should be possible that a shift in attention corresponds to a change in some of the components of the experience, the lower-level representations, without

---

[14] This is what happens in perceptual extinction.

radically changing the overall complex integrated representation. This would mean that recruiting certain biases could change which component representation is winning the competition and such change would be reflected in the integrated representation to a certain extent. I now discuss two cases that seem to fit with this picture.

Carrasco et al. (2004) have shown that attention affects the experienced contrast of a stimulus. More precisely, exogenously cueing a lower contrast stimulus caused the subject to perform at chance in determining which of two stimuli had higher contrast. The experimental task was to report the orientation of one of two Gabor patches that appeared as either higher or lower in contrast by pressing a keyboard button. Before each presentation, one of the two stimuli could be exogenously cued for attention. The striking finding is that attentional cueing effectively made the lower contrast stimulus look subjectively equivalent to the not-cued higher-contrast stimulus, to the effect that subjects performed at chance in the orientation detection task when the lower-contrast stimulus was cued, but not otherwise. This experiment clearly shows that a bottom-up attentional bias may change the level of contrast at which two stimuli are subjectively experienced as equal. In other words, the instantiation of attention by the representation of the cue stimulus increases the experienced contrast for that stimulus.

Now, the above experiment suggests that the contents of a bias, namely a spatial cue, may affect the contents of the lower-level representation that is part of the experience, namely the representation of contrast level. This seems to be a convincing case for the possibility of a causal relation between biases and experiences, of the type required by *causal* CP. However, this is a case of exogenous attentional cueing and, as such, even if one accepts that some contents of experience change in this case, it does not meet the requirements of the adequate causal schema for CP, which is the following (Stokes 2014): *Cognitive processes → Covert attentional shift → Perceptual experience.* In other words, in order to have evidence for *causal* CP, we would need a similar case involving endogenous attention.

The biases involved in the experiment above are indeed exogenous. But if a bottom-up bias can affect the phenomenal character of an experience in this way, in the context of biased competition, nothing prevents a top-down bias from doing the same. In fact, similar experimental results have been obtained with endogenous attentional cueing by Liu et al. (2009). In this second experiment, instead of a spatial cue at the target location, the authors used a central cue, presented at fixation, and a second cue, namely a peripheral rapid serial visual presentation task (RSVP), which consisted in a rapidly presented series of letters. Before the presentation of the target stimuli, i.e. the Gabor patches, subjects were asked to detect whether the letter X was among the RSVP letters.

This particular cue is supposed to engage voluntary covert attention at the target location, which can be considered a way of recruiting cognitive biases, since it requires a subject's recognition of the letters and motivation to attend to the letters. Once again, the perceived contrast, indirectly inferred from the subject's performance in detecting the higher/lower contrast stimulus, was modulated by attentional processes. This time, however, the instantiation of attention was driven by motivational and recognition biases. The same paradigm was applied with similar effects in Abrams et al. (2008, 2009). Hence, endogenous biases are able to alter the content of the experience, which is reflected in the phenomenal character of the experience of perceptual features such as contrast. If such biases can be considered cognitive, which is allowed in the competition view and supported by the results of the second experiment, the correct causal schema is met and, therefore, some attentional shifts are cases of *causal* CP.

The contrast experiments discussed above occurred in carefully controlled conditions. There are, however, more ordinary examples of experiences that may now be explained as cases of attentional *causal* CP. These cases are the aforementioned ambiguous or bi-stable images. Normally, such images admit of two or more interpretations that can correspond to noticeably different visual experiences. The two interpretations would typically alternate at a certain rate, but it is shown that the rate can be altered by certain factors. Meng and Tong (2004) showed that a voluntary effort of the subject could affect the switching rate between the two possible visual experiences of a Necker cube. Similarly, Liu et al. (2012) showed that subjects can exert a degree of voluntary control in the alternation between the two possible visual experiences of a spinning silhouette animation. Importantly, in both cases subjects were required to fixate on specific points of the image, meaning that there was no obvious change in the external stimulus.

Under the present framework these cases can be explained as cases in which the competition between two representations corresponding to the alternative experiences was affected by a motivational bias. Once again, we have a cognitive perceptual relation between the bias and the representation, which affects the contents of the experience without a change in stimulus. If the bias is absent, the pattern of alternation between the two experiences changes, meaning that the relation is also causal. Hence, these cases are instances of attentional *causal* CP. I come back to these examples in the later chapters.

Let us now proceed to discussing another form of cognitive penetrability introduced in Chap. 1, namely *semantic* CP. Once again, I restate the definition below:

Semantic CP: cognitive penetration occurs if there is a normative top-down relation between domain general information stored in the system and information processed locally by a subsystem.

Concerning *semantic* CP, in cases where the involvement of a cognitive bias modifies the content of the experience, such as the contrast case above, there could be a logical or otherwise normative relation between the bias and the experience. Since the bias can be itself a representation there may be a normative top-down relation between the contents of the biasing and the biased representations.[15] However, since the biasing representation has to be a high-level cognitive one and the biased representation has to be perceptual, the idea holds as long as one accepts that there could be a normative top-down relation between representations that may have different kinds of contents (e.g. conceptual vs. non-conceptual, see below).

---

[15] These are the representations that win out at the lower level as an effect of the bias from the higher level.

In biased competition, nothing prevents that a logical, rational or otherwise normative criterion holds between the high-level biasing representation and the low-level biased representation. If this is the case, assuming that the contents of beliefs are domain general and perceptual contents are domain specific, a shift in attention can be the result of domain general information conveyed by the top-down biases affecting domain specific processing in a normative way. Therefore, some attentional phenomena could in principle meet the requirements of *semantic* CP.[16]

Finally, let us turn to the third definition of cognitive penetration discussed in Chap. 1, namely *indirect non-conceptual* CP. As with the previous cases, I recall the definition below:

> **Indirect non-conceptual CP:** cognitive penetration occurs if there is a top-down causal
> (internal and mental) relation between: 1. a cognitive state with conceptual contents, 2. a
> top-down triggered process with non-conceptual contents and phenomenal character, and 3.
> a perceptual experience, where the non-conceptual contents of the experience are modified
> by the cognitive process (with conceptual content) in virtue of the intermediate process and
> without a change in the perceptual input to the system.

In Chap. 1, I discussed how this kind of penetrability is meant to address the problem of interacting mental states with different kinds of contents. In particular, this notion of CP should allow for the possibility that cognitive processes with conceptual contents, such as the orthodox accounts of propositional attitudes like beliefs and desires, could affect other mental processes, such as perceptual processes, which are typically thought to have a different kind of contents. The solution is to posit an indirect causal relation between the cognitive and the perceptual process. The relation is indirect because it is mediated by another process that sits in between. The mediator process is engendered by the high-level cognitive process and has the same kind of contents as the perceptual process.

Given the biased competition theory of attention, this kind of situation is completely acceptable. Since the competition is integrated across cognitive domains, both at the same and at different levels of processing, a higher-level bias, which can be a high-level cognitive representation, may steer the competition towards the selection of a lower-level representation, which then itself acts as a bias for another representation at the same level. Attention in this case can be said to be instantiated by both lower-level representations, in virtue of the integrated nature of biased competition.

The higher-level cognitive representation may have conceptual contents, for example it could be about the identity or category of an object, and the lower-level representations may have perceptual contents, for example they could be about the shape and size of the object. This possibility poses no serious problems since the meta-process of competition is not limited to representations with a specific kind of content. In fact, the biasing process concerns the architecture of the system rather than the contents of the system representations at different levels and, as such,

---

[16]For a clear computational outline of how intention can semantically affect visual processing through attention and thus penetrate perception, see Wu (2017).

representations at different levels and with different kinds of contents can bias each other as long as the right architectural requirements are met. The architectural constraints for top-down biasing can be met as long as the system allows for top-down connections and signal passing between different levels in the hierarchy.

One interesting point to note is the possible overlap between *semantic* CP and *indirect non-conceptual* CP. In *indirect non-conceptual* CP, we have the top-down relation between the high-level representation and a first low-level representation, call it r1, as well as the lateral relation between r1 and a second low-level representation, call it r2. While both these relations may be normative, they could be so according to different norms. Furthermore, the higher-level representation may be semantically related to r1, but r1 may be related to r2 by other non-normative means, for example by statistically reliable co-occurrence. It is not clear whether one should be prepared to consider such an occurrence as an instance of *semantic* CP. Regardless of this problem, instances of *indirect non-conceptual* CP can be engendered by biased competition, once the theory is assumed in the background.

However, it seems that in the competition view, the need for the mediating representation disappears. If there is a top-down relation between a high-level cognitive representation and a lower-level representation that is part of the experience, such relation can be direct. The high-level bias would cause the low-level representation to win the competition, i.e. instantiate attention, thereby modifying the overall contents of the experience. As I mentioned above, the relation is causal because if the high-level representation were not tokened, the experience would have different contents on that occasion. The removal of the intermediate step avoids the danger of regress to which the notion of *indirect non-conceptual* CP is exposed, as I pointed out in Chap. 1. The competition view allows for direct biasing relations among representations with different kinds of contents, as long as the adequate architectural constraints are met in the system. *Indirect non-conceptual* CP would then become a special case of *causal* CP, where the two *relata* of the cognitive-perceptual relation have different kinds of contents.

In this section, I argued that biased competition can instantiate the kind of relations required for most forms of cognitive penetrability discussed in Chap. 1. This possibility depends on a clarification of the nature of the phenomenon that we call attention, which is possible once the competition theory and the metacognitive view of attention have been assumed and motivated in the background. Attention is a property whose instantiation by a perceptual representation may change the content of a perceptual experience. The meta-process of competition that underlies the instantiation of attention may involve cognitive-perceptual causal relations without entailing a change in the input to perception. I now turn to discuss the last and most general form of CP among those introduced in Chap. 1, namely *consequentialist* CP, by focusing on the epistemic role of attention in perception and cognition.

6.4   The Epistemic Role of Attention

On the basis of the biased competition view, attention is a property that emerges from a metacognitive regulation process that can take place at every level of the processing hierarchy. Any shift in attention, be it stimulus-driven or cognitively driven, means that the winners among competing representations are changing. Competition does not select inputs to be represented; rather, it regulates representations. This should suffice to rule out any strong dismissive view of attention. Attention may occur whenever and wherever there is a need in the system for meta-cognitive regulation of representations. If attention is not secluded from perception and cognition, and it is instead an emergent property of the winners of an integrated competition process among representations at different levels of the hierarchy, this opens up the possibility that the cognitive processes act as biases for the competition among perceptual processes, and consequently, that attention qualifies as an instance of some varieties of cognitive penetrability, as I discussed above.

In this section, I examine how the metacognitive view allows us to recast the epistemic role of attention for the justification of perception-based beliefs. This issue is directly connected to the most general form of cognitive penetrability, namely *consequentialist* CP. As we have seen in Chap. 1, *consequentialist* CP occurs if a top-down cognitive-perceptual relation leads to one of three consequences: (1) theory-ladenness of empirical observations; (2) changes in the justificatory role of experience for beliefs; (3) dismissal of modular models of the mind. Here, I focus on the third consequence and, to facilitate the reading, I report an adapted definition of *consequentialist* CP from Chap. 1:

> **Consequentialist CP:** cognitive penetration occurs if a there is a top-down causal (internal and mental) relation between a cognitive state and a perceptual experience that leads to at least one of the three relevant consequences.[17]

Some authors have already noted that the problem of the epistemic role of attention is connected to many fundamental issues in the epistemology of perception (Lyons 2015; Machery 2015).[18] One of these issues concerns the question of whether perceptual experience can play a justificatory role for beliefs in the first place. Some authors reject this idea, while others embrace it on the basis of their views on the similarity or dissimilarity between contents of experiences and contents of beliefs as well as the nature of the relation between them. In what follows, I rely on the *phenomenal approach* to perceptual justification (Siegel 2012, 2013a, b, 2015; Siegel and Silins 2014, 2015; Silins 2016.

---

[17] Part of the remainder of this section is adapted from Marchi (2017).

[18] In particular, Machery writes: "if philosophers are primarily interested in the cognitive penetrability hypothesis for epistemological reasons, as suggested, it is strange to set aside the attention-mediated causal influence of belief, desires, emotions, etc. on perception, since the latter raises exactly the same kind of epistemological problems as a causal influence that would not be mediated by attention" (2015, p. 62, n4).

According to the *phenomenal approach*, perceptual experience can provide rational support[19] for certain perceptual beliefs, partly in virtue of its phenomenal character. In this general exploration of the epistemic role of attention, the precise nature of the justificatory relation is left unspecified. I assume that the *phenomenal approach* is correct and that a more detailed notion of justification consistent with this approach can be construed in both an internalist and an externalist fashion.[20]

The first issue I address concerns the necessity of attention for the justification of perceptual beliefs. Some authors frame the question of whether attention has a role to play in the justification of perceptual beliefs in terms of the counter-position between *attention needed* and *attention optional* views (Siegel and Silins 2014, 2015). Both views fall within the *phenomenal approach*. Where the two views diverge is on whether or not epistemically relevant experiences must be attentive. According to *attention needed* views, only perceptual experiences that are attended can play the appropriate justificatory role, while according to *attention optional* views, experiences that are unattended but retain their phenomenal character can still provide the appropriate justification in forming beliefs about what is being experienced, e.g. during change blindness (Siegel and Silins 2014, 2015). One first point to clarify is that if the instantiation of attention were necessary for conscious experience to arise in the first place (Prinz 2012; Dehaene et al. 2006), then *attention needed* views would be trivially true.

However, the necessity of attention for conscious experience is far from agreed upon. While Prinz (2012) holds that attention is both necessary and sufficient for conscious experience (see Chap. 5 for a more detailed outline of this view and an objection), Block (2007, 2012) champions the view that attention is neither necessary nor sufficient, and others have expressed doubts that both necessity and sufficiency are adequately supported by empirical data (Van Boxtel et al. 2010). Prinz's main claim is that attention makes representation available for working memory encoding. Thus, one would expect that attention operates or happens before working memory encoding. However, recent work on visual short-term memory, i.e. the memory system that allows a subject to rely for a limited time on visual information that is no longer available, suggests a different picture. Visual short-term memory can be divided into iconic memory and visual working memory. While the former has a high capacity and fast decay rate (about 500 ms), the latter has a low capacity and may last up to a few minutes. Recently, it has been proposed that an intermediate

---

[19] Specifically, the notion at play is that of *propositional justification* as used in Siegel and Silins (2014, 2015), according to which an experience can provide rational support for believing a proposition regardless of whether a subject uses the experience to form beliefs (Doxastic Justification). I leave open other important questions, such as, for example, whether experiences can do this by themselves or need auxiliary beliefs, i.e. whether the nature of the justification is immediate or not.

[20] Respective examples are *evidentialism*: experiences are evidence for belief; and *reliabilism*: experiences are among the reliable sources of evidence (Siegel 2013b; Steup 2014). However, see Ghijsen (2015, p. 8) for an account of why CP poses no problem for externalist accounts. Externalists may hold that that perceptual experience provides justification not in virtue of being a perceptual experience, but rather in virtue of being reliably caused, e.g. not being (badly) cognitively penetrated (see Ghijsen 2015, p. 27).

stage exists between the two, labeled *fragile visual short-term memory* (Vandenbroucke et al. 2011). Such an intermediate stage has both large capacity and a significant duration of several seconds (Sligte et al. 2008). Crucially, it has been shown that attentional manipulations affect information available in working memory but not information available in fragile visual short-term memory (Vandenbroucke et al. 2011). Going back to Prinz's view, it is only natural to think that if there is a stage in which representations are made available for working memory encoding, such a stage would be fragile visual short-term memory. However, if information encoded at such a stage is immune to different attentional manipulation, it is hard to understand how attention could possibly play the role of making representations available for working memory. If this were the case, one would expect to see attention play a larger role for information encoding in fragile visual short-term memory. However, while this data casts further doubt on Prinz's view on attention, by itself it is not enough to establish the necessity of attention for conscious experience or lack thereof. This latter hypothesis depends on whether one thinks that working memory encoding is necessary for conscious experience to arise. If it is and if attention is necessary for working memory encoding, then it is also necessary for conscious experience.

Returning to the problem of justification, assuming for now that attention need not be instantiated by a representation in order for it to enter phenomenally conscious experience, i.e. if one can have inattentive experiences, one can still ask whether attention is necessary for experience to play the appropriate justificatory role for beliefs. Proponents of *attention needed* views say that it is, whereas proponents of *attention optional* views hold that the justificatory role of such experience is preserved in the absence of attention, while attention might still need to be instantiated for conscious access or reportability of those experiences. I argue that the opposition between needed and optional views is based on an incorrect notion of attention linked to an indirect view, which is inconsistent with biased competition. With the new understanding of attention as a property that emerges from biased competition, I can clarify which aspects of these views are correct and which are incorrect. I start by discussing a dilemma faced by those who endorse both the *phenomenal approach* and the *attention optional* views.

The *phenomenal approach* is sometimes motivated by comparing the epistemic status of subjects who suffer from blindsight to that of normal perceivers. Here, one might have the intuition that even if blindsight subjects can sometimes form the same perceptual beliefs as normal subjects through different routes, such as unconscious processing, they are not in the same epistemic position as normal subjects in justifying those beliefs (Siegel and Silins 2014). Proponents of the *phenomenal approach* can explain this intuition. Since experience helps to justify beliefs partly in virtue of its phenomenal character, the phenomenal approach can be considered a version of phenomenal dogmatism: there must be something it is like for a subject to have an experience, in order for that experience to provide *prima facie* justification for a correspondent belief. It follows that the lack of phenomenal experience is enough to motivate why the blindsight subject is in a potentially worse epistemic position than a normal subject with respect to some beliefs she may form. If the blindsight subject and the normal subject both form the same belief that p but only the normal subject has a perceptual experience that p,[21] and the blindsight subject does not have justification from other sources for believing that p, under the phenomenal approach, the normal subject would be *prima facie* justified in believing that p while the blindsight subject would not.

Let us now go back to unilateral visual extinction. As discussed in the previous chapter, in extinction subjects retain a normal phenomenal experience of their impaired visual hemifield, but only in the absence of a competitor stimulus presented in the unimpaired hemifield. Much like blindsight, a proponent of the phenomenal approach may agree that subjects who suffer from extinction are not in the same epistemic position as normal subjects in forming perceptual beliefs about extinguished stimuli.[22] If this is correct, the problem is the following: when a competitor stimulus is present, what is diverted from the extinguished stimulus is attention, as I discussed in the previous chapter.

Yet, under the assumption that the instantiation of attention is not necessary for phenomenality, as I temporarily posited to avoid trivialization, one might hold that the extinction subject retains a phenomenal (and perhaps not accessed/attended) experience of the extinguished stimulus. However, if this is the case and if the *attention optional* view is correct, under the *phenomenal approach*, the extinction subject would be in the exact same epistemic position as a normal subject in forming beliefs about the extinguished stimulus, which is intuitively implausible. In other words, from the *attention optional* plus *phenomenal approach* it follows that an extinction subject can be in the exact same epistemic position as a normal subject, i.e. that both have the same rational support to justify perceptual beliefs based on their experience (which is not accessed by the extinction subject), since the only factor that changes between the two subjects is the instantiation of attention. This position, however, shares the same degree of intuitive implausibility that motivated the phenomenal approach in the first place.

At this point, one may retain *attention optional*, and say that the extinction subject has the same (unattended) phenomenal experience as the normal subject, but there is something other than attention (and phenomenal experience) that is missing in extinction and this further missing ingredient is what hinders the epistemic position of the subject. But if this were correct, the unimpaired (albeit unattended) phenomenal experience retained by the extinction subject would not be sufficient to attain the same degree of justification as a normal subject and this would threaten the *phenomenal approach*. Alternatively, one can retain the *phenomenal approach* and

---

[21] For the sake of simplicity, it may be assumed that the content of the experience and that of the belief are the same. See Siegel (2012).

[22] It is important to note that the extinction case is significantly different from cases of *inattentional* or *change blindness* discussed in Siegel and Silins (2014). In extinction subjects show the same impairments, e.g. shape crossing (Driver and Vuilleumiere 2001), as in neglect and the instantiation of attention is not affected by a separate task like counting the number of balls passing. Therefore, alternative explanations, e.g. involving failure of reportability, do not apply to extinction, whereas they do apply to inattentional and change blindness.

say that the extinction subject is not in the same epistemic position as a normal subject because he does not have the same phenomenal experience of the extinguished stimulus. But in this case, under the assumption that attention is the only thing that changes in extinction, it seems that attention is indeed necessary for the relevant kind of phenomenality, which leads to giving up *attention optional*. This option would apparently lead to the trivial truth of the *attention needed* view in the form of the instantiation of attention being necessary for having perceptual experiences in the first place. In what follows, I hope to offer a non-trivial solution to this problem.

One important feature of both the *attention optional* and the *attention needed* views is that, as a result of an indirect view of attention, they construe attention as something that is independent from perceptual experience itself (Siegel and Silins 2014). However, as I already argued, the attempt at constraining the role and locus of attention to specific places in the perceptual and cognitive hierarchy (as in the early/late-selection theories), which would be required to think about the processes that realize attention as independent from those that realize perceptual experience, is problematic. Under the metacognitive regulation view, competition is a regulatory process that operates at each level of the hierarchy and the kind of attention about which defenders of both *attention needed* and *attention optional* views have argued is a conscious manifestation of a property of relatively high-level representations, namely of those complex representations that underlie perceptual experience. I believe that the metacognitive view can help settle the debate between *attention necessary* and *attention optional* views without trivialization.

According to the metacognitive view, competitive regulation can happen at different levels of the processing hierarchy. In this picture, it is possible that in order for a representation to become integrated into the experience and thus to become phenomenally conscious, that representation must be winning the competition, and thereby be attended, at some of those levels, but not others. *Attention needed* and *attention optional* views need only clarify which among the different levels of the hierarchy, and thus of competition, they are respectively targeting. In particular, the *attention needed* view can maintain that in order for a low-level representation to be integrated into the experience, it must be attended. In this sense, attention is needed to enable phenomenology for that representation and, thus, its justificatory power that is allowed in the phenomenal approach. On the other hand, the *attention optional* view can maintain that a representation that is already integrated into the experience must be attended in order for it to be reportable or for a subject to exert the justificatory power of the experience, but they can also hold that the instantiation of attention by that representation is not needed in order for the experience to have its justificatory power in the first place.

To see how this construal serves both views, let us think about the extinction patient. When no competitor stimulus is presented, representations about the impaired hemifield can win the competition and thus instantiate the kind of attention that is needed to enable phenomenology for those representations. Nevertheless, even if this kind of attention is instantiated, and the subject has an experience of his otherwise impaired hemifield, she may be distracted by other factors and fail to subsequently report the stimulus just like a normal subject would. If so, the kind of attention that is not needed, the one leading to reportability, may not be instantiated by those representations that are already integrated into the experience. In this case, the subject may nonetheless have a non-reportable perceptual experience, which has justificatory power for certain beliefs, although the subject may never take advantage of that power.

On the other hand, when a competitor stimulus is present in the extinction subject's unimpaired hemifield, representations in the impaired hemifield cannot instantiate the kind of attention that is needed and, as a consequence, no experience arises from the stimulus presented in the impaired hemifield. This is consistent with the phenomenal nature of the impairments that arise in neglect and extinction (e.g. bisecting lines and comparing pictures), which seems to target the subjective appearance of the world. Hence, the subject is not justified in forming beliefs on the basis of an experience that she is not currently undergoing. However, this also implies that, at some levels, the instantiation of attention is indeed necessary for conscious phenomenology. This is a controversial claim, but it is endorsed by some prominent theories of consciousness (Dehaene et al. 2006; Prinz 2012).

Now, concerning *consequentialist* CP, if the above discussion is correct, it is easy to see that any high-level bias that can alter how competitive metacognitive regulation takes place at lower levels can affect how the kind of attention that is needed for perceptual justification is instantiated. Hence, a shift in attention that is caused by a cognitive bias can be an instance of *consequentialist* CP. Of course, the problem is much deeper than my tentative solution. For example, a proponent of the *attention needed* view might be unsatisfied by the restriction of the necessary kind of attention to the lower levels and might want to argue that higher-level kinds of attention are needed as well. Regardless of the complex ramifications of the issue, I hold that the competition view can offer a preliminary solution to the problem and shed light on the important role of attention in perceptual epistemology.

Another epistemic issue concerns the rationality or irrationality of the etiology of perceptual experiences. Siegel (2013a) argues that the etiology of an experience can be epistemically evaluable, i.e. it can be rational or irrational relative to more or less the same norms that apply to the etiology of belief. She holds that CP, if it occurs, can sometimes lead to experiences that have irrational etiologies providing less or no rational support for corresponding beliefs. Such experiences are *epistemically downgraded*. Siegel assimilates the etiology of a CP experience to that of rational or irrational belief and contrasts it to a-rational etiologies[23] of both experiences (e.g. hallucinations induced by a drug), and beliefs (e.g. god-zapped beliefs). According to the view I presented in the previous chapter and above, biased competition is a metacognitive process that constitutes an integral part of the etiology of those cognitive and perceptual processes that require optimization of a limited amount of processing resources. Given that perceptual experience is a product of some such processes, *a fortiori*, competition is among the factors that contribute to the etiology of experiences and, therefore, it affects the rational or irrational status of such etiology.

---

[23] Non-epistemically evaluable.

Siegel (2013a) writes that unconscious processes in "the basement of the mind" give rise to perceptual experiences and that those processes affect the rational role of the experience in supporting beliefs. This view is completely consistent with the metacognitive regulation view presented here. According to the metacognitive regulation view, competition is a built-in feature of the cognitive hierarchy that enables the proper unfolding of those very processes within a system with limited resources.

The competitive regulatory process from which attention emerges at any given level is sensitive to many sources of biases. While bottom-up biases, such as objective intensity or abruptness of perceptual stimulation, work independently of the subject's epistemic status, top-down (and perhaps lateral[24]) sources of biases can include epistemically evaluable cognitive processes such as the subject's current goals, desires, and beliefs. Importantly, even if partially driven by bottom-up biases, as I argued in the previous sections, competitive regulatory processes are meta-processes and they are still internal in an important sense. Hence, such processes qualify as the kind of unconscious processes that can affect the etiology of the experience since "the kind of rationally assessable etiologies of interest are internal to the subject's cognitive system" (Siegel 2013a, p. 711).

If a top-down bias that affects competitive metacognitive regulation at one or more levels underlying perceptual experience is the result of a cognitive process that can be rational or irrational, it seems that the etiology of the experience at that particular level inherits the rational or irrational status of the bias in virtue of the regulatory process. Therefore, going back to Siegel's original example, if Jill's belief that Jack is angry acts as a bias that determines how attention is instantiated at the relevant levels, with the result that Jill experiences Jack's face as angry,[25] competitive metacognitive regulation can lead to experiences with problematic etiologies and, thus, threaten their justificatory role. Again, such a case of biased competition with irrational biases is a case of *consequentialist* CP.

6.5   Summary and Conclusion

In this chapter, I have argued that competition is a meta-process that does not change the input to perception. This allows one to reject the dismissive attitude toward the role of attention for cognitive penetrability. I argued that the instantiation of attention may involve cognitive-perceptual relations that meet the requirements of all forms of CP introduced in Chap. 2. The biased competition theory of attention allows that an internal and mental relation between a cognitive bias and a perceptual representation is *causal* and can possibly be *normative*. Furthermore, it allows that

---

[24] See Siegel (2015) for a discussion of the epistemic evaluation of intra-perceptual etiologies.

[25] This can happen in several ways. For example, Jill may focus on only certain features of Jack's face or only on the darker locations of his face, etc. Importantly, according to the metacognitive regulation view, none of the available alternative explanations of her experience that involve attention can be construed as a pre-perceptual phenomenon.

the contents of the biasing and the biased states can be conceptual and non-conceptual respectively. Finally, the metacognitive view shows that attention has an important epistemic role to play for perceptual justification of belief and for the etiology of perceptual experience. Hence, shifts in the instantiation of attention may lead to some of the relevant epistemic consequences highlighted by *consequentialist* CP.

In the next chapter, I examine how the present discussion about the distinction between perception and cognition, attention and cognitive penetrability can be introduced in the increasingly popular framework of predictive coding. Predictive coding aims at being a unified theory of the mind based on one very clear fundamental principle: minimization of prediction error. I show that what has been said so far is not only consistent with the framework, but seems to follow from its adoption.

References

Abrams, J., Liu, T., & Carrasco, M. (2008). Endogenous, sustained attention alters contrast appearance. *Journal of Vision, 8*(6), 144.

Abrams, J., Barbot, A., & Carrasco, M. (2009). Endogenous attention alters the appearance of spatial frequency. *Journal of Vision, 9*(8), 131.

Block, N. (2007). Consciousness, accessibility, and the mesh between psychology and neuroscience. *Behavioral and Brain Sciences, 30*(5), 481–548.

Block, N. (2012). The grain of vision and the grain of attention. *Thought: A Journal of Philosophy, 1*(3), 170–184.

Carrasco, M., Ling, S., & Read, S. (2004). Attention alters appearance. *Nature Neuroscience, 7*, 308–313.

Connolly, K. (2017). Perceptual learning. In E. N. Zalta (Ed.), *The Stanford encyclopedia of philosophy*. https://plato.stanford.edu/entries/perceptual-learning/

Dehaene, S., Changeux, J.-P., Naccache, L., Sackur, J., & Sergent, C. (2006). Conscious, preconscious, and subliminal processing: A testable taxonomy. *Trends in Cognitive Sciences, 10*(5), 204–211.

Driver, J., & Vuilleumier, P. (2001). Perceptual awareness and its loss in unilateral neglect and extinction. *Cognition, 79*(1–2), 39–88.

Fernandez-Duque, D., Baird, J. A., & Posner, M. I. (2000a). Executive attention and metacognitive regulation. *Consciousness and Cognition, 9*(2), 288–307.

Fernandez-Duque, D., Baird, J. A., & Posner, M. I. (2000b). Awareness and metacognition. *Consciousness and Cognition, 9*(2), 324–326.

Firestone, C., & Scholl, B. J. (2015). Can you experience "top-down" effects on perception? The case of race categories and perceived lightness. *Psychonomic Bulletin and Review, 22*(3), 694–700.

Ghijsen, H. (2015). The real epistemic problem of cognitive penetration. *Philosophical Studies, 173*(6), 1457–1475.

Gibson, E. J. (1963). Perceptual learning. *Annual Review of Psychology, 14*, 29–56.

Gibson, E. J. (1969). *Principles of perceptual learning and development*. East Norwalk: Appleton-Century-Crofts.

Goldstone, R. L. (1998). Perceptual learning. *Annual Review of Psychology, 49*, 585–612.

Hohwy, J. (2015). Prediction error minimization, mental and developmental disorder, and statistical theories of consciousness. In R. J. Gennaro (Ed.), *Disturbed consciousness* (pp. 293–324). Cambridge, MA: MIT Press.

Kentridge, R. W., & Heywood, C. A. (2000). Metacognition and awareness. *Consciousness and Cognition, 9*(2 Pt 1), 308–312; discussion 324–326.

Koriat, A. (2007). Metacognition and consciousness. In P. D. Zelazo, M. Moscovitch, & E. Thompson (Eds.), *The Cambridge handbook of consciousness* (pp. 289–326). Cambridge: Cambridge University Press.

Liu, T., Abrams, J., & Carrasco, M. (2009). Voluntary attention enhances contrast appearance. *Psychological Science, 20*, 354–362.

Liu, C.-H., Tzeng, O. J. L., Hung, D. L., Tseng, P., & Juan, C.-H. (2012). Investigation of bistable perception with the "silhouette spinner": Sit still, spin the dancer with your will. *Vision Research, 60*, 34–39.

Lyons, J. (2015). Unencapsulated modules and perceptual judgment. In A. Raftopoulos & J. Zeimbekis (Eds.), *The cognitive penetrability of perception: New philosophical perspectives* (pp. 102–122). New York: Oxford University Press.

Machery, E. (2015). Cognitive penetrability: A no-progress report. In A. Raftopoulos & J. Zeimbekis (Eds.), *The cognitive penetrability of perception: New philosophical perspectives* (pp. 59–74). New York: Oxford University Press.

Macpherson, F. (2012). Cognitive penetration of colour experience: Rethinking the issue in light of an indirect mechanism. *Philosophy and Phenomenological Research, 84*(1), 24–62.

Marchi, F. (2015). Cognitive penetrability of social perception: A case for emotion recognition. *Review of Philosophy and Psychology, 6*(4), 617–620.

Marchi, F. (2017). Attention and cognitive penetrability: The epistemic consequences of attention as a form of metacognitive regulation. *Consciousness and Cognition, 47*, 48–62.

Meng, M., & Tong, F. (2004). Can attention selectively bias bistable perception? Differences between binocular rivalry and ambiguous figures. *Journal of Vision, 4*, 539–551.

Mole, C. (2015). Attention and cognitive penetration. In A. Raftopoulos & J. Zeimbekis (Eds.), *The cognitive penetrability of perception: New philosophical perspectives* (pp. 218–238). New York: Oxford University Press.

Moses, L. J., & Baird, J. A. (1999). Metacognition. In R. A. Wilson & F. C. Keil (Eds.), *The MIT encyclopedia of cognitive sciences* (pp. 533–535). Cambridge, MA: MIT Press.

Nelson, T. O., & Narens, L. (1990). Metamemory: A theoretical framework and new findings. In G. Bower (Ed.), *The psychology of learning and motivation* (Vol. 26). New York: Academic.

Prinz, J. J. (2012). *The conscious brain: How attention engenders experience*. New York: Oxford University Press.

Proust, J. (2007). Metacognition and metarepresentation: Is a self-directed theory of mind a precondition for metacognition? *Synthese, 159*, 271.

Pylyshyn, Z. W. (1999). Is vision continuous with cognition? The case for cognitive impenetrability of visual perception. *Behavioral and Brain Sciences, 22*(3), 341–365.

Raftopoulos, A. (2010). Ambiguous figures and representationalism. *Synthese, 181*(3), 489–514.

Reder, L. M., & Schunn, C. D. (1996). Metacognition does not imply awareness: Strategy choice is governed by implicit learning and memory. In L. M. Reder (Ed.), *Implicit memory and metacognition* (pp. 45–78). Mahwah: Lawrence Erlbaum.

Siegel, S. (2012). Cognitive penetrability and perceptual justification. *Nous, 46*(2), 201–222.

Siegel, S. (2013a). The epistemic impact of the etiology of experience. *Philosophical Studies, 162*(3), 697–722.

Siegel, S. (2013b). Can selection effects on experience influence its rational role? In T. Gendler & J. Hawthorne (Eds.), *Oxford studies in epistemology* (Vol. IV, pp. 240–270). Oxford: Oxford University Press.

Siegel, S. (2015). Epistemic evaluability and perceptual farce. In A. Raftopoulos & J. Zeimbekis (Eds.), *The cognitive penetrability of perception: New philosophical perspectives* (pp. 405–425). New York: Oxford University Press.

Siegel, S., & Silins, N. (2014). Consciousness, attention, and justification. In D. Dodd & E. Zardini (Eds.), *Scepticism and perceptual justification* (pp. 149–169). Oxford: Oxford University Press.

Siegel, S., & Silins, N. (2015). The epistemology of perception. In M. Matthen (Ed.), *The Oxford handbook of philosophy of perception* (pp. 781–811). Oxford: Oxford University Press.

Silins, N. (2016). Cognitive penetration and the epistemology of perception. *Philosophy Compass, 11*(1), 24–42.

Sligte, I. G., Scholte, H. S., & Lamme, V. A. F. (2008). Are there multiple visual short-term memory stores? *PLoS One, 3*(2), e1699.

Spehn, M. K., & Reder, L. M. (2000). The unconscious feeling of knowing: A commentary on Koriat's paper. *Consciousness and Cognition, 9*(2), 187–192.

Steup, M. (2014). Epistemology. In E. N. Zalta (ed.), *The Stanford encyclopedia of philosophy* (Spring 2014 Edition). http://platostanford.edu/archives/spr2014/entries/epistemology/

Stokes, D. (2014). Cognitive penetration and the perception of art. *Dialectica, 68*(1), 1–34.

Stokes, D. (2018). Attention and the cognitive penetrability of perception. *Australasian Journal of Philosophy, 96*(2), 303–318.

Van Boxtel, J. J. A., Tsuchiya, N., & Koch, C. (2010). Consciousness and attention: On sufficiency and necessity. *Frontiers in Psychology, 1*, 217.

Vandenbroucke, A. R., Sligte, I. G., & Lamme, V. A. F. (2011). Manipulations of attention dissociate fragile visual short-term memory from visual working memory. *Neuropsychologia, 49*, 1559–1568.

West, G. L., Anderson, A. A. K., Ferber, S., & Pratt, J. (2011). Electrophysiological evidence for biased competition in V1 for fear expressions. *Journal of Cognitive Neuroscience, 23*(11), 3410–3418.

Wu, W. (2017). Shaking up the mind's ground floor: The cognitive penetration of visual attention. *Journal of Philosophy, 114*(1), 5–32.

Chapter 7
Expectations and Predictions as a Model of the Mind

Abstract In this chapter, I discuss how each of the steps taken in this book to argue that attentional processes can generate cognitively penetrated perceptual experiences may be reconceived in the prediction error minimization framework. Section 7.1 introduces the framework of predictive processing in general and prediction error minimization (PEM) in particular. In Sect. 7.2, I argue that a distinction between perception and cognition can be established in PEM by adapting the action-resolution criterion proposed in Chap. 1 to the new framework. Section 7.3 discusses how the notion of cognitive penetrability can be understood in PEM without trivialization.

7.1 Predictive Processing: Fundamental Ideas

In the previous chapters, I first addressed the problem of how to draw a distinction between perception and cognition, which is required for a cogent notion of perception being cognitively penetrable. Second, I presented the biased competition theory of attention and argued in favor of its endorsement. Third, I investigated the role of attention in the interplay between perception and cognition. In this chapter, I discuss how these issues can be reconceived in the light of a predictive processing (henceforth PP) model of the mind. This topic is interesting because PP is one the most promising frameworks to model cognitive functions. Before proceeding, it will be helpful to offer an elucidation of the PP framework. This introduction has a general scope and focuses on the main theoretical aspects of the framework without delving into the formal computational details.

In cognitive science, the PP framework has become increasingly popular as an approach to modeling the mind that is inspired by and consistent with what we know about the neural organ. The notion of predictive processing subsumes several different computational approaches, each with its own set of algorithms. Spratling (2016) discusses five main versions of predictive processing and elucidates the computational differences between them. Despite the formal distinctions, however, the different versions of PP "share the common computational goal of fitting a model to data" (Spratling 2016, p. 5, online version).

At a general level, a PP computational system is distinguishable from a traditional sequential computer in one important respect. The traditional computer

© Springer Nature Switzerland AG 2020
F. Marchi, *The Attentional Shaping of Perceptual Experience*, Studies in Brain and Mind 16, https://doi.org/10.1007/978-3-030-33558-8_7

operates bottom-up by receiving inputs (external and internal if its architecture is complex enough) and performing operations on those inputs that provide outputs, which in turn can serve as inputs to other parts of the computer. This kind of computation can proceed in a serial fashion or in parallel. Each subsystem can be informationally encapsulated and have a specific function, but the fundamental temporal order of input-processing-output is preserved throughout the system. The traditional computer has no means to assess the incoming input before the input itself is provided.

A PP system, on the other hand, works in a proactive way. Such a system is endowed with a model of the external environment that it uses to generate expectations about incoming inputs, even before such inputs occur. When the input reaches the system, it is compared to the system's expectations and any mismatches between expectation and input generate an error signal – a prediction error. The error signal allows the system to update its model and achieve better predictions. It is in such a way that PP systems work by fitting a model to the data, since the better the model fit the better the predictions will be. Here I focus on the version of PP known as "prediction error minimization", or PEM for short (Hohwy 2013, 2014), which ambitiously aspires at offering a unified theory of the mind. The reason why I focus on PEM is that, to my knowledge, it is the only version of PP where the problems of attention and cognitive penetrability of perception have both received some significant discussion. Such a discussion is mainly due to the work of Hohwy (2012, 2013, 2014, 2017), on which this chapter relies.

The basic idea behind PEM is the same as other versions of PP. In the case of a cognitive processing system, such as the human brain, the system has to solve the problem of inferring the causes of its sensory inputs or, in other words, the causal structure of the environment in which the system finds itself and that is currently affecting the system. To solve this problem, the system needs to perform the fundamental task of minimizing prediction error. The way in which the human cognitive system achieves this goal is through perception and action, by which the system can fit an internal model of the world to the incoming data or actively seek new data to confirm the model.

The background assumptions of PEM set it quite apart from more traditional computational approaches to perception and cognition. Instead of analyzing the incoming signal in a purely bottom-up serial fashion, a PEM system forms *predictions* about how the evidence should be. Predictions are generated from the internal model and then compared to the actual evidence coming through the senses. If there is a mismatch between prediction and evidence, an error signal is generated and propagated into the system to revise the model and achieve better subsequent predictions. Once the model is updated, the error signals should typically decrease. This means that, in general, the goal of a PP system is to keep prediction error as low as possible. One can then conceive of the task of a cognitive predictive system as minimizing prediction error over long periods of time. As Hohwy writes: "the brain is an organ that on average and over time continually minimizes the error between the sensory input it predicts on the basis of its model of the world and the actual sensory input" (2014, p. 2).

Prediction error minimization is achieved through a process that approximates Bayesian inference. In perfect Bayesian inference, the posterior probability of a hypothesis that is supposed to explain the evidence, conditionalized on the actual evidence, is computed with iteration of Bayes' theorem from the likelihood of the evidence, the prior probability of the hypothesis (prior), and the prior probability of the evidence.[1] As Hohwy describes it:

> PEM is essentially inference to the best explanation, cast in (empirical, variational) Bayesian terms. The winning hypothesis about the world is the one with the highest posterior probability, that is, the hypothesis that best explains away the sensory input, in a context-dependent fashion [...]. (Hohwy 2014, p. 5)

Importantly, the cognitive system is not supposed to compute perfect Bayesian inference. Instead, it is supposed to be such that its operations, in the long run, will approximate Bayesian inference (Hohwy 2017). In other words, perfect inference is taken as a goal and different individual systems, or the same system on different occasions, can approach the goal through different routes.

What the system needs to get the PEM mechanism going is an internal generative model of the causal structure of the world, which sets the prior probabilities of the hypotheses, and the means to acquire new evidence used to test the hypotheses generated on the basis of the model. But how does a system acquire a generative model of the world? The answer is that the model is acquired through evolution and development. Gładziejewski (2016) nicely summarizes the development of PEM generative models:

> [...] causal-probabilistic regularities in the external world determine statistical patterns in the system's sensory input. The statistics of the incoming sensory signals serve as the only system-available "trace" of the causal-probabilistic structure of the external world. From the point of view of the predictive coding framework, our cognitive system uses the statistics of the input in order to build up an internal, skull-bound model of the external world that produces this input. [...] This model is generative in that it works as a sort of experience simulator [...]. That is, the internal model of the world constantly activates the system's sensory level top-down in a way that is supposed to (predictively) simulate the sensory activity produced by the external world. The better the simulation, the smaller the prediction error. (Gładziejewski 2016, p. 571)

By interacting with the world, a developing system can learn the likely patterns of stimuli occurrence in each context. But if successful interaction with the world requires prediction, and prediction requires a model that is acquired through interaction with the world, it looks like the framework is exposed to an objection of circularity. Proponents of PEM may reply that a biological system such as the human brain is already endowed with a basic generative model selected through evolution and neural development (Hohwy 2013, p. 63). Interaction with the world, coupled with an evolutionary driven fundamental model, shapes the system's expectations about its initial interactions with the world. Later, the parameters of the model can

---

[1] As I mentioned, this is an informal introduction to the basic ideas of PEM. For more technical details and formal treatments, see Friston (2005, 2010), Hohwy (2013, 2014), and Spratling (2016).

be set to reflect what is more likely to be encountered in a given situation or what are the more likely outcomes of an action.

Furthermore, the system can learn that some regularities in the world change at a rather fast pace, while other regularities remain stable for longer time periods, as well as how these different regularities interact with each other. A gust of wind is a regularity that happens at a very different timescale and localization from those of a planetary movement.

Since the world is structured into a hierarchy of regularities at different spatio-temporal resolutions,[2] an adequate model of the world should reflect such a hierarchy. The system needs to infer the causes of its sensory input where the causes of sensory inputs are regularities in the world. Such regularities can occur at different spatiotemporal scales and a good generative model of the world needs to reflect the spatiotemporal resolutions of the regularities that it represents. To adequately reflect the spatiotemporal variability of the causal structure of the world, the model has to be structured in a hierarchy of levels. Each level represents worldly regularities at different spatiotemporal resolutions. Kiebel et al. (2008) discuss how such a hierarchical model can be described for the human brain and understood in terms of PEM. A hierarchical model suffices to capture regularities that change at different timescales.

Hence, hypotheses based on the hierarchical generative model represent worldly regularities at different spatiotemporal resolutions (Hohwy 2013; Kiebel et al. 2008), where lower levels have higher resolution (track more localized and faster changing regularities), typically with greater detail, and higher levels have lower resolution, typically with less detail. The structure of the system's inferences is then thought to be hierarchical as well. Priors at lower levels are shaped by priors at higher levels. The eventual prediction error derived from testing hypotheses at lower levels is then propagated as high in the system as needed in order to minimize it.

As a toy illustration of the above point, suppose one enters a friend's living room and expects to find a red pillow on the sofa. For example, one might have seen such a pillow during a previous visit. Suppose that, instead of the red pillow, one finds a blue pillow. The mismatch between the evidence and expectation generates a prediction error signal that is propagated as high as the level of hypotheses about the color of the pillow and the model may be revised on the basis of the error signal with respect to the color of the pillow in the present context. But now suppose that instead of a blue pillow one finds an elephant sitting on the couch. This would generate a prediction error spike that may radically affect the model at many different levels and change what one knows about elephants and about one's friend quite considerably.

In the first case, the blue pillow, only the priors about sensory features of the object may be changed to accommodate prediction error, and many contextual priors already embedded in the model will be kept unchanged. In the second case, on

---

[2] Spatiotemporal resolution may be conceived as a property of representational contents at different levels of the hierarchy, whose individuation depends on the function that those representations are performing.

the other hand, much more established priors, such as those about elephants not living in human houses, are called into question, which correspond to context invariant beliefs that we have about the world. Thus, at first glance, the different spatio-temporal resolutions of hypotheses at different levels of the hierarchical model may allow the model to reflect the psychological notions of perception and belief. Perception would comprise hypotheses about regularities up to a certain spatiotem-poral resolution, mainly reflecting the current environmental context, while belief would comprise hypotheses about regularities that are context invariant or that can be generalized from one context to other similar contexts.[3]

To summarize, a predictive system generates hypotheses about the causes of its sensory inputs on the basis of its hierarchical model of the causal structure of the world. Once the system has generated such hypotheses it can compute the expected evidence that it would receive, given each hypothesis, in its current context. Expected evidence can then be compared to the actual evidence and if the system's predictive capacities are poor on that occasion, i.e. if the hypothesis generates a large amount of prediction error it may decide to switch to an alternative hypothesis that better explains the evidence, revising the overall hypotheses' landscape in the model. This mechanism, by which the system updates its model on the basis of the residual prediction error ensuing from the comparison between expectations and actual evidence, is known as *perceptual inference*. Perceptual inference is one of the two main building blocks of PEM. It is what allows the system to ensure that its own model of the world is accurate and to update the model in the light of unexpected evidence. Hohwy writes:

> Computationally, perception can then be described as empirical Bayesian inference, where priors are shaped through experience, development and evolution, and harnessed in the parameters of hierarchical statistical models of the causes of the sensory input. The best models are those with the best predictions passed down to lower levels, they have the high-est posterior probability and thus come to dominate perceptual inference. (Hohwy 2014, p. 262)

In addition to perceiving the world, an organism can typically act in its environ-ment and modify it to a certain degree to fulfill its needs. In PEM, this is modeled with a second type of inference, called *active inference*, which constitutes the other main building block of the framework. In active inference, the system may explore the world seeking new evidence that would validate its currently best hypotheses, or it can act upon the world in order to make a currently suboptimal hypothesis accu-rate. For example, one can move around an object to ensure that one has got the identity of the object right.

Action is a further way in which the system can minimize prediction error. Instead of revising its hypotheses to fit the sensory data, the system acts to change the data in such a way as to fit with the hypotheses. Where perceptual inference was concerned with fitting the model to the data, active inference is supposed to solve the opposite problem and fit the data to the model. As Hohwy puts it:

---

[3] I expand on this point in the next section.

[...] the model predictions will also be less erroneous the more the sensory input is made to fit the predictions. Given the basic idea that the main aim of the brain is to minimize prediction error, we should expect it to exploit this different direction of fit too. That is, we should expect that the brain minimizes prediction error by changing its position in the world and by changing the states of the world, both of which will change its sensory input. This can be captured in the expectation that the brain uses action to minimize prediction error. (Hohwy 2013, pp. 76–77)

Active inference works in much the same way as perceptual inference does, only with an opposite direction of fit (data to hypotheses). However, Hohwy points out that it would be a very inefficient practice for the brain to test arbitrary hypotheses through action. Testing the hypothesis that it is dark by closing one's eyes, he argues, would validate that hypothesis, but would be a bad practice for it would not minimize prediction error in the long run as it may lead to bumping into obstacles or even more dramatic consequences. Therefore, active inference should be performed on the basis of those hypotheses that have achieved the higher posterior probability in perceptual inference. A cycle is then established in which perceptual inference evaluates hypotheses in light of the data until it reaches a sufficiently low amount of prediction error. Active inference would then be recruited to gather new data under the expectations of how such data would change if the currently selected hypothesis were true. Active inference is a means by which the system can test its currently best hypotheses in order to increase its confidence in the adequacy of its perceptual inference.

Active inference may lead the system to form new hypotheses or to keep its current ones. For example, suppose one is looking at a familiar object from an entirely new angle and in a dimly lit room. This perceptual encounter with the object may provide the system with evidence that is inconsistent with the system's hypotheses about the usual properties of that object, such as shape and color. This would generate prediction error that the system needs to minimize. Now, in order to immediately minimize the error, the system could update its model in order to account for the new evidence. In general, since the object is familiar, this means that the prior probability of hypotheses about the object in the model were shaped by several previous encounters. For this reason, it would not be optimal for the system to change such hypotheses on the basis of one single encounter in which they no longer fit with the evidence. This may minimize prediction error now but lead to higher prediction error in the long run if the lack of fit on one occasion were due to contingent factors, such as bad lighting conditions, and not actual properties of the object.

Alternatively, the system may seek further and better evidence to test its original hypotheses without revising them. For example, one can move around the object or put it in better lighting conditions. However, the newly incoming data needs to undergo further perceptual inference in order to be compared to the system's expectations based on the original hypotheses. If the hypotheses are now a good fit for the new evidence then they may be kept, and if they are still a bad fit then the system now has good reason to revise them, perhaps concluding that what was thought to be a familiar object in the dim light was, in fact, a completely new one. Thus, the cycle between perceptual and active inference is continuous and, in normal conditions, it ensures that the system is selecting the hypotheses that best minimize prediction error in the long run.

Importantly, not all the system's hypotheses can be tested and validated through the same kind of actions. Some hypotheses may be put to the test by performing actions that are immediately available in one's everyday context, while other hypotheses need longer-term and carefully planned actions to be validated. For example, hypotheses about the color or shape of an object can be validated by gathering new sensory data, which may be done by simply looking in another direction or moving around. In other words, by performing simple actions in the world, hypotheses about shapes and colors of objects would be directly put to the test and kept or revised if needed.

But what about more stable and long-term properties of objects, such as their identity? What about hypotheses concerning abstract entities? What about hypotheses concerning macroscopic features of the world, such as the hypothesis that the earth revolves around the sun? If PEM has to be an exhaustive account of cognition, these features of the world, the very reliable long-term regularities, should also be reflected in the system's model of the world. They can be learned and incorporated in the system in the form of some high-level priors with low spatiotemporal resolution, i.e. with low sensitivity to local and short-term contextual changes, but they cannot typically be tested by performing simple and immediately available actions. There seems to be a boundary between hypotheses that can be tested through the kind of actions that are immediately available to one in an ordinary context and those that cannot be. I propose that such a boundary hinges on the notion of basic action discussed in Chap. 1. I expand on this point in the next section.

Striking a balance between perceptual and active inference is critical, because a successful predictive system must efficiently minimize PE not just at a given time, but also in the long run (Friston 2010; Hohwy 2013, 2017). In fact, as we have seen, it might be the case that a radical update of the model may help the system minimize prediction error now, while hindering its minimization capacities in subsequent tasks.

As a general example, let us assume that if the lighting conditions are poor, the evidence may be degraded. During perceptual and active inference in vision, if the evidence is degraded it is likely that, if a rather strong mismatch between the expectation and evidence occurs, with the consequence of a spike in prediction error, this could be due to noise rather than the actual inadequacy of the model. Under these circumstances, the system may either disregard such evidence and keep its model, or take the degraded evidence seriously and update the model accordingly. However, if the model has been developed in optimal conditions, a radical update in the light of degraded evidence would result in a faulty model that would be ill-suited for future prediction error minimization. An optimal strategy would be to disregard degraded evidence, preventing it from radically shifting the priors in the model, but this strategy is somewhat opposed to the usual and fundamental task of the system, i.e. prediction error minimization. Hence, in order to efficiently adopt this strategy only when needed, the system needs to know when the evidence should be expected to be degraded.

This raises the important problem of how the system may be able to evaluate the reliability of the evidence. In order to do so, the system needs a second-order model that reflects not the causal structure of the world, but rather the conditions under which the information about such a structure that is conveyed to the system is reliable. In more formal terms, the reliability of the evidence is called *precision*. Precision is defined as the inverse of the variability, or width, of a probability distribution. Expected precision for a given signal can be used as a measure of the estimated level of noise for that signal in the present sensory context. Optimizing the expectations of precision for any incoming information is a further fundamental task that the system must achieve in order to behave efficiently in the long run. In PEM, the optimization of precision expectation is identified with the role of attentional processes. The discussion of precision expectation concludes my overview of PEM's fundamental tenets. During the course of this chapter, I expand on this topic and its relation to the biased competition theory discussed in previous chapters. But first, let us examine how a distinction between perception and cognition can be drawn in PEM.

7.2   Perception and Cognition in PEM

As we have seen, a PEM system requires an internal generative model of the causal structure of the world, which is learned from interactions with the world during development and is initially based on some evolutionary driven "innate" priors. On the basis of the model, the system generates a hierarchy of hypotheses where those at higher levels provide top-down priors for those at lower levels. Hypotheses at different levels are about worldly causal regularities that occur at different spatio-temporal resolutions. During perceptual inference, the system receives sensory signals from the world that it can use as evidence to test its hypotheses about what it is currently presented with. If hypotheses at lower levels are inaccurate, an error signal is generated and propagated bottom-up through the system. The error signal serves as evidence for higher levels and the system may end up revising the model. On the other hand, the system can decide to perform active inference, i.e. act upon the world, and gather new evidence to confirm or disconfirm its hypotheses.

Whether or not the system decides to revise the model on the basis of the error signal depends on how reliable the error signal is considered to be. The reliability of the error signal depends on its level of noise, which is not constant in our world and context-dependent. However, the system cannot know the real precision of an incoming signal beforehand, but it can have expectations of precision in a given context based on previous inference performed in that context. Optimizing the expectations of precision and, thus, prioritizing or ignoring certain signals is, according to a key element of PEM, the task assigned to *attentional* processes in the model.

Following the basic tenets of PEM, there is no principled computational difference between the processes that take place at lower levels of the hierarchy and those that occur at higher levels (Hohwy 2013; Clark 2016). The difference is not in the processes themselves but in the spatiotemporal resolution of the causal regularities that those processes represent.

In other words, the same computational process, for example an iteration of Bayes' theorem, can, in principle, take place at different levels of the hierarchy. However, assuming that the system is trying to accurately model the causal structure of the world, the variables involved in processes at different levels will be mapped onto physical variables at different spatiotemporal timescales, i.e. they will represent different spatiotemporal phenomena (regularities). This means that the hierarchy proposed by PEM is continuous in the sense that there is no principled difference between kinds of processes at different levels.[4] Hohwy writes:

> *It seems the difference between percepts and concepts comes out in terms of a gradual movement from variance to invariance, via spatiotemporal scales of causal regularities. There is thus no categorical difference between them; percepts are maintained in detail-rich internal models with a short prediction horizon and concepts in more detail-poor models with longer prediction horizons.* (Hohwy 2013, p. 72)

This continuity provides the model with its powerful appeal of being a unified theory, but at the same time, it raises a question about the possibility of distinguishing between perception and cognition in a PEM processing hierarchy. Drawing such a distinction is only possible if one has a criterion for it that preserves the homogenous computational structure of a PEM hierarchy and is still able to differentiate processes at different levels on the basis of some of their properties. In Chap. 1, I introduced the action-resolution criterion (ARC) as a means of distinguishing between perception and cognition in a continuous processing hierarchy.

The hierarchy posited by PEM is one such hierarchy and now that we have a clearer picture of how active inference and perceptual inference work, we can adopt ARC to ground a distinction between perception and cognition in a PEM hierarchy. If all that changes between different levels of the hierarchy is their spatiotemporal resolution, the distinction between perceptual levels, corresponding, for example, to states of seeing, and cognitive levels, corresponding to doxastic states, must hinge on the spatiotemporal properties of hypotheses at those levels.

Now, one initial consideration is that there seems to be something in common between processes at a lower spatiotemporal resolution in PEM and doxastic states. Likewise, there seems to be something in common between processes at a higher spatiotemporal resolution in PEM and typical perceptual states. Some beliefs that we acquire during the course of our life endure for a very long time and are immune to change. In PEM's terminology this means that they have low spatiotemporal resolution. On the other hand, some processes that are typically considered perceptual change radically and very rapidly with minimal environmental or bodily changes. In PEM's terminology these would be processes that have high spatiotemporal resolution. Suppose one is inclined to say that processes that have high

---

[4]Whether the computed variables are continuous or discrete depends on the specific algorithms adopted in each different version of PEM.

resolution generate perceptions and processes that have low resolution generate cognitive states (beliefs, desires, etc.). The question now is where to draw the line between them or, in other words, how high the resolution should be for a process in the PEM hierarchy to be a typical instance of perception and how low the resolution should be for a process in the PEM hierarchy to be a typical instance of cognition.

To answer this question, one would need a criterion for identifying the set of hypotheses that have the adequate resolution for perception and the set of hypotheses that have the adequate resolution for cognition. I explore the possibility of using basic action as an adequate criterion to determine the resolution of each set in PEM. In Chap. 1, I argued that the spatiotemporal resolution of some processes of the system overlaps with the spatiotemporal resolution of basic actions and that, in virtue of the overlap, performing basic actions may affect how those processes unfold. I now apply the same line of reasoning to PEM's hierarchy of processes.

Basic actions are actions that do not have other actions as their causes or components, in PEM's terminology I use the term *basic active inference* to refer to active inference that involves only basic actions. The key to this idea is the following: while the whole predictive hierarchy represents worldly causal regularities at all those spatiotemporal resolutions that are relevant for a system's survival or that are allowed by a system's representational[5] capacities, whenever a system performs basic active inference, there is only a subset of hypotheses in the hierarchy that is affected by it. Hence, one can use basic active inference as a criterion to delimitate a subset of hypotheses in the system. The idea I want to explore is that hypotheses that are testable in basic active inference belong to perception and hypotheses that are not or cannot be tested in basic active inference belong to cognition. Let me now discuss the plausibility of this idea.

Suppose that one wants to confirm that there is mustard in the fridge and, in order to do so, one opens up the fridge and looks for mustard (performs active inference through a basic action). Once the fridge is open, there will be an array of sensory signals incoming to the system that will generate a spike of prediction error when compared to the previously valid set of hypotheses about what is directly presented in front of the system's sensory organs. The system will then minimize prediction error and adopt a new set of hypotheses with better predictive power in the present conditions. Not all levels of the hierarchy, however, will be affected in the same way, or at all, by the action of opening the fridge. For example, those levels whose hypotheses track regularities such as the taste of the mustard, the overall layout of the house, the current president of the USA or Earth's revolution around the sun will not be affected by the current active inference.

To say that certain hypotheses are directly affected by the performance of basic active inference is just to say that those hypotheses represent worldly causal

---

[5] I am assuming that there is a specific set of regularities that the system may represent in the generative model, given the system's sensory and cognitive *apparata*. This is a broad notion of representation (see Chap. 1), without commitments to any particular representational view. The problem of whether PEM systems have genuine representational capacities is still a matter of discussion. I discuss a view on representation that fits well with PEM later in the chapter.

regularities at the adequate spatiotemporal resolution for basic action.[6] This criterion allows for a significant degree of flexibility. Importantly, some hypotheses may
be identified as cognitive in one context and as perceptual in another context. The
hypotheses about the taste of the mustard, for example, will not be affected by the
basic actions of opening the fridge and visually searching for mustard in the fridge,
and, thus, they could be identified as cognitive hypotheses in that context. For example, one can have a belief about how the mustard of this particular brand tastes while
looking for it in the fridge. Nevertheless, such hypotheses may be tested by a subsequent basic action of tasting the mustard and, therefore, play a perceptual role in
that context.

This does not mean that all hypotheses at any spatiotemporal resolutions can
play both roles. There may be hypotheses that are at too low a resolution to be tested
in basic active inference and would therefore be invariably cognitive according to
such criterion. Which hypotheses can be tested in basic active inference depends on
the kind of organism in which the predictive system is embodied. Different organisms have different action possibilities, depending on their bodies and sensory
organs. For instance, by moving around, a bat could test hypotheses about the current distribution of ultrasound waves around it. This is possible for the bat in virtue
of its sensory apparatus and the same would not be possible for a human. Yet a
human may have beliefs about ultrasound waves, even if one cannot test them
directly by performing a basic action.

Given that only some of the system's hypotheses, which are typically about features of the current environment, will be affected by the performance of basic active
inference, one may call perception the set of those hypotheses. In this picture, perceptual hypotheses admit a degree of variation across different occasions, contexts,
and action possibilities of different organisms. However, there may be hypotheses
that are impossible to test through basic active inference and can therefore be considered as constituting an invariable basis of core cognition. I can now recast ARC
in PEM terms:

> **PEM-ARC:** Perception comprises hypotheses that can be tested through basic active infer-
> ence (active inference with only basic actions), in virtue of their spatiotemporal resolution
> and the natural constraints on the organism's body. Cognition comprises hypotheses at a
> lower spatiotemporal resolution than the resolution of basic active inference.

In order for PEM-ARC to be plausible at all, I need to show that it can at least capture some aspects of traditional distinctions between typical cognitive states such
as, for example, doxastic states like beliefs, and typical perceptual states such as, for
example, states of seeing.

It seems that some properties that are usually considered perceptual properties,
such as shapes and colors for vision or solidity for haptics, are adequately catego-
rized by PEM-ARC. Hypotheses about such regularities can be tested by performing

---

[6] For a characterization of basic actions, see Chap. 2. In a nutshell, basic actions are actions that do
not have other actions as antecedents or components and they may be construed as those actions
that may (but need not) have only motor intentions as their causes.

basic actions like rotating an object, turning on the lights, moving around the object or touching it. Hypotheses about other regularities, such as the current president of the USA or Earth's revolution, cannot be tested by performing any basic action, although they can be tested by performing a series of basic actions (complex action) or by employing some mediating tools, such as a newspaper or a telescope. Now the property of being the current president of the USA or rotating around the sun are not properties that are typically considered perceivable, but one may have beliefs about those properties with respect to a person or a planet. Thus, concerning these examples, PEM-ARC seems to fare well in categorizing some hypotheses as perceptual and some as cognitive.

One might argue that one can have beliefs about perceptual properties of objects. For example, one can believe that an object has a certain shape even when the object is not present. However, shape is a regularity which is at the adequate resolution for basic action and, therefore, hypotheses that represent such a regularity are perceptual according to PEM-ARC. These problematic cases are sometimes called perceptual beliefs and they may be considered borderline cases. The PEM description of such a case may be quite simple. Whenever one looks at an object there could be more than one hypothesis, with different priors, about some of its properties. For example, there could be a hypothesis about its current shape, a hypothesis about its usual shape, and a hypothesis about its original shape. The three hypotheses would have different resolutions: the hypothesis about the current shape of the object would be sensitive to minimal changes in the environment, which may be brought about by performing a basic action; the hypothesis about its usual shape would take more time to be revised; and the hypothesis about its original shape might never change. Only the first of these hypotheses seems to be directly affected by basic actions one can perform. Take the example of a pillow. By manipulating the pillow, one can change its current shape, thereby affecting the system's corresponding hypothesis without requiring the system to revise its hypotheses about its usual or original shape. Hence the system can form hypotheses at different resolutions about some properties of an object, which would correspond to perceptions of those properties and beliefs about those properties, depending on whether the resolution of the hypothesis overlaps with the resolution of basic action.

Of course, PEM-ARC has limitations and I have only discussed some examples of when it may perform adequately for a criterion to distinguish between perception and cognition in PEM. It may still fail in many other cases. Yet, even if PEM-ARC is rejected, it shows that processes at different stages of a continuous hierarchy may be distinguished into higher-order cognitive processes and lower-order perceptual processes on some of their features such as, for example, their spatiotemporal resolution. If such a distinction is, at least in principle, traceable in a PEM hierarchy, the important upshot for the rest of this chapter is that it makes sense to ask questions about the cognitive penetrability of perception in this framework.

7.3   Modularity and Cognitive Penetrability in PEM

In this section, I discuss how the ideas and problems that have animated the debate about cognitive penetrability may be discussed within the PEM framework. In order to do so, I start by addressing the issue of whether a modular subsystem can be characterized in a PEM system. If it turns out that there is no room for modularity in PEM, and by extension for impenetrability, then the issue will not be to show that there is in fact top-down penetrability in PEM, since this would be an implication of the framework, but rather to constrain the scope of penetrability to cases in which high-level cognition is actually involved.

It is immediately clear from the fundamental architecture that characterizes the PEM framework that standard notions of modularity and encapsulation are hardly applicable to the processing hierarchy of a PEM system. In previous chapters, I discussed Pylyshyn's early visual module, a specialized functional unit that is supposed to be encapsulated from all other domains of perception and cognition. Following Pylyshyn (1999), early vision functions by taking in inputs, processing them according to its own rules, and providing outputs to further and possibly unencapsulated processing stages. According to Fodor (1983), domain specificity and informational encapsulation are two of the fundamental and necessary features that characterize a "module". Domain specificity concerns the functional specialization of some processes and, for example, it can be conceived as a means by which to distinguish processes in different sensory modalities: visual, auditory, haptic, etc. Encapsulation, on the other hand, refers to the idea that functional units have their proprietary domain of information and do not take information from other parts of the system. For example, an informationally encapsulated visual system would not perform operations on information coming from a domain general memory system.

In a PEM hierarchy, functional specificity may be preserved to a certain degree on the basis of the contents of hypotheses at different levels of the processing hierarchy. For example, one could say that vision and audition involve hypotheses that are supposed to represent different kinds of worldly regularities and that such hypotheses are functionally specific. However, this point is not trivial because it is still a matter of discussion how the contents of hypotheses in a PEM hierarchy should be characterized. I leave it open whether it is possible to distinguish between contents of a PEM hierarchy in such a way that preserves functional specificity.

Providing an answer would require examining the formal detail of different PEM models, which is beyond the scope of the present discussion. I would just like to point out that some regularities of the world, for example the sound waves that can be picked up by the human auditory system, have some statistical or spatiotemporal properties that are quite different from other regularities of the world, for example the light waves that can be picked up by the human visual system. If this is so, the different statistical properties of the two kinds of regularities would be reflected in the mathematical contents of the PEM model by which we describe auditory and visual perceptual inference and, thus, functional specificity may still be preserved in the model.

But what about encapsulation? One fundamental feature of a PEM hierarchy is that prior probabilities of hypotheses at each level of the hierarchy are shaped by prior probabilities at the levels above. In other words, in order for the model to generate a hierarchy of hypotheses that reflects the learned statistical regularities of the world, there can be no individual processing level that is isolated from all other levels of the hierarchy. As we have seen, the posterior probability of a hypothesis at any level is computed on the basis of the prior probability of that hypothesis and the likelihood of the evidence given that hypothesis.

The prior probability of a hypothesis, however, depends on a set of environmental and developmental constraints at different spatiotemporal resolutions that the system has learned and internalized in its generative model over time. Such constraints span the whole hierarchy and, thus, the prior probability of a given hypothesis at a certain level depends on other hypotheses at different levels and relies on information that is computed elsewhere in the system. Therefore, it looks like the idea of informational encapsulation does not fit well in a PEM architecture.

Accordingly, the natural way to go is to think that each level of the hierarchy is sensitive to prior probabilities computed at the levels above and that, in virtue of this feature of the model, some widespread top-down penetrability has to be expected in a PEM system. Hohwy (2013, 2017) is one of the authors who has devoted the most attention to the possible implications of PEM for the debate about CP.[7] In what follows I shall rely mainly on his well-developed discussion of these issues. Hohwy (2013) agrees that the PEM framework is bound to admit some kind of penetrability. He writes:

> The framework says that perceptual experience depends on top-down prediction of sensory input, so it seems to imply that if the predictions change then the perceptual inference will change too, even if the input stays the same. (Hohwy 2013, p. 117)

However, he clarifies that the story cannot be so simple. He specifies that even if perceptual inference is guided by top-down predictions, it is also constrained by the bottom-up error signal. Not all predictions are equally powerful in minimizing prediction error at a given time and, consequently, not all predictions are capable of significantly determining perceptual inference when sensory stimulation occurs. This is because the error signals supervise the inferential process in such a way that only those hypotheses that adequately minimize it could be chosen as the new parameters of the model. It thus seems that, even if the influence of top-down predictions is crucial in the model, the mechanism of perceptual inference does not allow for all top-down predictions to affect perceptual inference to the same degree.

Suppose, as a toy example, that I own a cat and, while at home, I expect to see it sleeping on my living-room couch as it usually does. When I check the couch, I instead find a dog lying on it. Now, this will generate a prediction error that my system has to minimize. Suppose, for simplicity, that no further action is taken except for looking at the animal sleeping on my couch. The system has good reasons

---

[7] But see the Special Issue of *Consciousness and Cognition* (Newen et al. 2017) for a collection of papers on the topic.

to expect said animal to be a cat and, therefore, the hypothesis with the highest prior probability should be the cat hypotheses. If CP in PEM were so radical as one is initially and intuitively led to think from the architecture of the model, the high prior probability of the cat hypothesis would be the determinant factor for the outcome of the ongoing Bayesian inference which would make me see my cat instead of the dog. However, this is not the case. Applying Bayes' rule, when sensory evidence is taken into account, the likelihood of the dog-evidence in the light of the cat hypothesis is so low that the posterior probability of the cat hypothesis ends up being abysmal. The system needs to select a different hypothesis and, in normal circumstances, the dog hypothesis will end up having the highest posterior probability among the available alternatives.

Hence, contrary to the previous intuitive conclusion about penetrability in the framework, it seems that the very nature of the framework's mechanisms, which are supervised by the evidence and the ensuing prediction error, excludes any genuine case of CP.

Hohwy (2013) finds this conclusion to be too restrictive. This view, he says, overly simplifies the mechanism, without considering the role of noise in perceptual inference and uncertainty about the evidences. In poor lighting conditions or in the middle of a fog, the system might expect the evidence to be unreliable, while, on other occasions, the evidence might be so ambiguous as to underdetermine perceptual inference. If the system expects the evidence to be unreliable, it might decide not to minimize the eventual prediction error, which may be considered too noisy, and not to revise its model of the world in light of the evidence. Likewise, if the evidence is ambiguous, two or more different hypotheses may have the same likelihood. In other words, in these two cases, the system would end up selecting the hypothesis that has the highest prior, which, in turn, might be affected by a whole array of cognitive factors.

In a PEM architecture, nothing prevents that, in such cases, priors that are determined very high-up in the hierarchy, namely at the cognitive level corresponding to established beliefs and desires, end up shaping the priors all the way down to the levels corresponding to traditional perceptual contents such as shapes and colors. If this is the case, there is room for interesting CP in PEM under conditions of mounting uncertainty. Hohwy (2013) writes:

> This gives a principled class of cases for which we should expect interesting cases of cognitive penetrability to emerge. When uncertainty is high, we should expect an increase in the ability of ever higher-level prior beliefs to determine conscious experience. (Hohwy 2013, p. 124)

I expand on Hohwy's notion of mounting uncertainty and his analysis of CP in PEM in the next sections. For the moment, let us adopt CP under mounting uncertainty as an interesting and somewhat constrained notion of CP in a framework where top-down processing is a widespread architectural feature.

Even with this notion at hand, however, it remains to be discussed whether perceptual inference under mounting uncertainty, and the ensuing increased relevance assigned by the system to its model's priors, does actually involve processes that can be genuinely characterized as perceptual or cognitive. Without a way of deciding whether the prior that acts as the penetrating state is indeed cognitive and the infer- ence that is drawn on the basis of such prior concerns perceptual hypotheses, one cannot be sure that CP actually occurs in PEM.

This problem has been recently raised by Macpherson (2017) who argues that whether PEM entails the occurrence of CP is no straightforward matter and requires a clear specification of both the version of PEM and the notion of CP that are at stake. She focuses on the question of whether PEM actually involves cognitive states or a distinction between perception and cognition at all. She holds that both these aspects are necessary requirements of CP. Macpherson defines cognitive states as doxastic states. In basic versions of PEM, she argues, there is no clarity as to whether higher levels of the processing hierarchy should be considered as corre- sponding to doxastic states and in some of the available specifications of the model (e.g. Clark 2013), the whole distinction between perception and cognition seems to be rejected. If there is no involvement of cognitive states in PEM's perceptual infer- ence or if there is no distinction at all between perception and cognition in PEM, there is no room for a notion of CP[8] that could be tied to the traditional debate in any interesting sense.

On one possible reading, what PEM theorists mean when they talk about the continuity between perception and cognition, and the ensuing rejection of a distinc- tion between them, is that processes taking place at lower levels in the hierarchy are no different in kind from processes that take place at higher levels in the hierarchy; they are all processes that approximate Bayesian inference. As I have already dis- cussed, this does not entail that we cannot trace a sensible distinction between more general categories, such as perception and cognition, that comprise subsets of these processes. The PEM version of the action-resolution criterion (PEM-ARC) that I discussed in the previous section provides an example of how this issue may be settled. According to the present proposal, the resolution of the processes at differ- ent levels is the key to divide them according to the two categories and the discrimi- nant factor is whether the resolution is adequate for the kind of basic actions that the organism in which the system is embodied can perform.

The idea, as I already presented it, is that only hypotheses at certain spatiotem- poral resolutions can be tested by basic active inference. But even assuming that PEM-ARC helps us to establish a resolution-based distinction in a continuous pro- cessing system, is it really the case that processes that belong to cognition according to PEM-ARC correspond to doxastic states, as required by Macpherson's analysis? This remains a thorny and open question for PEM theorists. As Macpherson points out, it is not clear whether different versions of PEM admit of something like dox- astic states at all. Even if I cannot settle the issue here,[9] I argue that PEM-ARC can still provide us with some guidelines for answering the question positively.

---

[8] Things become even more complicated if one distinguishes between penetrability of early vision and penetrability of experience. For present purposes, this can be considered as a parallel issue and I shall leave it aside. I refer the reader to Macpherson (2017) for further details.

[9] But see Hohwy (2017) for a helpful distinction between the notion of "folk psychological" belief and Bayesian "belief".

Therefore, it seems that it is possible to devise a non-trivial notion of CP that is consistent with and maybe even entailed by some versions of PEM, provided that its scope is constrained to cases of mounting uncertainty and that it meets two requirements: 1. a distinction between perception and cognition is kept, and 2. something corresponding to a doxastic state is involved. We may call this *PEM* CP and define it as follows:

> **PEM CP:** In a predictive hierarchy, CP occurs when high uncertainty allows for a low-resolution high-level cognitive prior to fully determine the selection of a high-resolution perceptual hypothesis as the one that best minimizes prediction error in the present context, even in the light of contrasting evidence.

This definition captures the idea that, even if there is always a degree of top-down modulation in perceptual inference, if the evidence is weighted in the same way as the prior, the outcome of the inference is determined by the world and the internal model to a similar extent. When there is high uncertainty about the evidence, however, the system may assign a higher weight to the prior and refrain from revising the model, even in the light of some significant prediction error. The outcome of perceptual inference in such a case would be fully determined by the prior and, provided that the prior is high-level enough to be cognitive, this would be a case of CP in PEM.[10]

For example, the prior probability of the hypothesis that there is a tree in front of my house is at a lower resolution than basic active inference, because for any basic action I can immediately perform, the prior would typically not be affected. Hence, such a hypothesis could be considered cognitive according to PEM-ARC and it would correspond to a belief about a tree being in front of my house. If there is in fact a tree in front of my house, we might assume the prior probability of the hypothesis to be pretty high. Suppose that, when looking out of the window during a foggy dusk, I visually experience the tree outline in the fog. However, unbeknownst to me, the tree had been cut down the previous day. This case would qualify as an instance of PEM-CP, if the experience corresponds to the selection of a lower-level hypothesis about the tree's outline, which is fully determined by the prior of the cognitive belief-like hypothesis. The evidence, which could be consistent with low-level hypotheses about both the tree outline and, for example, about some pattern of refraction of light in the fog, is weighted less in inference due to the high uncertainty in the perceiving conditions.

---

[10] See Clark (2016, pp. 50–51) for the pervasiveness of top-down trumping of sensory signals under high expectations. Hohwy (2013) adds conditions of uncertainty. Hence, there may actually be two cases of *PEM* CP (if CP is considered as equal to top-down trumping): 1. high uncertainty, and 2. strongly established prior. However, I consider 2 to be less interesting for my purposes in this book. The reason is that it requires learning over time, while the threatening cases of CP are more online cases which are reflected by the conditions in 1.

7.4   Summary and Conclusion

In this chapter, I have introduced the PEM framework as one of the more widely endorsed and promising frameworks in cognitive science. I have discussed the general framework, without delving into specific applications and I have used it to recast the discussion in the previous chapters in a new form, thereby arriving at a sensible and interesting definition of CP within the framework. Now that we have a definition of CP in PEM, it remains to be seen how such a phenomenon may arise in the PEM processing hierarchy, i.e. by which mechanism can a low-resolution prior affect a higher resolution hypothesis under mounting uncertainty. I argue that attentional processes can actually engender PEM-CP and, if they can, it will be interesting to explore what sort of cases of perception we might expect to be penetrated in this way. But before discussing this point, I need to introduce in greater detail how attentional processes are modeled in PEM and how this relates to biased competition and to the metacognitive view of attention introduced in previous chapters.

References

Clark, A. (2013). Whatever next? Predictive brains, situated agents, and the future of cognitive science. *Brain and Behavioral Sciences, 36*(3), 181–204.
Clark, A. (2016). *Surfing uncertainty*. Oxford: Oxford University Press.
Fodor, J. A. (1983). *The modularity of mind*. Cambridge, MA: MIT Press.
Friston, K. (2005). A theory of cortical responses. *Philosophical Transactions of the Royal Society of London. Series B: Biological Sciences, 360*(1456), 815–836.
Friston, K. (2010). The free-energy principle: A unified brain theory? *Nature Reviews Neuroscience, 11*(2), 127–138.
Gładziejewski, P. (2016). Predictive coding and representationalism. *Synthese, 193*(2), 559–582.
Hohwy, J. (2012). Attention and conscious perception in the hypothesis testing brain. *Frontiers in Psychology, 3*, 96.
Hohwy, J. (2013). *The predictive mind*. Oxford: Oxford University Press.
Hohwy, J. (2014). The self-evidencing brain. *Nous, 50*(2), 259–285.
Hohwy, J. (2017). Priors in perception: Top-down modulation, Bayesian perceptual learning rate, and prediction error minimization. *Consciousness and Cognition, 47*, 75–85.
Kiebel, S. J., Daunizeau, J., & Friston, K. J. (2008). A hierarchy of time-scales and the brain. *PLoS Computational Biology, 4*(11), e1000209–e1000212.
Macpherson, F. (2017). The relationship between cognitive penetration and predictive coding. *Consciousness and Cognition, 47*, 6–16.
Newen, A., Marchi, F., & Brössel, P. (Eds.). (2017). Cognitive penetration and predictive coding. *Consciousness and Cognition, 47*, 1–112.
Pylyshyn, Z. W. (1999). Is vision continuous with cognition? The case for cognitive impenetrability of visual perception. *Behavioral and Brain Sciences, 22*(3), 341–365.
Spratling, M. W. (2016). A review of predictive coding algorithms. *Brain and Cognition, 112*, 92–97.

Chapter 8
A Predictive-Processing Model of Attentional Cognitive Penetration

Abstract This chapter examines how the PEM framework introduced in the previous chapter may be applied, even in its more general form, to model attentional cognitive penetration. Section 8.1 argues that the biased competition theory of attention and the metacognitive view presented in Chaps. 3 and 4 are compatible with PEM. In Sect. 8.2, I discuss how attentional cognitive penetrability can be modeled in PEM. Finally, in Sect. 8.3, I examine two studies that, when provided with a PEM interpretation, qualify as cases of attentional cognitive penetration.

8.1 Attention in PEM: Precision, Competition, and Metacognitive Regulation

In this section, I argue that the PEM model of attentional processes supports the metacognitive view and the biased competition theory on which the metacognitive view relies. The present discussion allows me to highlight a more specific sense in which attentional processes are metacognitive.

One of the interesting attempts at modeling attentional processes in a predictive framework has been proposed by Rao and Ballard (2005). According to them, and in line with the basic tenets of PEM, a system can learn the statistical properties of objects[1] it encounters and form a generative model for those properties. With the generative model at hand, the system can form predictions about the expected properties of an object. If the predictions are not completely fulfilled, for example if the target object is partially occluded, prediction error will ensue. Attentional processes constitute a means for tuning such prediction error in order to retain a coherent interpretation of the stimulus based on the model. Rao and Ballard write:

> We discussed how attention emerges in such networks as a consequence of selective filtering of predictive error signals. This allows the network to "focus attention" on a single object or "switch attention" to another object without using an explicit "spotlight of attention". (Rao and Ballard 2005, p. 566)

Such filtering of error signals can parse visual objects into foreground and background or highlight different objects on the basis of the consistency of their expected

---

[1] Their treatment focuses on visual objects and specifically images.

F. Marchi, *The Attentional Shaping of Perceptual Experience*, Studies in Brain and Mind 16, https://doi.org/10.1007/978-3-030-33558-8_8

properties and the model. This filtering process works on both the available and expected properties of stimuli and, as such, it achieves the fundamental selective and modulatory functions that are typically associated with attentional processes (see Chap. 3). Rao and Ballard offer a specific computational model for this kind of attentional processes. They discuss how their model can be related to the "where" and "what" cortical visual pathways (Goodale and Milner 1992) and adequately account for object-based and spatial-based attention without involving any specific attentional spotlight.

The idea of "selective filtering of predictive error signals" has been developed by other proponents of predictive coding and it has received a more general formulation in PEM through the works of Feldman and Friston (2010) and Hohwy (2012, 2013). According to these authors, attention emerges from the need of the system to optimize expected precisions for sensory signals and error signals: "The basic idea we pursue is that attention entails estimating uncertainty during hierarchical inference about the causes of sensory input" (Feldman and Friston 2010, p. 1).

As I mentioned, uncertainty can be formalized as the width or *variance* of a probability distribution and its inverse is *precision*. Therefore, optimizing expected precision gives the system an estimation of uncertainty in its current inferences. It is crucial to understand that the need for optimization of expected precision in PEM's Bayesian inference rests on the assumption that the level of noise in the world is not constant. If the system could simply assume a constant level of noise for a given sensory channel, it would not need to assess the reliability of sensory and error signals coming through that channel. But in a world such as ours, the level of noise tends to change and the system needs to reliably estimate noise magnitude in its inferences at any time.

In order to estimate the level of noise, the system may rely on several factors. One of the most important of these factors is the acquired knowledge about noise patterns in a given environment at a given time. For example, an open space in broad daylight would normally generate less noisy signals than a forest in a foggy night. The learned statistical regularities of noise patterns can be decomposed into other internal and external factors that are driven by assumptions deriving from learning. For example, these factors may include: perceptual cues, under the assumption that cued locations yield more precise signals; stimulus intensity, under the assumption that stronger signals have a higher signal-to-noise ratio; and internal motivations, under the assumption that, for example, prediction errors ensuing from hypotheses about desired objects are more precise. In general, there are many top-down and bottom-up elements that may drive how precise a given sensory signal or error signal are expected to be.

On this point, Hohwy (2012) remarks that the system cannot pre-assess the absolute precision of incoming signals, because such a value is state-dependent and the states of the world on which it depends may vary from time to time. The system can solve this problem by estimating noise with a further second-order Bayesian inference. Much like first-order perceptual inference, second-order inference is guided by knowledge about learned statistical regularities. The difference is that in first-order inference such regularities concern the cause of sensory input and in second-order inference these regularities concern patterns of noise in different contexts. Hohwy writes:

> In general, the precision weighting should depend on prior learning of regularities in the actual levels of noise in the states of the world and the system itself (e.g., learning leading to internal representations of the regularity that sensory precision tends to decline at dusk). There is then a (second order) perceptual inference problem because the magnitude of precision cannot be measured absolutely. It must be assessed in the light of precision expectations. The consequence is that generative models must somehow embody expectations for the precision of prediction error, in a context dependent fashion. (Hohwy 2012, p. 4)

Perceptual and active inference would lead to poor behavioral results in a world where levels of noise can vary from context to context and is not reliably estimated for incoming signals. In order to evaluate the variables (distributions) that are compared in perceptual inference, a PEM system needs to develop expectations about the levels of noise in the context in which the inference is being performed. In other words, the system needs to estimate the precision of the values of interest, namely predictions (expected distributions) or evidence (actual distributions and consequent error signals). To achieve this task, the system performs the second-order statistical inference that shapes its expectations of precision. One aim of the system is to optimize such second-order inference and, thereby, its precision expectations, by learning about patterns of noise in different contexts. Optimization of precision expectations is PEM's version of attentional processes. Hohwy summarizes these points nicely in the following way:

> Putting all this together under the prediction error minimization approach we get the following picture. (i) To achieve confident and efficient perceptual inference, prediction error minimization should aim for precision. (ii) Precision is achievable only if we generate expectations for the precisions of prediction errors. (iii) Precision expectations must be based in an internal model of precisions in the world. (Hohwy 2013, p. 65)

As I described it in Chap. 3, the primary function of attentional processes is to optimize processing resource allocation in a limited capacity system. It seems that optimization of precision expectations is a reliable way of performing this function. Hence, there is good reason to think that optimization of precision expectations in PEM and the underlying second-order Bayesian inference map onto what are typically considered to be attentional processes. One important clarification is that, in principle, the need to optimize precision expectations in PEM does not arise from the limited capacities of a processing system but from the system taking into account the variable level of noise in the environment. As such, the PEM notion of attentional processes seems more inclusive than the notion I outlined before, for such processes may be needed in predictive systems with, possibly, unlimited processing resources.

However, if devoting too much processing resources to noisy signals would be inefficient in a system with unlimited resources, it would be even more pressing to avoid such a situation in a system with limited resources. In this respect, if PEM is a good model for biological systems, optimization of precision expectations is the way in which such systems ensure that their limited resources are devoted to what they expect to be the most relevant tasks, i.e. the signals that are expected to be less noisy. Hence, optimization of precision expectations can be considered as an efficient way in which a system can optimize allocation of its processing resources and, therefore, it is directly linked to the primary function of attentional processes.

Furthermore, Clark (2016, pp. 74–76) suggests that the differences between different kinds of attention, e.g. feature-based vs. spatial, can be explained by optimization of precisions at different levels of the predictive hierarchy which concerns different hypotheses, e.g. object identity vs. object location. This consideration allows the PEM framework to account for the varieties of attentional phenomena discussed in Chap. 4.

In the previous chapters, I argued that optimization of processing resources allocation is achieved through biased competitive selection. And that attention is the property of a representation of *"being the current winner of the competition"*. One can now ask whether optimization of precision expectations is a good model for biased competition. This topic has already been addressed in the literature and has received a positive answer in PEM (Feldman and Friston 2010) and in other versions of predictive coding alike (Spratling 2008). Furthermore, Feldman and Friston claim that it emerges naturally from their model:

> *[...] there is no tension between biased competition and predictive coding [...] the characteristic behaviors of biased competition emerge naturally under predictive coding. The key thing that reconciles these two theories is to realize that predictive coding can be generalized to cover both states and precisions and that (state-dependent) precision is itself optimized.* (Feldman and Friston 2010, p. 17)

Thus, the competition view seems to fall naturally in line with PEM,[2] where the task of the system is always taken to be that of settling on the hypothesis with the highest posterior probability among the alternatives. Furthermore, since optimization of precision expectations is dependent on both contextual cues and knowledge about the expected level of noise, it shows the adequate sensitivity to both bottom-up and top-down biases as required by the biased competition theory. Optimization of expected precision can thus be considered as a computational model of biased competition. If competition is modeled as optimization of precision expectation, attention would be the property of a signal or hypothesis of *"being expected to have higher precision than the competing signals or hypotheses"*.

In the view I presented in Chap. 3, attention was conceived as a property of representations. One question that arises here is whether this claim can be preserved in PEM. There is an ongoing discussion on the problem of whether PEM admits of representations and what sorts of representations there might be (see, for example, Wiese 2017). I cannot settle this issue here, but since the answer to the question about attention being a property of representations in PEM hangs on the kind of representations that one is prepared to admit, as an example, I shall mention a view on representations that is, at least, consistent with this claim. The view in question has been proposed by Egan (2014). She argues that mental representations are characterized by their mathematical content. Mathematical content depends on a specific function-theoretic description of a cognitive mechanism. Once one has specified the

---

[2] On this point, see also Clark (2016, p. 38 and pp. 60–61).

mathematical function that the system computes in order to carry out a certain cognitive task in a given context, the kind of representational contents that one can ascribe to the system are the mathematical contents allowed by that function, its arguments and values. In PEM, the function-theoretic characterization revolves around Bayesian inference and the arguments and values are probability distributions.

Under Egan's account of representational contents, it makes perfect sense to say that attention is a property of representations in PEM. According to Egan (2014), the representational contents that are part of the theory are the mathematical values of the function by which a cognitive mechanism is described. Attention can be described as a property of the mathematical values involved in Bayesian inference. In PEM, such values are probability distributions and attention is the property of the value that is expected to be more precise in the current environment. As such, attention is a property of the representational contents that are admissible in PEM. I do not claim that PEM theorists are committed to accept Egan's view. However, her account shows that PEM can admit of genuine representations and that attention can be a property of those representations. The upshot is that PEM's account of attention is consistent with the idea that attention is a property of representations that emerges from biased competition among them.

As I mentioned above, the need for optimization of expected precision does not arise in PEM from the strict resource limitations of a system. In principle, a system with unlimited resources would still need to optimize precision expectations, if it operates in a world with variable levels of noise:

> Attentional competition is then not a matter somehow of intrinsically limited processing resources [...]. It is a matter of optimal Bayesian inference where only one model of the causal regularities in the world can best explain away the incoming signal, given prior learning, and expectations of state-dependent levels of noise. (Hohwy 2012, p. 7)

Here one might worry that a good model for a system with unlimited resources cannot be, at the same time, a good model for a system with limited resources. However, if one addresses this point from the opposite perspective, the worry disappears. PEM is a theory inspired by the brain. As such, the model aims at describing systems with limited resources. Even if optimization of expected precisions is not specifically tied to resource limitations, it still provides a mechanism for efficient resource management. For example, precision expectations can determine which among many available error signals need to be prioritized for further processing (minimization). Now, a model with an efficient built-in mechanism for resource management can be applied to a system with unlimited resources with good results, albeit not the other way around. Thus, nothing prevents optimization of expected precision from being a plausible model for biased competition in systems with limited resources.

Let us now turn to the instantiation of attention. Attention is considered to be an emergent property in both biased competition (Desimone and Duncan 1995) and PEM (Feldman and Friston 2010). Attention would emerge from the process of competition in all systems that survive by minimizing prediction error in a world with varying levels of noise, although such systems may minimize prediction error by different means and in different ways, depending on their specific evolutionary history and contingencies. An interesting upshot of this claim is that if attention were modeled as a consequence of optimization of precision expectations, there would not be any need for the instantiation of attention in a world with constant levels of noise. In such a world, the system may take priors, likelihoods, and evidence, the basic elements of perceptual inference, at face value and perform its computations without weighting them for precision.

However, rather than saying that such a world would be devoid of attention, it is perhaps more correct to say that such a world would have a form of attention that is as constant as its level of noise, or, in other words, the instantiation of attention would depend on other properties of signals and hypotheses and not on the expected levels of noise in a given context. One could speculate that the behavior of a system living in such a noise-constant world would display a much lower degree of flexibility. In fact, the possibility of optimizing expected precisions and, thus, prioritizing certain signals does not just allow the system to behave efficiently, but allows it to behave efficiently to different degrees. In other words, a competition process in which the winners are not predetermined allows for individual variability in behavior and for the fact that different systems may minimize prediction error by different means, driven by different sources of bias and to different degrees of success.

So far, I have argued that optimization of precision expectations is a good model for the primary function of the fundamental attentional process of biased competition. It remains to be seen whether it is also a good model for the metacognitive view. The question here is whether optimization of precision expectations is a meta-process in PEM. The first thing to note is that if attention is modeled as a property emerging from optimization of expected precision, there is a deeper sense in which the processes that cause its instantiation may be considered to be metacognitive. First of all, expected precision is a second-order statistical value that is associated with first-order values such as priors, likelihoods, and evidence. As such, expected precision does not specifically concern the regularities that those first-order values stand for. On this topic, Feldman and Friston write: "attention is more concerned with optimizing the uncertainty or precision of probabilistic representations, rather than what is being represented" (2010, p. 1). Thus, the process of optimization of precision expectations seems to be a meta-process in much the same way as I have argued that biased competition is.

Furthermore, optimization of precision expectations specifically relies on the knowledge that the system has acquired in development about how much noise is to be expected in a certain context and for what signals. If the system moves to a new context, it needs to learn the new patterns of noise and, therefore, we might expect optimization of precision expectation in the new context to improve over time. If applied to a process that regulates other processes within the system, these two features, namely relying on acquired knowledge and improvement over time that is parallel to knowledge acquisition, are among the typical traits of a genuine metacognitive process (Fernandez-Duque et al. 2000). Hence, optimization of precision expectations is a regulative process that shows some hallmarks of metacognition. For this reason, PEM's account of attentional processes is a good model for the metacognitive view proposed in the previous chapter.

8.2   Attentional Cognitive Penetration in PEM

To conclude my discussion of how the problems that I have previously addressed in this book may be cast in the PEM framework, it remains to be discussed whether attention can engender cognitive penetration in PEM. I have clarified how cognitive penetration and attention are to be understood in PEM. Cognitive penetration is perceptual inference under mounting uncertainty, when the system weights the cognitive prior more than perceptual evidence, and attention is a property of signals and hypotheses that emerges from the process of optimization of precision expectations. The question about the relation between attentional processes and cognitive penetration can thus be rephrased as whether optimization of precision expectation can cause perceptual inference under mounting uncertainty. Phrased in this way, however, the question is borderline trivial, because optimization of precision expectations serves the specific function of assessing how much uncertainty should be expected in the current context. It follows that if some internal or external factors cause the system to expect less precise signals, the inferences that the system will draw in that context will have higher uncertainty and cognitive penetration will likely occur.

Perhaps there is a way to make this claim less trivial. In a recent paper, Hohwy (2017) refines his analysis and argues that the extent of CP that we should expect in perceptual inference is tied to the learning rate of the system on that particular occasion. The learning rate refers to the weighting assigned to prediction error in inference and it represents how much the system is ready to learn from the evidence, by updating its priors.

Some of Hohwy's considerations are similar to those introduced in the previous sections. In order to perform perceptual inference in a noisy world, the system needs to know when to trust the evidence and when instead to rely on its prior knowledge. If the system relies on the evidence to update the model it has a high learning rate; if, instead, it keeps its prior knowledge, ignoring the evidence, it has a low learning rate. Now, it is obvious that one should expect higher top-down modulation in the case of low learning rate, i.e. when the system does not trust the evidence too much. In normal conditions, many of the cases in which the system distrusts the evidence, and thus has a low learning rate, would be cases in which uncertainty is high and incoming sensory and error signals are expected to be imprecise. This ties the notion of learning rate to precision expectations and to the previously introduced idea of CP under mounting uncertainty. However, Hohwy claims that a low learning rate means greater top-down modulation in inference, but top-down modulation should not be directly equated with CP. He writes:

> It is initially tempting to equate top-down modulation with CP, and bottom-up modulation with cognitive impenetrability. This would deliver a clear definition and quantification: the degree of penetrability and impenetrability would simply be determined by the learning rate. [...] However, there are at least two objections to this initial attempt at a Bayesian conception of cognitive penetrability. The first objection is that the account does not have the resources to address the substance of the cognitive penetrability debate, which concerns top-down penetration by fairly high-level cognitive beliefs. [...] The second objection is that the account is both too liberal and too demanding. (Hohwy 2017, p. 77)

The way to provide a more interesting account of CP is to look at deviations from the optimal Bayesian learning rate, which could be high or low. On each instance of perceptual inference, there is an optimal Bayesian learning rate that a perfect Bayesian computer would adopt. However, a system that approximates Bayesian inference, such as the human brain, allows for a great deal of individual variability, meaning that, even if it can perform inferences and minimize prediction error in the long run, it does not do so by implementing perfect Bayes. This makes the whole account more plausible since biological systems are not required to perform perfect probabilistic inference. On the other hand, this means that, at any given time, there could be deviations from the optimal learning rate.

In a constant world, such deviations would tend to zero in the long run. But in a changeable world it may be the case that the system never manages to adopt the perfect learning rate, even if it would tend to move closer to it over time, if the environment remains relatively stable. Hohwy suggests that cognitive penetrability happens when the learning rate is lower than the optimal Bayesian learning rate and the decrease is driven by a prior that is high-level enough to be considered cognitive. Now, he mentions that there are computational methods that could, in principle, be used to assess, in each case of perceptual inference, how high-level are the priors driving such inference.[3] However, here I rely on the action-resolution criterion (PEM-ARC) to achieve the same result.

The initial question of this section, namely whether attentional processes can engender cognitive penetration in PEM, can now be rephrased in a more interesting way as the questions of whether optimization of precision expectation can affect the learning rate of the system and eventually engender deviations from the optimal learning rate, and how this may happen. Providing an answer to these two questions sheds light on what relations can hold between a cognitive state and a perceptual process in PEM.

The answer to the first question is positive: the learning rate of the system depends on the precision that the system assigns to its hypotheses and error signals. Now, to answer the second question, CP would happen if expectations of precision are driven by a high-enough prior and if they lower the learning rate below the optimal one. Since nothing prevents this from being the case, optimization of precision expectations can in principle be a way in which CP is brought about in PEM. However, it is important to note that not all instances of top-down modulation of precision expectations would be instances of CP. There could be cases in which the learning rate is not altered or in which it is raised by the process that causes the instantiation of attention. This means that attentional processes can work to counteract CP.

To provide an example, suppose that the system finds itself in a new environment. Such an environment may share some similarities with previous environments that the system has interacted with. Now the system might choose to adopt previously learned regularities about noise in similar environments to optimize its expectations of precision for signals in the new environment, or it may choose to

---

[3] For example, by employing a hierarchical Gaussian filter (Hohwy 2017).

start anew and learn the current patterns of noise from scratch, under the assumption that new contexts require new learning. The strategy that the system adopts in the new context will radically affect its precision expectations and therefore the system's learning rate, possibly lowering it and allowing for a large amount of CP.

However, the choice between the two strategies is not obvious and there is no strategy that is better in general. The assumptions that support each strategy are both valid and both strategies may lead to better long-term prediction error minimization. For example, it may be that the system is inexperienced and has too small a sample of previously encountered similar environments to reliably infer the patterns of noise in the new context. In this case, it should adhere to the second strategy and acquire the patterns of noise from scratch. But a system that has yet to optimize its precision expectations for the new context may be led to expect imprecise signals even if the signals are in fact precise. This would be a deviation from the optimal learning rate in which the system is driven to expect higher uncertainty than necessary and, therefore, to lower the learning rate too much, thus opening the door to CP.

If what I have been saying so far is correct, cognitive penetration occurs when the system deviates from the optimal learning rate and this can be caused by transient suboptimal attempts at optimizing precision expectations. Here, one could argue that if this is the case, CP is the hallmark of a failure of perception or, in other words, it occurs when the system cannot perform its task (inferences) efficiently and accurately. However, such a conclusion is too simplistic. Both strategies in the above example could lead to success in the long run. In other words, large amounts of CP do not entail that the system is behaving maladaptively. Suppose, for example, that the environment is very dynamic; in this case, to keep precision expectation fixed for too long could be dangerous. Therefore, the best strategy would be to update precision expectations often and this allows for the possibility of more deviations from the optimal learning rate and thus more CP.

This section was specifically meant to address the relationship between attentional processes and CP in PEM. I have established that optimization of precision expectations, when leading to deviations from the optimal Bayesian learning rate, can be one of the ways in which CP happens in PEM. I can now discuss how this relates to my argument for the possibility of attentional penetration concerning the various notions of CP addressed in Chaps. 2 and 4.[4] This point becomes more relevant if we consider how attentional processes in PEM map perfectly onto biased competition and the metacognitive view.

Let me start by clarifying that I do not discuss *indirect non-conceptual* CP because it is beyond the scope of this work to specify how the conceptual vs. non-conceptual distinction may be drawn in PEM. But what about the other three forms of CP addressed in previous chapters? Concerning *consequentialist* CP, it seems that deviations from the optimal learning rate, especially on the lower end of the spectrum, would make a subject more resilient to the acquisition of novel knowledge from experience. In fact, the system could disregard evidence expected to be

---

[4] Please refer to those chapters for the full formulation of each definition.

very imprecise. If such evidence could be part of the usually reliable process that leads to the formation of new perceptual beliefs, in the form of updated high-level priors, such a process could be undermined or be considered less reliable on some occasions as a result of how precision expectations are optimized. In this sense, CP in PEM, when implemented through attentional processes, could be epistemically pernicious and, therefore, it satisfies the definition of *consequentialist* CP.

Concerning *causal* CP, when a suboptimal learning rate is a consequence of optimization of expected precision, the internal and mental relation between the high-level prior and the low-level values whose expected precision is determined by the prior is causal because, if the prior were not recruited, the learning rate would not have decreased. Now, whether such top-down relation is a relation among contents remains an open question that I cannot settle here, because, as I said, it is not clear how the contents of hypotheses and priors in perceptual inference should be construed. However, if Egan (2014) is right and the only proper representational contents of a computational model of cognitive functions are mathematical contents, then the relation at stake seems indeed to be a relation among contents. Therefore, attentional CP in PEM meets the requirements of *causal* CP.

Concerning *semantic* CP, it seems that in PEM nothing prevents that there be a rule for what priors should be recruited for a given inference. For example, priors concerning the learned regularity that evidence gathered in the condition of poor illumination must be expected to be less precise should be allowed to be recruited only for optimizing precision expectations in visual perceptual inference, because the same may not be true for other sensory modalities. Thus, there could be a normative relation between the high-level prior and the low-level values that figure in the inference and the requirements of *semantic* CP would be met. To see whether such rules are, in fact, required or ever actually in place would require a further specification of the formal details of PEM that is beyond the scope of this work. Here I limit the claim to PEM being, at least, compatible with *semantic* CP.

In conclusion, a deviation from the optimal learning rate that is brought about by attentional processes in PEM is an instance of CP that meets the requirements of *causal* CP and is consistent with *consequentialist* CP and *semantic* CP. The upshot is that further work on the topic of the interactions between perception and cognition in PEM will be directly relevant for most of the issues discussed in the traditional debate about CP in general.

8.3   Precision and Uncertainty: The Case of Bi-Stable Images

To conclude this chapter, I would like to rethink in the PEM framework some of the examples of perceptual phenomena that have been ruled out as possible instances of CP in the traditional debate, and that can now be recruited as evidence for attentional CP. As we have seen, these examples concern cases in which the stimulation conditions are optimal, but the stimulus is inherently ambiguous and which meet the adequate causal schema[5] for genuine CP (Stokes 2014). Under such conditions, it is possible that the predictive system ends up with two competing hypotheses that generate the same amount of prediction error. In other words, the same stimulus provides strong evidence for two competing models of the world that may significantly differ with respect to one or more of their constituent hypotheses. In such a case, if we assume that the prior probability of the competing hypotheses is the same, the system would end up in a condition similar to that of mounting uncertainty, but not depending on a high absolute level of noise, since we can assume the two signals to be equally precise. I call this condition "perfect ambiguity". This is precisely what would happen in the case of a bi-stable image, where the gaze direction of the viewer is held fixed. If the evidence allows for two stable interpretations, then there are two hypotheses in the model that explain away and generate the same amount of prediction error.

Even in such a condition, however, the system may still have different expectations of precision for one of the two possible error signals that are generated by testing each of the two competing hypotheses. The idea is that by assigning different precision expectations (weights) for each of the signals in a case of perfect ambiguity, the system would settle for one hypothesis at a time and, thus, avoid a dangerous stall. This may correspond to a deviation from the optimal learning rate for that particular perceptual encounter, but this is further proof that such deviations are not always the worse option, because the stall generated by an unresolved ambiguity can be potentially more dangerous for the system.

Concerning the relevance of such cases for cognitive penetrability, it is crucial to assess whether the factors that bias precision expectations in this condition are in fact cognitive and whether the level at which the relevant precision expectations play their role is perceptual, which could be achieved with the help of PEM-ARC. If this were the case, we would have a cognitive bias determining the processing of one or more perceptual levels by altering precision expectations for that level. In other words, we would have a clear case of attentional cognitive penetration in PEM.

As I mentioned, in order for perfect ambiguity to occur, one needs two error signals that are generated from two competing hypotheses in the light of the same evidence, as in bi-stable images. In usual conditions, one is free to look at different parts of a bi-stable image and this means that the stimulus can be sampled differently through basic active inference. As we have seen, active inference consists in an exploration and sampling of the perceptual environment in order to get new evidence to better minimize prediction error. Supposing that the image in question admits of two interpretations, the samples that the system obtains by looking and focusing on different parts of the bi-stable image would provide better evidence for one of two competing hypotheses corresponding to each interpretation respectively. In other words, one of the two error signals generated by one of the hypotheses becomes lower than the other with each sampling. Even if we do not know the exact level or levels of the hierarchy that are involved in the processing of a bi-stable

---

[5] Cognitive process → Covert attentional shift → Perceptual experience.

image, since basic active inference is capable of determining the relevant hypothesis on which the system eventually settles, we can already establish that such hypothesis is in fact at a perceptual level according to PEM-ARC.

However, suppose that basic active inference is constrained, for example by keeping gaze fixation at the center of the image.[6] This means that the sample evidence available to the system is the same and this would then be a case of perfect ambiguity. In this case, a subject presented with a bi-stable image may still have two competing hypotheses and two different error signals coming from each of these hypotheses. Given the discussion in the previous sections, the alternation between the two possible percepts in these cases can be explained by the system's higher precision expectations for one of the two error signals at a time. The system settles for the hypothesis that better minimizes the error signal that is currently deemed more precise. In other words, since optimizing precision expectations is PEM's attentional process, the currently dominant hypothesis, which minimizes the prioritized error signal, would be the one instantiating attention. Nevertheless, since the evidence still supports the competing hypothesis as well, it cannot be easily disregarded, and after a certain amount of time, if no further bias is provided, the expectation of precision may switch and the concurrent hypothesis may become dominant. Now, if a cognitive bias can affect the alternation rate between the two hypotheses, we would have a very good example of how PEM's explanation of what happens in these cases involves attentional cognitive penetration.

One can show that the alternation between the two visual interpretations of an ambiguous display is sensitive to subjective volition (Leopold and Logothetis 1999). In other words, a subject is capable of voluntarily altering the rate of the switching between the two interpretations of a bi-stable display, if so instructed. In PEM terms, a volitional state tracks some spatiotemporal regularities that are not directly affected by basic active inference. In fact, a subject may perform a series of basic actions in order to fulfill a desire, which is a paradigmatic volitional state, and this would be impossible if the wished-for state of the world that is tracked by the desire were to change by each basic action performed. Hence, since volitional states seem to be at a different and lower spatiotemporal resolution than basic action, we can consider them to be cognitive states according to PEM-ARC.[7] Thus, a case in which volition affects the alternation between the interpretations of a bi-stable image under conditions of perfect ambiguity would meet all the requirements for a clear instance of attentional cognitive penetration of perceptual experience in PEM.

Liu et al. (2012) investigated the role of voluntary control in a bi-stable display. The experimenters had subjects look at the "spinning silhouette" animation, which is composed of the silhouette of a dancer rotating on a central axis. Importantly, the silhouette may be perceived as rotating either clockwise or counter-clockwise, which corresponds to a major phenomenological change in one's perceptual experience of the image.

---

[6] In a concrete example, this may be achieved by requiring subjects to look at a fixation cross.

[7] Furthermore, Hohwy et al. (2008) discuss how other high-level factors, such as our knowledge that there can only be one object at one place at a time, may bias the competition between hypotheses during bi-stable perception.

In this experiment, subjects were required to fixate on specific points of the image. Experimenters were interested in the rate at which subjects' experience of the dancer's direction of movement switched. In one condition, they informed subjects about the display's inherent bi-stability and asked them to voluntarily switch the perceived direction of movement as much as possible. The experimenters found that a voluntary effort of the subjects to switch the image as much as possible almost doubled the rate of the switching itself. Does this case qualify as attentional cognitive penetration? It seems so, insofar as it meets all the requirements that I have been narrowing down in the previous sections, namely sameness of stimulus and gaze fixation,[8] different perceptual experience, and voluntary and cognitively driven control over the instantiation of attention. The explanation would be that the cognitive bias provided by the instruction would be to always favor the non-dominant percept, which would generate a faster than normal alternation of the competing hypotheses. However, an objector might argue that the stimulus in question was a rather complex one, since the movement in the display might affect bottom-up how attention is instantiated.

Meng and Tong (2004) show similar results with an immobile and simpler stimulus, namely a Necker cube. In this experiment, again, subjects were required to look at a fixation cross and instructed to try to: "1) 'just look at the cube passively'; (2) 'attempt to perceive the cube from the top view for as long as possible' (i.e., as if seen from above); and (3) 'attempt to perceive the cube from the bottom view for as long as possible'" (Meng and Tong 2004, p. 541). Moreover, in each of these cases, there were three possible fixation locations in the image, for a total of nine conditions. As in the experiment above, subjects were able to significantly affect the dominance duration of each of the two possible visual interpretations of the Necker cube. Critically, experimenters also investigated whether the same voluntary control over the alternations of the two percepts could be exerted by subjects in conditions of binocular rivalry. What they found is that, in binocular rivalry, subjects were capable of voluntarily affecting the alternation rate to a much lower degree.

These results are important for two reasons. First, they show that covert attentional modulation of bi-stable images happened independently of fixation changes. Second, the comparison with binocular rivalry shows that when the available evidence is different, i.e. consisting of two different stimuli, the instantiation of attention is much more driven by the properties of those stimuli and no significant volitional modulation is found. The reason for this difference is that in bi-stable perception the evidence available for both visual interpretations of the stimulus is the same, whereas in binocular rivalry there are two stimuli and two corresponding sources of evidence that are incompatible with one another. The two sources of evidence available in rivalry act as bottom-up biases in favor of each of the stimuli in turn. Hence, it is plausible to assume that, when volitional control occurs, what allows for it to occur is the availability of the same evidence for both interpretations and that the switching rate in such cases is itself largely independent from the properties of the stimulus and only sensitive to top-down factors.

---

[8] Eye movements were monitored.

The bi-stable perception cases illustrated here tick all the boxes for attentional cognitive penetration. Furthermore, in the Meng and Tong case, the learning rate is plausibly lowered below the optimal. Voluntarily holding on to a percept means that the subject is refusing to take into account evidence accumulating in favor of the alternative percept. The optimal learning rate in cases of perfect ambiguity may be represented by a roughly equal switch rate. Altering the switching rate means altering the learning rate. Thus, higher-level cognitive states can change perceptual experience by means of influencing expectations of precision and learning rate at perceptual levels of the PEM processing hierarchy. This means that attentional CP occurs in the examples discussed, given that PEM's explanation of these cases is right.

8.4   Summary and Conclusion

I argued that all the arguments provided in the book in favor of the possibility of cognitively penetrated experiences engendered by attentional processes can be consistently reconceived in the prediction error minimization framework. I have examined how a distinction between perception and cognition can be drawn in PEM and how cognitive penetrability has to be understood in the framework. Furthermore, I addressed PEM's model of attentional processes and its compatibility with the biased competition theory and the metacognitive view. Finally, I discussed how a clear case of attentional cognitive penetrability can be described with the avail of the theoretical tools of the PEM framework and how experimental evidence supports the occurrence of attentional cognitive penetration under uncertainty in a PEM interpretation of the results.

References

Clark, A. (2016). *Surfing uncertainty*. Oxford: Oxford University Press.

Desimone, R., & Duncan, J. (1995). Neural mechanisms of selective visual attention. *Annual Review of Neuroscience, 18*, 193–222.

Egan, F. (2014). How to think about mental content. *Philosophical Studies, 170*(1), 115–135.

Feldman, H., & Friston, K. J. (2010). Attention, uncertainty, and free-energy. *Frontiers in Human Neuroscience, 4*, 1–23.

Fernandez-Duque, D., Baird, J. A., & Posner, M. I. (2000). Executive attention and metacognitive regulation. *Consciousness and Cognition, 9*(2), 288–307.

Goodale, M. A., & Milner, A. D. (1992). Separate visual pathways for perception and action. *Trends in Neurosciences, 15*(1), 20–25.

Hohwy, J. (2012). Attention and conscious perception in the hypothesis testing brain. *Frontiers in Psychology, 3*, 96.

Hohwy, J. (2013). *The predictive mind*. Oxford: Oxford University Press.

Hohwy, J. (2017). Priors in perception: Top-down modulation, Bayesian perceptual learning rate, and prediction error minimization. *Consciousness and Cognition, 47*, 75–85.

Hohwy, J., Roepstorff, A., & Friston, K. (2008). Predictive coding explains binocular rivalry: An epistemological review. *Cognition, 108*(3), 687–701.

Leopold, D. A., & Logothetis, N. K. (1999). Multistable phenomena: Changing views in perception. *Trends in Cognitive Sciences, 3*(7), 254–264.

Liu, C.-H., Tzeng, O. J. L., Hung, D. L., Tseng, P., & Juan, C.-H. (2012). Investigation of bistable perception with the "silhouette spinner": Sit still, spin the dancer with your will. *Vision Research, 60*, 34–39.

Meng, M., & Tong, F. (2004). Can attention selectively bias bistable perception? Differences between binocular rivalry and ambiguous figures. *Journal of Vision, 4*, 539–551.

Rao, R. P. N., & Ballard, D. H. (2005). Probabilistic models of attention based on iconic representations and predictive coding. In L. Itti, G. Rees, & J. Tsotsos (Eds.), *Neurobiology of attention* (pp. 553–561). Amsterdam: Elsevier.

Spratling, M. W. (2008). Reconciling predictive coding and biased competition models of cortical function. *Frontiers in Computational Neuroscience, 2*(4), 1–8.

Stokes, D. (2014). Cognitive penetration and the perception of art. *Dialectica, 68*(1), 1–34.

Wiese, W. (2017). What are the contents of representations in predictive processing? *Phenomenology and the Cognitive Sciences, 16*(4), 715–736.

Conclusion

Retracing the Steps

In this book, I set out to seek an answer to the following question:

> *Under what conditions, if at all, do changes in perceptual experience that are driven by high-level cognitive states and mediated by attentional processes, constitute genuine cases of cognitive penetration?*

This research question is connected to three sets of problems that I discussed in turn, before concluding that the answer to it is positive.

1. Problems regarding whether and how a distinction between perception and cognition can be established.
2. Problems regarding what it means for a perceptual experience to be cognitively penetrated and what kinds of cognitive penetrability we are interested in.
3. Problems regarding what is attention and how attentional processes unfold.

Concerning the first set of problems, namely whether and how a distinction between perception and cognition can be established, I discussed established ways of distinguishing between perception and cognition by relying on format or kind of processing. I further argued that perception and cognition may be kept separate even in a system where the format and the kind of processing is the same at all levels of the hierarchy, by relying on the overlap between the spatiotemporal resolution of perception and that of basic action.

Concerning the second set of problems, namely what it means for a perceptual experience to be cognitively penetrated and what kinds of cognitive penetrability are we interested in, I presented the accounts of cognitive penetrability that have been most extensively discussed in the contemporary debate and formulated four definitions based on these accounts. I examined the problems that would arise from the truth of the cognitive penetrability hypothesis and discussed three radical consequences that it could have for epistemology, cognitive architecture, and scientific observation.

© Springer Nature Switzerland AG 2020
F. Marchi, *The Attentional Shaping of Perceptual Experience*, Studies in Brain and Mind 16, https://doi.org/10.1007/978-3-030-33558-8

Concerning the third set of problems, namely what is attention and how attentional processes unfold, I defended the view that attention is a property of representations that engage in competitive interactions with one another. I rejected the dismissal of attentional processes as one of the ways in which a perceptual experience could be shaped by cognition. I argued that attentional processes are processes of *biased competition* and that the latter are metacognitive processes. The instantiation of attention as a result of these processes can be driven by cognitive factors and generate cognitively penetrated experiences.

Finally, I presented the *prediction error minimization* framework as a way of modeling perception and cognition that allows us to describe in detail how attentional cognitive penetration unfolds. The upshot is that we should expect cognitive penetrability in general and attentional cognitive penetrability in particular, under conditions of uncertainty or ambiguity in sensory evidence. This poses some clear limits on the range of experiences that can be cognitively penetrable through attentional processes in any interesting sense.

Attention Shapes Experience: Should We Be Worried?

As I have discussed throughout the book, the cognitive penetrability of perceptual experience is thought to have radical and mostly undesirable consequences for several domains of cognitive science. How can one evaluate scientific theories if observation is *theory-laden*? How can one justify a belief on the basis of a perceptual experience, if that experience could already be shaped by that very same belief? I have argued that attentional processes, which are tied to the limited resources available to the physical vehicles of perceptual and cognitive processing, and are thus among the most fundamental processes of the mind, can generate cognitively penetrated experiences. Does this mean that the undesirable consequences of cognitive penetrability are widespread and unavoidable?

Fortunately for our epistemology and scientific theorizing, this is not the case. In the picture I presented, cognitive penetrability is an exception to an otherwise reliable hierarchy of processes that runs from sensory input to belief formation. Cognitive penetrability, even when it is brought about by attentional processes, may happen under conditions of mounting uncertainty and perfect ambiguity. But if the perceptual stimulus is not ambiguous and the perceiving conditions are optimal, the view I proposed does not predict cognitive penetration. Even assuming that the *prediction error minimization* framework will yield a clear and complete account of perception and cognition, the overwhelming presence of top-down modulation in a *prediction error minimization* model of the mind does not entail that there is any dangerous penetration under normal perceiving conditions.

As long as the world itself is allowed to supervise the inferences that the system takes, i.e. as long as the evidence is considered reliable by the system, the system's prior knowledge will not radically determine the outcome of the system's inferences, although it always plays a role of top-down modulation of prior probabilities at each step of the prediction error minimization process.

The same is true for the attentional case. Attentional cognitive penetrability should be expected when the system is not sure about how to treat the evidence. This may happen when there is a radical shift of context or the evidence is gathered in such conditions that the system expects it to be poorly informative and imprecise. In this picture, cognitive penetrability, more than a threat to the reliability of perception, is a backup plan that allows the system to rely more on what it has learned about the world, which has ensured its efficient behavior up to the current point in time, than on new information.

Hence, in conditions where the evidence is expected to be gathered under optimal conditions, such as in carefully controlled experiments or in good perceptual environments, there is no reason to expect dangerous cognitive penetrability to happen. This ensures that evaluation of scientific theories and perceptual epistemology are not threatened by the possibility of cognitive penetration, even if one accepts that attentional processes are among those that can cause cognitive penetration to occur.

The outlook for future research should be to clearly define under which circumstances cognitive penetrability should be expected to happen. Furthermore, the discussion should focus not only on its possible negative consequences but also on the positive ones. One question that immediately arises is the following: under what circumstances does the cognitive penetrability of perceptual experience prevent the system from adopting maladaptive behavior? This question taps into the relation between perceptual experience and action. If experience typically serves as a guide for action, then the possibility of experience being shaped by background cognitive states could cause the system to behave in a more conservative way under conditions of uncertainty. To my knowledge, this point has not been addressed to a sufficient extent and it could provide interesting new developments for the long-standing debate about the interactions between perception and cognition.

Printed in the United States
By Bookmasters